They Know Us Better Than We Know Ourselves

They Know Us Better Than We Know Ourselves

The History and Politics of Alien Abduction

Bridget Brown

NEW YORK UNIVERSITY PRESS
New York and London

NEW YORK UNIVERSITY PRESS
New York and London
www.nyupress.org

© 2007 by New York University
All rights reserved

Library of Congress Cataloging-in-Publication Data
Brown, Bridget, Ph. D.
They know us better than we know ourselves : the history and
politics of alien abduction / Bridget Brown.
p. cm.
Includes bibliographical references and index.
ISBN-13: 978-0-8147-9921-5 (cloth : alk. paper)
ISBN-10: 0-8147-9921-3 (cloth : alk. paper)
ISBN-13: 978-0-8147-9922-2 (pbk. : alk. paper)
ISBN-10: 0-8147-9922-1 (pbk. : alk. paper)
1. Alien abduction. I. Title.
BF2050.B76 2007
001.942—dc22   2007006143

New York University Press books are printed on acid-free paper,
and their binding materials are chosen for strength and durability.

Manufactured in the United States of America
c 10 9 8 7 6 5 4 3 2 1
p 10 9 8 7 6 5 4 3 2 1

Contents

	Acknowledgments	vii
	Introduction	1
1	Elusive Shreds of Memory: The Trauma and Recovery of Alien Abduction	21
2	The Invisible Epidemic: Abduction Traumatists	37
3	Good Subjects: Submitting to the Alien	52
4	My Body Is Not My Own: The Intimate Invasion of Alien Technology	70
5	An Ongoing and Systematic Breeding Experiment	83
6	They Have the Secrets: Conspiracy Theory as Alternative History	100
7	This Is Worse Than Friggin' Aliens: Conspiracy Theory and the War against Citizens	121
8	Look and See What You Have Done: Abductees and the Burden of Global Consciousness	142
9	You Have a Sensitivity: The Limits of Chosenness	160
10	Reality Gets Exploded: Abductee Culture, Abductee Belief	177
	Conclusion: Alien Abduction and the New Face of Terror	207
	Notes	211
	Bibliography	239
	Index	243
	About the Author	247

Acknowledgments

First, thanks to the abductees who were, for the most part, extremely willing and helpful participants in this project. I am grateful also to the folks at The Center for UFO Studies for complete access to their fabulous archive.

I also offer my profuse thanks to many willing and astute readers. These include Andrew Ross, Lisa Duggan, Toby Miller, and Cyrus Patell of New York University. Thanks also to my colleagues Sandie Friedman, Rebekah Kowal, Leslie Paris, and Deborah Williams. And to Peter Knight, coordinator of the conspiracy cultures conference held at King Alfred University, at which a version of chapter 4 was presented in 1998, and editor of *Conspiracy Nation: The Politics of Paranoia in Postwar America* (NYU Press, 2002), in which a related version of chapter 4 appears. And to Eric Zinner and Emily Park at NYU Press for their patience and faith in the project.

I dedicate this book to my family and friends for their support during the long haul, for the innumerable alien cartoons, articles, photographs, and related ephemera they sent me, as well as for the endless opportunities to discuss my project and fine-tune my arguments. And finally, to my husband, Lawrence Lipkin.

Introduction

> The salient characteristic of the traumatic event is its power to inspire helplessness and fear. —Judith Herman[1]

> It starts with fear and opens up into exploration.
> —Jean, alleged alien abductee

Welcome to SPACE

In the summer of 1999 Henry, one of the alleged alien abductees I interviewed for this project, invited me to attend a meeting of the SPACE (Search Project for Aspects of Close Encounters) support group for abductees and other experiencers of paranormal phenomena. Henry has been facilitating such SPACE meetings since 1992. SPACE's Statement of Purpose, as it appears in the organization's newsletter, the *SPACE Explorer*, reads:

> The support and research group gives UFO experiencers a chance to share openly in a comfortable social setting and to explore experiences on the unknown frontier of close encounters. This interactive and proactive program tries to help by providing understanding; caring support; nonjudgmental, meaningful feedback unencumbered by belief systems; and professional resources. In our search for truth, we hope to encourage experiencers toward real empowerment by overcoming fears; creating new life skills; nurturing transformation; and, for those who wish, conducting proactive interaction with the unknown.

The meeting that I attended took place in the apartment of a member who lives in a doorman building on the Upper East Side of New York City and focused on open sharing with other experiencers. I was struck by the sense of fellowship among attendees. There were eighteen people at the meeting I attended, including me. Attendees were asked to bring

Introduction

Fig. 1. SPACE Explorer newsletter cover. SPACE Explorer 8, no. 4 (winter 2000), I issue 6.

snacks for a mid-meeting refreshment break. I contributed a bag of tortilla chips, was introduced, and the conversation began. Attendees began by swapping possibly alien-related ailments and experiences: does anyone have headaches? Experience lucent dreams? Remote viewing? Does anyone see fire flies? Blue beams? People considered these questions and reported related experiences. The conversation organized itself around the ways in which things "bleed through" from different realities and dimensions for the people in attendance. Tanya, whose story I discuss further in chapter 7, contributed that, in her experience, the alien facets of her own identity occasionally bleed through for others to see. One other member of the group—a woman in her late sixties who lives in the West Village—shared several stories of conscious, waking "breakthroughs," episodes during which she sees things while walking down the street or sitting in a restaurant, things that others simply do not see. To me, an outside observer, such accounts sounded delusional. Yet here in this "comfortable social setting" they were met with, as promised, "non-judgmental feedback."

The conversation then turned to alien abduction specifically, to how people do and should deal with their mysterious experiences. Reiterating the ongoing debate between widely published alien abduction experts Budd Hopkins and John Mack—a debate over the central meaning and purpose of abduction that I have traced throughout this project—SPACE members discussed whether they should "remain victims" or use their abduction-related suffering to, in the words of one attendee, "transform into something totally powerful." In this conversation an interesting sort of factionalism emerged. Several attendees who were new to the group spoke in New Age/twelve-step parlance characteristic of John Mack and the "large group transformational work" he has done.[2] They argued, in line with Mack, that powerful transformation can occur through trauma. Barbara, an attractive young woman with a glow of affluence and West Coast good health, advocated dealing with the alien abductor/victimizers by "releasing, surrendering the ego, and . . . [coming] into higher consciousness." She implored the group to try to meet the enemy with love and positive energy for the greater good of humankind.

Her suggestion was met with some nods, some bewildered silence, and some resistance. Jim, an older gentleman wearing a ponytail, was particularly unimpressed with her suggestion due to his belief that it is really the very human members of our government that are the enemy. The government, he stressed, would merely laugh at such expressions of love and forgiveness. Conflict cannot be resolved through benevolent and positive thought, he argued, when the powers that be operate on the "CYA" principle—cover your ass. But Barbara was not easily daunted. She suggested that if "we as a group"—abductees, victims— forgave the government for what it had done, maybe conflict would be resolved: the government would admit past wrongs and we would all "move to a higher level." Her thinking exemplifies the sort of blurring between private and public, or social, "healing" in which abductees often engage. Barbara offered in support of her suggestion the story of a two-time rape victim who is stronger, better than ever as a consequence of her trauma. Making the common and always troubling equation between alleged abductees and rape victims, she proposed to the skeptical hostess of the meeting, Sylvia, that she and others "give them"—aliens, government, whatever forces conspire to oppress us—"what they need with your heart," in a sort of collective act of redemptive submission. Both Jim and Sylvia, more inclined toward the view espoused by Budd Hopkins that the real and present threat of abduction must be met with equal doses of self-defense and self-healing, were unconvinced. For starters, Jim noted that, "some of us can't do that. It's too painful." Sylvia added, shifting back again from aliens to the government as culprit, "I can't forgive the government" citing the things the government had done to citizens with "LSD and Agent Orange."

In many ways the conversation from the SPACE meeting with which I open, and the meeting in general, contains and exemplifies most of the features of belief in alien abduction that I will discuss in the chapters that follow. A number of interpretive camps have emerged among those who espouse and profit from the "ET hypothesis," or the argument that actual extraterrestrial aliens regularly and repeatedly abduct humans. I tack back and forth between these approaches throughout this book. They include the New Age argument that alien abduction is a mode of spiritual transformation; the so-called "realist" argument that alien abduction is simply physical and emotional victimization to be treated therapeutically; and the conspiracy theory argument that alien abduction is the product of human-alien conspiracy and government deception. So too did the conversation at the SPACE meeting reflect many of the central anxieties to which abductees give voice in their accounts, including the struggle with the possibilities and limitations of victim identity based on certain ideas about trauma; the quest to locate various "powers that be" in the alien; the struggle for control of knowledge, both of one's self and of one's world; and the unsettling belief that the body is the site of that struggle.

The unique ways in which stories of abduction by extraterrestrials give expression to these anxieties is of central concern to me throughout the chapters that follow. I seek to offer a critical but respectful reading of alien abduction as a terrestrial phenomenon rooted in the social, cultural, and political history of the United States in the late twentieth century. In other words, I do not believe in aliens. I do believe though that alleged alien abductees believe passionately in their own accounts, and that these accounts must be taken seriously for what they tell us about the dual sense of peril and possibility felt by many Americans. Abductees and the experts who treat them offer sobering counterpoints to narratives about the democratic possibilities of the Space Age, the Cold War, the Information Age, and globalization. The story of abduction by extraterrestrials is the story of biotechnological progress told from the perspective of the anesthetized patient; of military-industrial advancement told from the perspective of the species struggling to avoid extinction on a polluted planet; of national progress and imperialism told by the citizen betrayed and colonized by his or her own government. Through their accounts alleged abductees express a pervasive sense of anxiety about and disenfranchisement from the projects of national technical, scientific, and social progress in America since the 1960s. In the following chapters I look at how abductees grapple with new information about the state of themselves, their planet, their nation; with new views of the body, new views of the earth, newly revealed truths about the national past and present. Accounts of abduction by aliens demonstrate how for some these new views, and the new self-knowledge they supposedly facilitate, are more often confusing and disturbing than enlightening and reassuring.

The alien abduction scenario also offers a telling revision of the story of human-alien contact itself that bears our attention. Unlike the sort of large-scale military conflict posited in *The War of the Worlds*–type science fictions, alien invasion is redefined in abduction accounts as profoundly intimate, a physical, sexual, and psychological invasion of self. Steven Spielberg's *Close Encounters of the Third Kind* (1977)—a film that intensified popular interest in UFOs and their alien occupants during the 1970s—suggested that aliens might actually be in the business of abducting human beings. Yet contact itself is cast in that film as a spiritually expansive exercise in cross-cultural, intergalactic communication. And while the first accounts of abduction by aliens had appeared by the 1970s, the types of stories about human-alien contact that captivated the popular consciousness were those, like *Close Encounters*, that pondered the religious or spiritual implications of contact with an extraterrestrial other. Erich Von Daniken's *Chariots of the Gods* (1974) exemplifies this trend. In this best-selling book, and others that followed profitably in its footsteps, Von Daniken argued that aliens were in fact responsible for the birth of the great ancient civilizations. His work, and other work like it during this period, underscored the obvious similarities between alleged extraterrestrials (or "ancient astronauts") and traditional gods, all believed to exert some degree of control on humanity from above, or beyond, humanity itself. And like most theories of extraterrestrial life up to that point, it helped blur the lines between science and religious belief.[3]

Close Encounters of the Fourth Kind, a term that "ufologists" have come to use to describe alien abduction, are, in contrast, characterized by unwilling capture and violation. Spiritual transformation comes, if at all, as the result of such violation. While some abductees do claim to feel a sense of connection with their alien captors, it is a forced connection more akin to Stockholm Syndrome than communion. The abducting aliens—a species known amongst believers as Greys—are consistently described not as gods, but as clinicians, their power defined by their superior knowledge and intellect, their ability ultimately, in the words of best-selling author and alleged abductee Whitley Strieber, to "know us better than we know ourselves."[4] Produced mostly since the 1980s, accounts of alien abduction suggest not the wonder and possibility of close encounters, but rather the sense, perhaps best expressed by the 1980s and 1990s alien entity the Borg, that "resistance is futile."[5]

Ultimately, what follows is a somewhat schizophrenic reading of the alien abduction phenomenon. I will argue that the phenomenon is symptomatic of a historical period during which people have come to feel increasingly divested of the ability or authority to know what is real or true about themselves and the world in which they live. At the same time, and also in reaction to a variety of social and historical forces, they feel increasingly unsure whom to blame for their feelings of confusion or disempowerment. The alien abduction phenomenon provides a narrative outlet for various and interrelated cultural anxieties, while the abducting alien offers a location and source for those anxieties.

I will also argue, however, that while alien abduction narratives express very real feelings of disempowerment, abductees transform their powerlessness into a bounded status that enables them to be heard, if only in the real and virtual communities in which they participate. In contrast to the profound passivity, even paralysis, that abductees describe experiencing during their alleged abductions, the vigor of their involvement in the process of making meaning of, and producing their own stories about, alien abduction was quite marked in the people who agreed to share their experiences with me. The alien abduction phenomenon can help us think about how people left out of certain narratives of progress create their own stories and fashion truths that square with their own experience of the world. In each chapter I consider the extent to which the belief in abduction by aliens offers abductees a type of agency, a method for critiquing existing power structures. I also look, however, at what is problematic about a belief system in which agency is acquired through the belief in one's own victimization and oppression.

Explaining Alien Abduction: Beyond Belief, beyond Psychology

If abducting extraterrestrials do not exist, how are we to understand the shared belief that they do? How should we make sense of these accounts? There is a vast, burgeoning body of literature that offers "believing" accounts of alien abduction, and an equally expansive body that sets about the task of actively "debunking" the phenomenon. Yet there are still relatively few books that seek to understand and explain it as a terrestrial phenomenon worth our attention. Those that do tend to situate the phenomenon—or the related phenomenon of belief in UFOs and aliens—at the intersection of psychology and religion, or myth, questioning the degree to which such belief may be internally or externally motivated.

Two key studies written during the 1950s aptly sought to explain belief in UFOs and their alien occupants as social-psychological phenomena. Carl Jung suggested in 1959 that belief in UFOs was the product of a collective unconscious, part a product of individual psychology, part myth. Written before the emergence of belief in alien abduction, Jung's psycho-social reading of belief in flying saucers, *Flying Saucers: A Myth of Things Seen in the Sky,* argues that while reports of UFO sightings are sincere, they are the products not of actual events but of subconscious mental processes.[6] Jung's reading of UFOs is still one of the most provocative readings available for its effort to theorize the connections between individual and collective experience and imagination. The Jungian framework is, however, committed to tracing universalities and similarities understood to transcend history.

This method is particularly pervasive in folkloric explanations of extraterrestrials, such as Thomas Bullard's "UFO Abduction Reports: The Supernatural Kidnap Narrative Returns in Technical Guise."[7] Somewhat paradoxically, existing historical explanations of the belief in aliens are also limited by their own somewhat ahistorical definitions of myth. Two such historical treatments of the UFO myth have more recently been published by Smithsonian Institution Press, *Watch the Skies! A Chronicle of the Flying Saucer Myth,* by Curtis Peebles (1994), and *UFO Crash at Roswell: The Genesis of a Modern Myth,* by Benson Saler, Charles A. Ziegler, and Charles B. Moore (1997).[8] *The UFO Crash at Roswell,* for example, is concerned with proving that Roswell is "a narrative that deals with transcendental issues such as why and how the world and humankind came to be in their present form," and seems unconcerned with understanding the particular cultural and historical uses of belief in aliens, or with exploring who may be served or disserved by this myth.[9] Such approaches ultimately fail to account for both the historical specificity and contexts of belief in extraterrestrials, and continue to distract us from more difficult questions about their cultural meanings and historical uses.

Social psychologist Leon Festinger was more interested than Jung in understanding the connection between belief and human behavior. Festinger, famous for his theory of cognitive dissonance, studied a UFO cult who had prophesied the end of the world. He determined that when prophesy failed, the group actually became even more deeply invested in their beliefs. Festinger wrote in *When Prophesy Fails* (1954) that, "A man with a conviction is a hard man to change. Tell him you disagree and he turns away. Show him facts or figures and he questions your sources. Appeal to logic and he fails to see your point."[10] Festinger's conclusions resonate with William James's observations, made a half century earlier, about the psychology of belief. As long ago as the turn of the twentieth century James grappled with the complexities of "belief in an unseen order" and "the psychological peculiarities" of such an "attitude." James did well to point out that the "objects" of our consciousness "elicit from us a reaction; and the reaction due to things of thought is notoriously in many cases as strong as that due to sensible presences. It may be even stronger."[11] In other words, nonmaterial ideas, beliefs, and presences may illicit in us very real reactions, emotions, and behaviors. As the accounts of the alleged abductees that follow suggest, the pain of alien abduction is indeed real because it has real effects.

Neither Jung nor Festinger considered accounts of extraterrestrial abduction specifically; these accounts would appear roughly a decade later, during the 1960s. Jung and Festinger did, however, lay the intellectual groundwork for the idea that legitimate scholarly (that is, skeptical) inquiry into belief in human-alien contact needed to be rooted in consideration of human psychology. Decades later, many of the small cohort of scholars seeking to explain the alien abduction phenomenon proceed from this same assumption. In *Hystories: Hysterical Epidemics and Modern Media* (1997), Elaine Showalter combines psychology with literary and cultural analysis in her treatment of alien abduction and other phenomena that she believes are related "psychogenic diseases," such as Satanic ritual abuse, "Gulf War Syndrome," and Chronic Fatigue Syndrome.[12] Showalter does consider the rootedness of this belief in a historical moment, albeit the too broadly defined "fin de siecle." However, her analysis remains strictly textual, and of the texts she reads, her emphasis remains on literature, the least likely source of images and narratives for the greatest number of people. Showalter argues that we blame external sources such as aliens, Satanists, and even our parents, for problems that are rooted in the individual psyche. Ultimately, however, she gives short shrift to those external sources of anxiety and disempowerment that may be at the source of individual psychic suffering. By arguing that belief in alien abduction is a type of modern hysteria, Showalter pathologizes alleged abductees and thus fails to consider how belief in abduction may be a means for expressing social suffering.

Like her predecessors Jung and Festinger, psychologist Susan A. Clancy argues in *Abducted: How People Come to Believe They Were Kidnapped by Aliens* (2005) that stories of alien abduction, both terrifying and comforting, serve a quasi-religious purpose. As such they are indeed a means through which people find meaning in their lives.[13] But as a psychologist Clancy is less interested in elaborating on what meaning, precisely, they find through these accounts than on analyzing and synthesizing research findings. Clancy maps out the ways in which a variety of physiological and psychological factors—from sleep paralysis to fantasy-proneness—may work together to produce people who claim extraterrestrial kidnap. Certainly she stops short of looking closely at the stories themselves, short of delving into their details. I will argue here that it is crucial to do so in order to tease out the particular shared anxieties to which they give expression, and perhaps even less obviously, to unearth the critiques of contemporary American life that I believe lie hidden in such accounts.

Recent work on conspiracy theory in general offers a useful way out of this bind, accounting for alternative belief systems as not just the products of individual and social psychology, but as means through which people come to understand the effects of power in their lives. Both Jodi Dean and Peter Knight, Dean in a book-length treatment of the alien abduction phenomenon, Knight in chapters within larger treatments of conspiracy theory in general, offer critical, interdisciplinary considerations of alien abduction conspiracy theory. They treat it as a complex cultural phenomenon shaped by both popular discourse and the material realities of people's everyday lives.

Dean's book *Aliens in America: Conspiracy Cultures from Outerspace to Cyberspace* (1998) is the only book-length, cultural studies treatment of alien abduction to date. Dean makes a number of excellent and timely arguments in her book, some of which clearly complement those I will make here. She argues, for example, that the abducting alien functions as "an icon for some difficult social problems, particularly those located around the fault lines of truth, reality, and reasonableness."[14] Yet while Dean calls for, and performs, a "broader, more multilayered and interdisciplinary analysis" of alien abduction than, say, Showalter, she too backs away from historical analysis, relying on generalizations about "society at the end of the millennium." She relies too heavily on "virtuality" and the emergence of the Internet as the source of the confusion and contest over truth that abductees enact, and does not sufficiently historicize "virtuality," or the emergence of computer and communications technologies within the broader contexts of the Cold War, postindustrialism, or globalization. And while she does seek to include the voices of abductees in her project, overall they are eclipsed by her highly theoretical argument about "life in cyberia."

Knight has contributed two books to the nascent literature on contemporary conspiracy theory. In *Conspiracy Culture from Kennedy to the X Files* (2000), he treats alien abduction as part of a more broadly defined cultural phenomenon of "Body Panic." *Conspiracy Nation: The Politics of Paranoia in Postwar America* (2002), a collection of essays, includes a section on alien abduction conspiracy theories. In each case Knight's work as both author and editor is emblematic of, and instrumental in, the move to take conspiracy theory more seriously, not as a hobby of the marginal and deluded, but as "part of the everyday struggle," in Knight's words, "to make sense of a rapidly changing world."[15]

I feel great affinity with the work of both Dean and Knight, with the ways in which each has begun to open up the possibility of viewing the alien abduction phenomenon as historical and political, rooted, as it is, in culture and lived experience. Indeed, throughout the following chapters I read accounts of alien abduction as alternative popular histories of the last forty years or so. I will argue throughout that these accounts, if read closely, act as what historian George Lipsitz calls "grassroots theorizing about complicated realities."[16]

In order to do so I spend a great deal of time considering both written and oral accounts of alien abduction. My analysis is based first on a critical examination of the voluminous popular literature on the subject, including mass-marketed, published accounts of alien abduction, self-published literature produced by abductees and conspiracy theorists, organization newsletters, and online accounts of alien abduction and related phenomena. As I note in chapter 3, there is a lot to be learned from reading between the lines of alien abduction stories about how abductees talk about the conditions of their lives outside of their alleged experiences. I also assume that the stories we tell ourselves about our place in the world—including our memories of a shared past and imagined future—are shaped by our interactions with mass culture and mass media. I look too, then, at how the belief in abduction by extraterrestrials is constituted by and through popular culture, in print, film, and television.[17]

Who Are the Abductees? And Why Alien Abduction?

Unlike any of the literature that precedes it, this book also draws on interviews with alleged alien abductees from the New York City area.[18] I look only at American abductees and read abduction largely as an American phenomenon. Belief in abduction by aliens has certainly spread outside of the United States, yet alien abduction as it has come to be defined through the popular literature is an American export, spread like other mass-produced cultural forms.[19] I have also chosen to limit my ethnographic research to the greater New York City area. I did so largely out of curiosity: like most people outside of the community of UFO believers, I assumed that alien abduction took place only in great rural expanses, and that alleged abductees were exclusively white, rural or suburban, and lower middle class. I was surprised to learn that there is a thriving culture of alleged alien abductees in and around New York City.

My informants range in age from around thirty to sixty-five, although over half of them are in their forties. Two are married, three divorced, and six single. Four have children, and each of those four believes that his or her children too have probably been abducted. My informants live in Greenwich Village and the Upper West Side of Manhattan, Ozone Park in Queens, Co-op City in the Bronx, Bay Ridge and Cobble Hill in Brooklyn, northern New Jersey, and the south shore of Long Island. The people around whose stories this project is structured are, as a group, fairly diverse in terms of gender, race, and ethnic background. I suspect, however, that this is more a function of the metropolitan location I have chosen for my study than anything else: the popular literature on the subject does indeed paint a picture of a largely white, middle- to lower middle-class cohort. Of the eleven people I interviewed, five are female, six male. Indeed I had to make a special effort to seek out female abductees, despite Budd Hopkins's warning that men do not often come forward because "it's not macho to be a powerless victim." Not only was this not the case, but, as I discuss in chapters 1 to 3, alien abduction seems to be a cultural form somewhat unique in its capacity to let men express feelings of victimization and vulnerability.

One of my informants was African American, and another one Latino. Of the white abductees I interviewed, one was Irish-American, one Italian-American, one of Greek descent, three of mixed northern European descent, one of German-Jewish and one of Eastern European Jewish descent. Believing experts suggest abductees come from all classes and professions and that those with money or status to lose simply do not come forward—they have too much at stake. This may be true. While I did not gather data about economic status, my informants hold a variety of types of jobs, including counselor, therapist, graphic artist, musician, and mail carrier. One works in retail, one for a major television network, and one is a journalist for a local newspaper syndicate. A number have been through several jobs and careers. While none appear to be wealthy, neither do they appear to be members of any clearly defined underclass. Ideologically, the alleged abductees with whom I spoke do for the most part share an interest in "alternative" beliefs: in New Age culture, alternative science, the occult, or conspiracy theory. So too did a number of them come of age during the 1960s and 1970s. They typically take a suspicious view of the "powers that be," but have either never been involved in direct political action, or have grown disenchanted with and dropped out of political activism. They seem now, in general, to prefer the support group or hypnosis session—the rather more instant gratification of self-work—to the incrementalism of collective action toward social and political change.

Through interviews with abductees, as well as observation of the therapeutic subcultures that have arisen to address this perceived collective trauma, I have been able to explore what it is in these science-fictional scenarios that speaks to the everyday experience of so many individuals, and what is at stake for those who believe. My interviews with abductees have, I hope, enabled me to attend to the realness of traumatic and terrorizing feelings grappled with by abductees while at the same time treating the abductees as alternative or popular historians of the age in which we live. Throughout the following chapters I will consider the extent to which abductees, through their varied cultural practice, may resist and rewrite official or dominant narratives about technology, authority, and the future.

I read the copious available accounts of alien abduction—accounts shared in books, during interviews, at conferences, on message boards—seeking to understand the ways in which they both reflect and revise more dominant versions of a shared historical past and present. I also grapple throughout with the question of what alien abduction stories do that is different than more directly politicized stories of, for example, victimization and trauma. I read them alongside other chronicles of contemporary life with which they are imbricated, drawn from magazines, newspapers, television, and film produced since the 1960s, accounts with which they are implicitly or explicitly in conversation. I hope in this manner to situate the sense of disempowerment that pervades accounts of abduction by extraterrestrials: disempowerment in the face of unseen forces, including the experts perceived to control and manage us through their command of intelligence, knowledge, technology, and scientific principle; and the real and imagined governments understood to control and manage all spheres of human activity.

The question remains: why aliens? More specifically, why do we need alien abduction as a means to express the various anxieties I have outlined when other cultural texts do similar work? First, aliens—or at the least the allegedly abduction-minded alien "Grey" species—are remarkably versatile symbols that seem capable of taking on numerous meanings. Throughout this book I consider how, in the context of accounts of abduction alone, they most often stand in for doctors, therapists, clinicians, and bureaucrats; more broadly they represent the forces of scientific/technical progress; and even more broadly, the gamut of powers that are perceived to control and/or oppress us. In all instances they are godlike in their omniscience and omnipotence. So too are they technically savvy; their power is consistently believed to be based in their superior intellect.

Accounts of alien abduction are avenues through which some people work through deeply ambivalent, oftentimes confusing feelings about the extent to which knowledge equals power in contemporary American life. In fact, the power struggle that occurs in most accounts of abduction by aliens is a struggle not between the haves and the have-nots, but the knows and the know-nots. Knowledge is seen both as elusive and desirable, and as a complex and volatile commodity: to have too little is bad; to have too much is perhaps worse. To believe that someone else —another class of individuals, here personified as another race of entities entirely—has access to the sort of knowledge that drives human (read American) progress consistently leaves alleged abductees in the role of hapless, resourceless victims. This perceived power imbalance is brought to life in accounts of alien abduction through the raw, forced physical encounter between alien and human. The sometimes disabling impact of otherwise abstract social forces is manifested through the alien abduction scenario. Because such alleged close encounters are brought to bear on individual human bodies, the effects of such forces are paradoxically rendered more real, and certainly more intimate, through the otherworldly scenario of extraterrestrial capture and violation. So too do such accounts provide a means for expressing amorphous feelings of suffering and victimization that may in fact be rooted in unsatisfying domestic or personal lives.

Furthermore, because alien abduction posits an especially extraordinary story of victimization and suffering, it grabs our attention; it gets people heard, if not believed. It offers a fantastic, intriguing, otherworldly rendering of why many people feel at best alienated, at worst traumatized, by the knotty realities of everyday life. At the same time that accounts of abduction by aliens are terrifying, they are also immensely interesting. And as the epigraph with which I open this chapter suggests, for many alleged abductees what begins with fear opens up into exploration.

In the following chapters I offer cultural and historical explanations for these widely reported feelings of terror, vulnerability, and powerlessness, as well as chosenness and elation, in the face of allegedly forced and repeated confrontation with an alien other. Chapters 1 through 3 examine how the story of abduction by aliens mediates the complexity of personal history, memory, and self. Chapters 1 and 2, "Elusive Shreds of Memory" and "The Invisible Epidemic," examine the way in which the eclectic coalition of experts who "treat" abductees, and abductees themselves, have framed alien abduction as psychological trauma, abductees as victims, and abduction experts as those capable, like the aliens themselves, of controlling the simultaneously painful and relieving process of confronting the past. "Elusive Shreds" explores how it is that abduction came to be understood as a traumatic experience in need of therapeutic "unlocking." It also considers the history of abduction experts, their investment in unlocking the "truth" of alien abduction, and their increasingly unquestioned reliance on hypnosis as the method with which to do so. "The Invisible Epidemic" goes on to examine the power dynamic that exists between alleged abductees and the self-styled experts who treat them, considering the abuses of power that may occur in the often voyeuristic process of retrieving memories of alien abduction. In this chapter I also begin trying to understand what it is about the horrifying but precise memory of abduction by aliens that is so compelling to people struggling with murkier personal and social uncertainties.

Chapter 3, "Good Subjects," turns to abductees in an effort to understand their investment in the hypnotherapeutic process, the role that they have played in fashioning their own submission and identity as victims to extraordinary, extraterrestrial forces. In this chapter I consider the tension between what is included in and what is left out of alien abduction narratives, for while such accounts are rife with the fantastic details of sexual and other physical violation, mundane details of suffering and anxiety are underplayed or omitted.

I turn my attention to the content of alien abduction accounts, to those details "revealed," usually under hypnosis, in chapters 4 through 9. I look into what specific cultural and social forces abductees feel are violating them, and how those forces get mapped onto the abducting alien. In chapters 4 and 5, "My Body is Not My Own" and "An Ongoing and Systematic Breeding Experiment," I explore the most commonly reported feature of alien abduction: the claim that abductees have been rendered powerless by their alien captors and subjected to invasive physical and more specifically, reproductive, procedures. I read this facet of abduction accounts alongside other contemporaneous accounts of the encroachment of reproductive technologies. In most accounts, inability to control one's body includes inability to control sexual function and desire as well as what is perceived to be one's biological destiny. Yet as in chapters 1 and 2, abductee feelings about such repeated violation are characterized by ambiguity, and so I also explore the somewhat narcissistic conclusion reached by many alleged abductees that the abducting aliens "need" them.

Alleged alien abductees who are also conspiracy theorists generally share with others the fundamental belief that they have been physically captured and experimented upon by extraterrestrial entities involved in some sort of ongoing research project. These abductees go on, however, to implicate human elites for allowing, sanctioning, or participating in such human experimentation; they insist on the connection between the sort of biological engineering discussed in my last chapter and a more large-scale project in social engineering. These abductees are the focus of chapters 6 and 7, "They Have the Secrets" and "This Is Worse Than Friggin' Aliens." Dismissed by some in the abduction community as "the paranoids," conspiracy theorist abductees believe that alien abduction is the product of a set of conspiracies involving not just extraterrestrials, but also a complex hierarchy of humans. These are most often elite groups of humans representing a monstrous cross-section of a postwar military-scientific-intelligence complex with whom the aliens are believed to be in league. While early chapters look at the difficulty of establishing stable, reliable accounts of one's personal history, conspiracy theories of alien abduction grapple with the impossibility of doing the same on a collective, national, or global scale.

In "They Have the Secrets" I look broadly at conspiracy culture and specifically at the extent to which believers in alien abduction are or are not a part of that culture. In so doing I examine how the history of political cover-up and revelation during the 1970s and 1980s fueled conspiracy theories of alien abduction and conspiracy theory in general, most especially through the revelation of those abuses of state power that were enacted on the bodies of American citizens. "This Is Worse Than Friggin' Aliens" goes on to look at the more extreme end of alien abduction conspiracy theory, referred to by some as the Dark Side Hypothesis. In this chapter I examine how the Dark Side Hypothesis takes the idea of personal violation by the powers that be to an extreme, personalizing the broad abuses of power detailed more generally in other conspiracy theories.

Chapters 8 and 9, like chapters 4 and 5, explore alien abduction as a means through which people confront how technological progress makes us rethink our status as humans. More specifically, I consider how heightened awareness of our culpability in the earth's destruction has come to be understood by many abductees as a central facet of the abduction experience. "Look and See What You Have Done" considers how this particular narrative has taken shape in stories of contact with aliens since the 1950s, but also in other contemporary cultural narratives about the state of the planet and our place on the planet in an era that includes both the Space Age and cultural, political, and economic globalization. I take a short detour through sometimes overlapping, sometimes contradictory Space Age and environmentalist discourses about planet Earth in order to lay bare the various uses to which the view of Earth from space, and the personification of the earth that emerges simultaneously, were put during the 1960s and 1970s, which are the decades during which the alien abduction phenomenon emerged and took shape.

In "You Have a Sensitivity," I return to contemporary accounts of alien abduction. In these accounts, published during the 1980s and 1990s, the reported visions of global apocalypse are more graphic, and the lessons imparted by extraterrestrials about human culpability in environmental disaster are more punishing. I consider how the awe, confusion, and anxiety that come with a newly expanded view of the state of the planet detailed in chapter 8, in addition to the sense born of globalization that power is diffuse and difficult to locate, is manifested in and through these accounts. Throughout this chapter I also consider how and why alleged abductees express deep ambivalence about having been "chosen" to spread the word about human degradation of the planet. I conclude chapter 9 by revisiting the problematic and related notion (a notion set forth by SPACE member Barbara at the beginning of this chapter) that individual and collective transformation can only be achieved through pain, and question the efficacy of this belief.

My final chapter, "Reality Gets Exploded" focuses exclusively on the cultural practice of the New York area abductees whom I interviewed for this project. I argue here that by participating in the cultural practice of being an alien abductee, alleged abductees become agents in the social drama of alien abduction; they discover human interaction, fellowship, support, and a means of self-expression. Whether privately or publicly, all of the people whom I interviewed for this chapter devote some part of their lives to the fairly enthusiastic consideration of what alien abduction means to them and how they think the phenomenon will affect the world at large. They also become participants in a collective project that seeks to revise mainstream notions of reality itself. I question ultimately the extent to which the agency they gain through abductee identity, or belief in the alternate realities they suggest, is empowering or enabling to my informants.

If alien abductees act as alternative historians, as I argue they do, what are we to make of the escalation of such popular historical revisionism during the 1980s and 1990s? The alien abduction phenomenon emerged during the 1960s and 1970s, but it boomed in the 1980s and early 1990s as increasing numbers of alleged abductees came forward, and the abduction phenomenon entered popular consciousness through the escalating media attention it received.[20] As such, the bulk of written accounts offer their revisionist histories of the last forty years from the perspective of the late Cold War, Reagan-Bush years, and tell us as much about the changing cultural climate of those years of conservative political and social retrenchment as they do about the historical events they narrate.

Surely a revival of interest in aliens in general, signaled by the rise in interest in abduction specifically, paralleled Ronald Reagan's revival of Cold War anxieties through the us-versus-them rhetoric of the "evil empire" and the very real reinvigoration of the arms race. Reagan used this rhetoric in part to redraw clear-cut lines between good and evil, us and them, lines perceived by conservatives to have been blurred to ill effect by the new social movements of the 1960s and 1970s. Abductees and other conspiracy theorists demonstrate how profound and complicated this blurring was: while they are clearly compelled by the neatness of the Manichean distinctions between good and evil, a patriotic nationalist "us" of the sort invoked by Reagan is no longer viable; in fact, conspiracy theorists turn that model on its head, suggesting that the interests of the state are most often sinister and oppressive. In the end alien abductee accounts of life in late twentieth-century America point to the dissonance that exists for many between the conditions of their own lives and dominant accounts of a shared American past and present.

So too does one see alleged abductees grappling with the Reaganist suggestion that the social movements of the 1960s and 1970s had failed, having exerted not a progressive but a deleterious effect on the nation. According to this conservative logic, collective action was at once futile and destructive. The return to more liberal, or at least moderate, ideology during the Clinton administration signaled not a reinvigoration of protest and activism but rather a call to "heal" and unify, to set aside differences and move forward as a nation. On the one hand, abductees—especially the conspiricists among them—voice cynicism about this narrative of national healing. Their accounts insist on the continued existence of social hierarchies and power imbalances, and especially on state abuses of power even in an era of political decentralization. At the same time, the abduction phenomenon is in large part, I argue, the result of this redirection of dissent, this defusing of the impulse to collective action and social protest. My interviews with alleged abductees in particular suggest that they can often only express dissent and social displeasure through the fantastic, dramatic, otherworldly scenario of abduction by aliens.

And even within that scenario, the possibility of asserting one's will in protest is constantly called into question. Since the earliest accounts of abduction by aliens, alleged abductees have tried to talk back to their captors and object to forced "procedures." Barney Hill—whose story was featured in *The Interrupted Journey: Two Lost Hours Aboard a Flying Saucer* (1966), the first "true" published account of abduction by extraterrestrials—remarked, recalling an abduction experience, "I don't want them to operate on me."[21] In 1987 Strieber claimed to have asserted more forcefully, "I'm not going to let you do an operation on me. You have absolutely no right." In Strieber's account the aliens supposedly responded, "We do have a right." In each case protest is met with puzzlement and palliatives at best, at worst with the invocation of total authority. Strieber is horrified by this bold assertion of power: "Five enormous words. Stunning words. We do have a right. Who gave it to them? By what progress of ethics had they arrived at that conclusion?"[22] Abductees rehearse again and again the difference between the right to protest and the ability to effect change over the conditions of one's own disempowerment. They theorize, ultimately, that power does operate on us whether we want it to or not.

1

Elusive Shreds of Memory
The Trauma and Recovery of Alien Abduction

Alien abduction expert Budd Hopkins estimates that he has worked with roughly seven hundred people, helping them to uncover the otherwise unfaceable details of their multiple abductions by aliens. Hopkins is the author of three popular books on alien abduction, *Missing Time* (1981), *Intruders: The Incredible Visitations at Copley Woods* (1987), and *Witnessed: The True Story of the Brooklyn Bridge UFO Abductions* (1996). He has played a central role in reinvigorating interest in the topic, manifested in the boom in accounts of abduction to emerge during the 1980s and 1990s. He now runs the Intruders Foundation, an online clearinghouse for information about alien abduction. He is a fixture on UFO lecture circuits and runs a New York City support group that many of the area abductees I have interviewed attend. He is, according to his promotional materials, "generally regarded as the world's leading authority on the UFO abduction phenomenon," and has appeared on the *Today Show*, *Oprah*, *Good Morning America*, *Roseanne*, and on numerous television specials on alien abduction from the more sensational series *Sightings* to the sober and high-minded PBS series *Nova*. His book *Missing Time* was made into a television movie starring Mare Winningham; Hopkins was played by Richard Crenna.

I first saw Hopkins speak at the 1994 Whole Life Expo, "The World's Largest Exposition for Holistic Health, Personal Growth, and Positive Living," in New York City. I was curious then about what exactly aliens had to do with "personal growth and positive living" and to see how abduction experts positioned themselves among UFO investigators, who have traditionally been more interested in outer space than the inner space of the human psyche. The "UFOs and the Coming Millennium" panel provided just the sort of overview of ufology celebrities that I had hoped to find. The emcee was Trish McCannon, a Pleiedian

22 | *Elusive Shreds of Memory*

Fig. 2. *Intruders* cover. Budd Hopkins, *Intruders: The Incredible Visitations at Copley Woods* (Ballantine, 1987).

contactee and multidimensional channeller. Also on the panel were Fred Bell, former NASA engineer and speaker on ET technologies; Bob Dean, ex-soldier devoted to exposing the government cover-up of ET knowledge—the "cosmic Watergate" I discuss at length in chapters 6 and 7; Mike Rogers, friend of Travis Walton, the abductee featured in the 1993 film *Fire in the Sky*; and Vance Davis, a "decorated Army Intelligence Specialist who went AWOL before the Gulf War in 1990 with five other high level operatives after they received warnings about forthcoming Earth Changes along with Alien Visitation Craft and the aliens that control them."[1]

These panelists spoke confidently and authoritatively about the "end of one great cycle and the beginning of the next," of the role in our lives of an elaborate hierarchy of alien races involved, for better for worse, in our inevitable march toward apocalypse. They spoke with a kind of heady paranoia about the lies and deceit of both aliens and the government and the conspiracy among the "forces of dark" to bombard humans with ELFs, or extra-low frequency waves, that make us tired, disoriented, and ultimately powerless in the face of our enemies. These ufologists seemed engaged in a discourse of aliens and otherness that came from a number of places: from science fiction, from eco-apocalyptic atomic age and millennial anxiety, from conspiracy theories that posit all occurrences as interrelated parts of a larger, covert plan. Then it was Hopkins's turn to speak. Hopkins looks sort of rumpled and avuncular—a cross between character actors Hal Holbrook and Alan Alda. In the midst of this fantastic millennialism, Hopkins presents himself as an oasis, if not of reason then of reasonableness. Unlike his other panelists, he insisted, he did not KNOW what was going to happen to any of us; he knew nothing of prophesy or the coming millennium; unlike the others, he was not primarily interested in aliens, but in people. Hopkins maintained that he was less concerned with the existence of a "cosmic Watergate" than with treating and healing people who claim to have been abducted and traumatized by aliens. It is his mission, he declared to the capacity crowd, to "make these people whole again."

I interviewed Hopkins in May 1998 in the well-appointed Chelsea apartment he shares with his wife and two large-eyed, hairless, and suspiciously alien-looking cats. Hopkins spent most of our over-two-hour interview defending his position that alien abductions are real events, dismissing point by point various "debunking" arguments that have been made against him. He also went out of his way to discredit other experts whom he accuses of "having an agenda." In contrast, he tries to position himself—as in his performance at the Whole Life Expo—as a man of reason. He insists that his approach in his books is evidence-driven: if he "discovers something important" he writes a book. "Data comes in," Hopkins notes, "and I look at it as objectively as possible." He roughly groups other camps into "New Age, Christian, paranoid/government-blaming, and cults." In contrast, he claims not to impose an interpretation. According to Hopkins "there are many ways in which people understand what happened to them in order to cope and survive," and he likes "to leave their coping styles in place."

During our interview Hopkins also explained how he—an abstract painter of some standing in the art world—has become one of the foremost authorities on alien abduction. In 1964 Hopkins had a UFO sighting that initiated his interest in UFOs. In 1976 he wrote an article for the *Village Voice* about UFOs. After the *Voice* article Hopkins began to look into the claims of alleged alien abductees and, realizing that certain skills were required to get at the "truth" of the abduction experience, an experience that seemed almost always to be buried in amnesia, he entered what he calls a "seven-year apprenticeship" with a number of psychiatrists and psychologists, during which he learned about hypnotherapy and "gathered evidence." In 1983 he began hypnotizing alleged abductees himself. Now he is busy year round "interviewing" some of the hundreds of possible abductees he receives letters from, performing hypnotic regressions, and facilitating a support group that meets in his apartment every two months or so.

Hopkins claims that for years—with several notable exceptions including the Hill and Andreasson cases, which I discuss below—few abductees came forward, because of shame. He suggests that many investigators and scientists were guilty of perpetuating a sort of collective denial that kept abductees quiet mostly as a result of "fear of allowing such an unknown into our life." Once materials became available about alien abduction in the 1980s—including his own books—more and more abductees began to come forward. Hopkins notes that "unless there is an infrastructure of organizations and investigators [abduction] is not a 'phenomenon.'" If people don't know what to call it, he explains, it goes unrecorded.[2]

I agree with Hopkins on this last point, though he and I surely interpret its meaning differently. Hopkins means that members of this quasi-professional network serve the critical function of helping otherwise isolated and miserable individuals locate the extraterrestrial source of their anxiety, confront the hidden trauma of alien violation, and move on. I believe, and will seek to argue here, that this community of experts has played a central role in creating and shaping the abduction phenomenon. They have done so in large part because of the authority and legitimacy the hypnotherapeutic process confers on them through their ability to "treat" abductees, whom they have helped render victims in need of their assistance. They have built careers on their supposed aptitude at revealing "hidden truths" about people's pasts, "truths" that are held up as evidence of the actual existence of aliens, particularly juicy and titillating evidence that has made its way into best-selling books or highly rated television talk shows. At the same time such experts are, I will argue, guilty of ignoring or eliding the very terrestrial sources of suffering that abductees talk about, both directly and indirectly, when they talk about their abduction by aliens. In this chapter and the next, I examine the way in which the eclectic coalition of experts who "treat" abductees have framed alien abduction as a psychological trauma, abductees as victims, and abduction experts as those capable, like the aliens themselves, of controlling the simultaneously painful and relieving process of confronting the past.

The Charisma of Hypnosis: The Postwar Context

Since the 1960s a growing coalition of UFO investigators, psychologists, psychiatrists, and noncredentialed therapists who use hypnosis to treat alien abduction as repressed trauma have helped construct the compelling notion that most of us are walking time bombs of buried information in need of release through the proper therapeutic methods. According to this quasi-professional community, one need only find the right hypnotist, or investigator, or therapist to unlock the truth about one's individual past, which may indeed include repeated abduction by extraterrestrials. Many abductees acknowledge that if they had not contacted an expert such as Budd Hopkins, they might never have fully realized their hidden personal histories as alien abductees. Indeed, since the first account of a human abduction was published in 1966, the story of abduction has been about people seeking the help of those who were deemed capable of accessing parts of their pasts to which they themselves lacked access.

The Interrupted Journey: Two Lost Hours Aboard a Flying Saucer, written by UFO investigator John Fuller and published by Dial Press in 1966, acts as a sort of origin story in alien abduction discourse. The first published and mass-distributed account of abduction by aliens, it tells the story of Betty and Barney Hill, an interracial couple living in New Hampshire who claimed to have encountered a UFO while driving home from a trip to Canada in 1961.[3] The Hills' story is referred to in almost all subsequent published accounts of abduction, and served as a conversational touchstone in most of the interviews I conducted with New York area abductees. *The Interrupted Journey* contains many of the features that would come to distinguish abduction accounts from previous stories of UFO or alien contact. These include the decision made by most abductees to seek therapeutic treatment for their alleged contact with extraterrestrials. As its subtitle suggests, *The Interrupted Journey* is fundamentally concerned with the theme of retrieving or reconstructing lost time. The day after their purported encounter with a UFO the Hills became aware that they had "lost" two hours during that trip; they could remember nothing between seeing the UFO and driving along a particular stretch of New England highway. In the wake of this experience, Betty began to have long, detailed nightmares about being taken on board the UFO and examined by aliens. Barney developed insomnia and his ulcer became aggravated. He also began to worry about a mysterious ring of warts around his groin that appeared after they had returned home from the trip. Betty became driven by a desire to know whether her dreams were really memories of an actual, forgotten event. She became determined to "know one way or the other because . . . well maybe my dreams are something that really happened."[4] Likewise, Barney asked a friend, referring to his UFO sighting, "How do I *know* that this thing happened? How do I *know* that I wasn't just seeing things?"[5] And so, like thousands of alleged alien abductees to follow, the Hills set out to find answers that would relieve them both of "crippling anxiety" and the unbearable burden of uncertainty.

In order to determine whether her experience was "illusion, hallucination, dream, or reality," Betty Hill first turned to members of the UFO investigative community already in place in the early 1960s for help.[6] Walter Webb of the National Investigations Committee on Aerial Phenomena (NICAP) was dispatched to handle this intriguing new type of case. At his urging the Hills decided to retrace their original journey. As Fuller writes, "the compulsion grew in both of them that they must return to the scene of the incident, as Walter Webb had suggested, and relive the experience trying to recapture the elusive shreds of memory."[7] Betty in particular believed that retaking the trip from Montreal to their home in Portsmouth, New Hampshire, would "spark a chain of memory that would suddenly bring back their recall."[8] When repeated reenactments of their mysterious trip failed to jog their memory, which remained frustratingly elusive, the Hills decided to seek the help of a hypnotist.

The Hills decision to seek certainty through the retrieval of lost time was made at a time when ideas about the nature of memory and its relationship to truth were at issue in both popular and political culture. Hypnosis—long a popular form of stage entertainment—gained increasing visibility and credibility in the wake of World War II. U.S. intelligence agencies including the Office of Strategic Services (OSS) and the Central Intelligence Agency (CIA) dabbled with hypnosis (under the broader rubric of "mind control" and "brainwashing") as possible means through which the United States might seek to sabotage enemies. Though efforts to create unwitting assassins through such means neither succeeded nor gained much credibility within the national security state as a whole, the notion that expert agents might control and manipulate an individual's mind and memory was a powerful one. *The Manchurian Candidate*—both Richard Condon's best-selling 1959 novel and John Frankenthaler's 1962 film—widely popularized this notion.[9]

On a less sinister but no less intriguing level, the process of unearthing and treating trauma through memory was also already in place in the national project of healing a nation in the wake of war. In *Interrupted Journey*, Fuller credits family friend Major James MacDonald, an Air Force intelligence officer who had just recently retired from active duty, with suggesting hypnosis as "a way to penetrate the unyielding curtain that began to descend" when Barney tried to recall what happened after he exited the car to view the descending UFO. MacDonald, it seems, could testify to the credibility of hypnosis which, under "controlled medical conditions" could "produce some strikingly dramatic results in the rehabilitation of servicemen suffering from war neuroses."[10] MacDonald's suggestion was supported by another military man and member of the Hills' church group, Captain Ben Swett from Pease Air Force Base. Swett, according to Fuller, was "well known for his study of hypnosis."[11] Finally Barney's psychiatrist, with whom he had been exploring the possible emotional and social problems of being an interracial couple, and of being subjected to racism, also suggested consultation with a hypnotist. It was Barney's psychiatrist who referred the Hills to Dr. Benjamin Simon, a Boston psychiatrist and neurologist. Simon came to his interest in hypnosis through the treatment of "military psychiatric disorders" during World War II. Fuller goes to great lengths to establish Simon's credibility and legitimacy. Fuller notes with special interest that Simon had served as advisor to, and appeared in, a 1946 documentary about the psychiatric treatment of war veterans called *Let There Be Light,* directed by John Huston. Marshalling military and scientific authority, Fuller makes his case for the legitimacy of hypnosis as a *therapeutic* tool. He equates the Hills with sufferers of war neuroses, quoting Major MacDonald who "reasoned the Hills had experienced a violent trauma much like shell shock." Fuller thus argues that the Hills ought to be taken seriously—more seriously in many respects than other historically female "hysterics" whose stories had also been in circulation for over a century, and to whom I return later in this chapter.[12] More interested in the extraordinary possibilities of extraterrestrial trauma, both Fuller and Simon fail to pursue the original psychiatrist's suggestion that the Hills' sense of trauma might be related somehow to the daily challenge of living as an interracial couple in a racist society.

What Fuller also omits, presumably in the effort to make his project and his clients seem more credible, is that Betty herself initiated hypnosis for several reasons. In her initial letter to Major Donald Keyhoe of NICAP, she indicates, "We are considering the possibility of a competent psychiatrist who uses hypnotism." Reflecting back on her decision, Betty Hill states that as a "professionally trained social worker," she knew of cases in which "hypnosis had been used to remove amnesia," and had been "used by dentists" so that their patients would not feel pain. Finally, hypnosis was "often the subject of TV programs." The example she gives—mentioned nowhere in *The Interrupted Journey*—is a show she has seen in which "a group of people would be put into a light trance and told this blank wall had a window and if they looked out the window they would see a UFO fly by. Each one told, in great excitement, a glowing account of his 'UFO sighting.'" It is unclear whether Betty saw this show before or after her own alleged abduction. It is, in either case, a puzzling example to give in support of the legitimacy of hypnosis to reveal "truth," indicating as it does the suggestibility of people under hypnosis, the suggestibility in particular of people to claims of having seen UFOs. Perhaps this ambiguity—the traces of the possibility that Betty may have desired to tell, with great excitement, her own glowing account of a UFO sighting—is what made Fuller decide to omit references to Betty's interest in hypnosis.[13] If so, this can be read as the first of many such omissions by UFO investigators in the name of making subjects look "normal": that is, as if they could have no earthly motive for reporting UFO contact.

The Hills' hypnotist, Dr. Simon, has an interesting presence in Fuller's book. The book opens with a forward written by him, in which he characterizes himself as "a reluctant member of the dramatis personae."[14] Simon defends his use of hypnosis as an effective tool with which to "unlock the door to the hidden room (the amnesia)," and yet he is clearly concerned about a common misunderstanding readers will have about the nature of the "truth" as revealed through hypnosis. He wants to counter the tendency to "envelop hypnosis with an arcane charisma, and the practitioner with the robe of Merlin."[15] He wants to clarify that,

> the charisma of hypnosis has tended to foster the belief that hypnosis is the magical and royal road to truth. In one sense this is so, but it must be understood that hypnosis is a pathway to the truth as it is felt, and understood by the patient. The truth is what he believes to be the truth, and this may or may not be consonant with the ultimate non-personal truth.[16]

Dr. Simon would thus "orient his treatment to the recall of the patient's experiences and their . . . thinking and feeling—not to the establishment of the reality or non-reality of unidentified objects."[17] While Simon continually underscored distinctions between subjective and objective reality, subsequent hypnotists have been more than happy to don the robe of Merlin, and to assist those such as Betty and Barney Hill with the daunting task of separating "illusion, hallucination, dream, or reality." Many have, since the *The Interrupted Journey,* enthusiastically cultivated the "archane charisma" of hypnosis in the treatment of alleged alien abductees, helping them navigate the blurry line between "truth as it is felt" and "the ultimate non-personal truth" and at the same time exploiting its very ambiguity.[18]

The notion that bits and pieces of one's past could be retrieved whole and intact by a certain class of expert took hold of the popular imagination just as the notion of a stable, unified truth seemed to be disintegrating on a number of cultural fronts. By the 1960s and 1970s photography, film, and perhaps most especially television (by virtue of its popularity and ubiquity) had already begun to trouble any easy sense that one could distinguish reality from simulation. Postmodern thinking posited identity and subjectivity itself as complex and fragmented, troubling any easy notion of a single, stable self. And emerging ideas about multiculturalism increasingly suggested that multiple, diverse perspectives needed to be attended to in accounts of history and social reality. The idea that one could, through a process as simple as hypnosis, retrieve "what really happened," reassemble "elusive shreds of memory," and reconstitute shattered selves must indeed have been comforting in this turbulent context. And yet at the same time, the self that is recuperated via hypnosis was not and is not whole and unified, but reconstructed. Hence the ongoing debate and inconclusivity about the type of truth offered by hypnotists: we want to see it as restoring a true self, but that true self is itself a reconstruction or simulation, indeed more akin to a fragmented, postmodern notion of subjectivity.

Nonetheless, hypnotherapists, alongside other, more legitimate psychotherapists, came to fill a sort of quasi-religious void, as traditional religious practice began to decline during the 1960s and 1970s.[19] Yet while hypnotherapists may act as latter-day shamans, they position themselves not as magicians, but as men of science. It is in fashioning themselves as men of science and reason—as therapists rather than magicians—that they have had the best chances of gaining credibility in the culture at large, a culture in which science has come for many to stand as its own de facto truth. Abduction hypnotherapists working in the murky medium of memory—up to and including Budd Hopkins—claim scientific credibility in order to bolster their own truth claims. With one foot in psychoanalysis and one foot in vaudeville, they have shored up power and prestige, at least within the community of UFO/alien believers, by claiming access to knowledge—to reality and truth itself—that alleged abductees themselves lack.

"I Certainly Hope That Dr. Simon Isn't Really a Spaceman!" Therapist as Alien/Alien as Therapist

The process of undergoing hypnosis, as performed in alien abduction narratives, involves relinquishing self-control, both emotionally and physically. People who enter hypnotherapy to retrieve information about their abduction experiences tacitly agree to submit to the therapist and so the dominance of the doctor and the dominance of the aliens whose abuses abductees recount are often interchangeable. What is both intriguing and disturbing to an outsider like me is that so many abductees not only consent to this form of external control—routinely giving over power to authority—but also intuit the analogy between controlling doctors and controlling aliens. Perhaps the most telling line in *The Interrupted Journey* is spoken by Betty after hearing the tapes of their hypnotic regressions. As Fuller renders the scene, "In the elevator going down, they were alone for the first time, with a measurable recall of the incident now thoroughly in their minds. The first thing that Betty could say was in reference to Dr. Simon. 'I certainly,' Betty laughed, 'hope that Dr. Simon isn't really a spaceman!'"[20]

The Hills also confuse their captors and Simon during hypnosis. Trying to describe the feeling of dissociation upon being taken from the car, he reports, "it was much like being put into hypnosis by Dr. Simon. I knew the leader was there, yet I felt there was a complete separation of his words and his presence."[21] In one particularly interesting exchange between Simon and Barney, Simon tries to press Barney to admit that his "memories" are not really of experiences, but of the dreams Betty has relayed to him. Simon asks "from whom did you learn about this experience? You didn't really have it, did you?" Barney responds, "I was hypnotized." Simon asks, "you were hypnotized. By whom?" To which Barney answers, "Dr. Simon . . . I was hypnotized by Dr. Simon. . . . He made me go back to September 19, 1961. . . . he told me I would relate this, and I related this."[22] During repeated hypnotic sessions the Hills learn more about hypnosis, and what they learn ironically confirms what they already suspected—that they themselves have little control over their own memory, little access to the details of their own personal history.

In case after case therapists are described as aliens, aliens as therapists, the two forces collapsing into one another, equally in control of the patient, and in particular of the process of remembering and forgetting. Fuller notes that "during hypnosis the incidents described in the trance can be wiped from conscious memory. Conversely, on instruction from the doctor, they can be recalled."[23] Simon's job is to allow the Hills to remember, and then to "make sure that the amnesia was reinstated after each session."[24] As Fuller describes the process, the Hills' recall "may be turned on and off at will at the instruction of the operator."[25] At the same time that the Hills are rendered "tape recorders" to be operated by Simon, he also in fact tape records their sessions. As Fuller notes, after the first few sessions, "only the doctor was aware of what had been uncovered."[26] In the interest of protecting them from knowing too much, too soon, Simon does not allow them to hear or know what memories he has released.

As in most accounts of alien abduction to follow, the Hills' alien captors are described as entities who, like hypnotherapists, manipulate memory, and control and ameliorate pain and anxiety through the induction of a hypnotic state. In contrast to the therapists, however, the aliens are consistently described as deeply invested in making their subjects forget. Though in Fuller's words, "the door to the forgotten time period begins to swing open" during hypnosis, the Hills both report that they are not supposed to remember.[27] Betty tries to explain to Simon that "that's the whole point. They don't want you to know what has happened. They want you to forget all about it."[28] Betty suggests that the aliens have made her afraid of remembering when she speculates (still under hypnosis) that "maybe it was the fear of remembering it too. It was something about the way he said it was better to forget it. Almost like a threat."[29] Barney too reveals a fear of remembering, suggesting that his captor left him with the sense that he would "know if ever (he) had gone too far by revealing something." He had been told to forget, and that "you have to forget it, you will forget it, and it can only cause great harm that can be meted out to you if you do not forget."[30]

Likewise, the syntax of hypnotism suggests domination of the subject by verbal command. Throughout the book, in transcripts of various sessions, we hear Simon instructing the Hills, "you will not remember anything that has transpired here until I tell you to recall it"; "you will not be troubled by anything you remember"; "you will remember everything"; and "I'll see to it that you don't have that anxiety again."[31] The last directive in particular suggests a godlike level of control, not only over the Hills' memory, but also over their emotion. The therapeutic gesture is at once comforting—the therapist takes anxiety away—and chilling in the level of external control it suggests.

In early accounts of alien abduction, the struggle over memory takes place, then, between the alien and the hypnotherapist, the latter positioning himself as heroic champion of memory/truth. The abductee is merely present: a physical vessel into whom information may be placed, and from whom information may be retrieved. The mental and physical passivity of the abductee body is even more pronounced in the next book-length treatment of alien abduction, *The Andreasson Affair: The Documented Investigation of a Woman's Abduction Aboard a UFO*

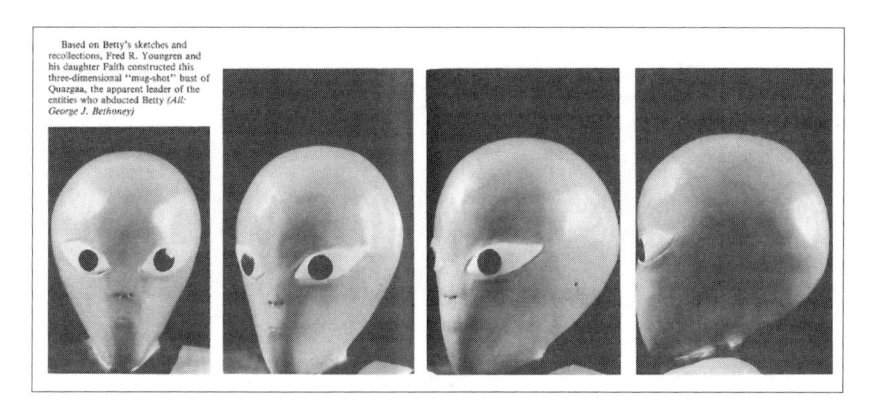

Fig. 3. Quazgaa mug-shot. Raymond Fowler, *The Andreasson Affair* (Englewood Cliffs, NJ: Prentice Hall, 1979), 92–93.

(1979). Written by UFO investigator Raymond Fowler, *The Andreasson Affair* too consists largely of transcripts of hypnotic regressions.[32] The book opens with Fowler's justification of the hypnotic process, and an assertion that the hypnotist who treated Betty Andreasson and her daughter Becky, was "a well recognized expert in the practical use of hypnosis."[33] While Fowler remains somewhat ambiguous about the nature of the truths revealed under hypnosis, his caution is outweighed by his sense of wonder at the potential revelations to come from this project. While he initially contends that the truths unlocked in hypnosis are truth "as he or she believes the truth to be," he later contradicts himself when he asserts that, "deep trance hypnosis, properly administered by a skillful hypnotist, can produce near-total recall for everything a subject has ever experienced. In this trance state, a person must tell the truth."[34] Structuring the text around transcripts of hypnotic sessions, as in the Hill case, is meant to lend veracity to otherwise incredible memories that are unlocked. The technology of the tape recorder itself—its ability to capture and freeze accounts of the truth—is also presented as evidence of the truthfulness of the claims made. By simply transcribing the content of these tapes, Fowler, like other experts who use the same format, assumes the position of objective witness: demanding just the facts, he can only dutifully report the details that emerge about nasal and ocular probes, cities of crystal, and extended dialogues with an alien captor named Quazgaa who informs Andreasson of her role in determining the future of the human race.

Though early abduction hypnotherapists sought legitimacy for their studies by equating alleged abductees to male victims of shell shock, so too did they participate in the longer history of exploiting female hysteria with its sexual overtones of physical control through mental domination. The nineteenth-century clinical interest in female hysteria functioned in a similar manner, authorizing the public diagnosis and "treatment" of hysterics (usually women) by doctors (always men) such as Jean-Martin Charcot. Charcot, the director of Salpetriere Hospital in Paris in the late nineteenth century, took an avid interest in female hysteria, theorizing that the symptoms of hysteria were real, the result of neurological weakness originating, as the word itself suggests, in the womb. Charcot championed hypnosis as a method for the observation and classification of hysterics and their symptoms, and, in fact, believed that only hysterics could be hypnotized.

While female hysterics were listened to carefully by doctors such as Charcot during this period, they were also held up as exotic objects of scientific interest, often for public consumption. Charcot exemplified this approach to female hysteria in Tuesday lectures at Salpetriere Hospital, which featured live, theatrical demonstrations of female hysteria, as well as of Charcot's "observation, description, and classification."[35] Over a century later, Andreasson and her daughter are likewise held up as both objects of curiosity, and as female subjects out of control, in need of pseudo-scientific analysis and interpretation.

Fowler's objective posturing elides the complex, and in this case deeply gendered, nature of power relations at play during the hypnotic sessions. He writes about Andreasson's relinquishment of individual control in the name of scientific investigation with giddiness, while control over Andreasson's thoughts and memories are manifested even more explicitly than control over the Hills had been in *Interrupted Journey*, in control over her body. During fourteen sessions, both Betty Andreasson and her daughter Becky were hypnotized by Dr. Edelstein; each hypnotic session was attended by at least three male investigators. Present at each session were hypnotist Harold Edelstein, Fowler, and one or more of three Mutual UFO Network investigators in town to investigate the case, Fred Youngren, Jules Vaillancourt, and Joseph Santangelo.[36] Throughout the book Fowler registers his awe at Edelstein's ability to control the actions and emotions of his subjects. He reports, describing Edelstein's methods, that, "he once pointed his finger at Betty to show us her reaction: she went out like a light, and her body went limp like a rag doll."[37] He marvels at how "Betty and Becky relived their traumatic experience in great detail. They each expressed natural apprehension, fear, wonder, concern, pain, and joy." He adds later that the women, "were turned off and on like biological tape recorders! It was fascinating to see a practical demonstration of the mind's remarkable facilities for storing memory."[38] They are reduced to disembodied "minds" at best, and at worst to inanimate tape recorders and rag dolls.

The sexual overtones of the hypnotherapeutic process are especially thick in *The Andreasson Affair*. As Edelstein probes his subjects, the session dialogue sounds at times as if it were taken from a phone sex transcript. He first relaxes Betty, adding "you will have nothing to fear" and then asks "did they have to tie you down in order to perform the examination? . . . Were you strapped down, or were you held?"[39] Fowler observes that Andreasson was "deeply under the influence of Harold's soft but firm voice" as he says, "deeper and deeper . . . let yourself go. Deeper and deeper."[40] Fowler reflects that as she relived her buried trauma, "her suffering and ecstasy would be contagious."[41] Like an attendee at Charcot's Tuesday lectures, the reader of the abduction narrative is thus drawn in, a voyeur, willingly exposing him or herself to the contagion of abductee suffering and ecstasy.

Fowler concludes his inquiry into the affair with a question that has been taken up with gusto by subsequent abduction investigators. Fowler asks,

> If we accept such cases at full face value, one overriding question emerges: How many UFO abductees are there? How many like Becky and Betty Luca [the name of Andreasson's second husband] have "lost" a few hours of time and had information locked into their minds for future release: Others may exist like her, primed subconsciously with knowledge and messages from an extraterrestrial civilization.[42]

Having made the speculative leap to accepting accounts of alien abduction at "full face value," Fowler presses even further, asking "What would happen if this information dam were to burst into the conscious mind of thousands of people all over the planet?" What if each of us is, like Betty, a "loaded bomb"? Fowler himself has gone on to explore this proposition in two subsequent books, *The Andreasson Affair Phase II* (1985), and *The Watchers: The Secret Design behind UFO Abductions* (1990). Indeed some version of this "what if" question has driven all subsequent accounts of abduction, summoning abductees to offer up testimony of their own experiences, and invigorating popular interest in accounts of abduction through the 1980s and 1990s. I turn to these accounts in my next chapter, and to the volatile context of debates over memory that fueled them during the 1980s. In the following two chapters I continue to examine the alien abduction phenomenon as a site for the struggle to lay claim to personal histories, personal histories shaped by a shared and deeply felt sense of trauma and victimization.

2

The Invisible Epidemic
Abduction Traumatists

In *Missing Time*, Budd Hopkins relays the story of Virginia, an alleged abductee who recalls having a large gash in her leg as a child, a wound that bled a lot but was not especially painful. What confounds Virginia as she recalls the incident is that her family has no memory of it at all. So too does Hopkins's subject Philip report a scar of mysterious origin. When Philip asked his mother about it, she "could not remember anything about it either."[1] Hopkins seems perplexed by these incidents, asserting that "it is against everything we would normally expect that [Virginia and Philip's parents] have no idea at all of [their] origin."[2] He simply cannot fathom that the parents of young children might forget, or at least forget some of the details of, their child getting a cut: "I asked [Virginia's mother] if she remembered actually witnessing the accident . . . and she answered no. . . . Her recollections were admittedly —and strangely—vague."[3] Faced with the messy realities of both parenting and memory, Hopkins concludes that "more than a mere dollop of forgetfulness was stirred in from outside." More believable to Hopkins—and indeed to Virginia and Philip as well—is the alien thesis: "If the causes of their wounds were as Virginia and Philip recall them through hypnosis—incisions made by remote-control, robotlike machinery inside a UFO," he offers reassuringly, "then everything falls into place."[4]

In such stories, vague but disturbing incidents from our pasts are more satisfyingly told as tales of extraterrestrial, robotic violation. In such revisionist personal histories, intangible and remote sources of suffering are made tangible. New memories, retrieved via hypnosis, challenge older, murkier accounts. The alien abduction experts who are the subject of this chapter struggle to weave the strands of uncertainty about abductees' personal histories into ironclad narratives that prove the existence of aliens. The absence of precise memory in their subjects creates a lacuna to be filled with the stable—if otherworldly—figure of the alien. This chapter examines how, through the diagnosis and treatment of alien abduction as trauma, the abduction traumatists sought during the 1980s and early 1990s to medicalize and thus legitimize the phenomenon. So too does it interrogate the power dynamic that exists between alleged abductees and the self-styled experts who treat them, considering the abuses of power that may occur in the often voyeuristic process of retrieving memories of alien abduction.

Repressed Memory, Repressed History

During the 1980s memory itself seemed to be on trial in a variety of cultural locations. Popular interest in alien abduction boomed in the midst of, and in part as a result of, widespread anxiety and contention about memory; about its ability to reveal past trauma, to stand as evidence, to empower victims, to heal a variety of hurts. Indeed the 1980s were fraught with tension, conflict, and debate over the reliability of memory, the relationship between memory and history, and the relationship between memory and truth. Dominant accounts of the past—both individual and collective—were challenged on a number of levels in the culture at large. The social movements of the 1960s and 1970s had challenged easy acceptance of dominant, hierarchical accounts of the historical past; increasingly scholars revised accounts of historical events to include social histories and first-person accounts of the past. So too did the feminist movement challenge easy acceptance of patriarchal accounts of personal and family histories. The impetus to reclaim the voices of those who had historically been silenced was just one more factor in the emergence of what journalist Debbie Nathan characterizes as a "social panic" over the murkiness of memory during the 1980s as increasing numbers of people claimed to retrieve memories that had long been repressed.[5] The impetus to "believe the victims" of long hidden or repressed abuse—most often sexual abuse, most often of females—contributed to a cultural acceptance, even embrace, of new accounts of both personal and collective history. These various factors, this complex web of social forces, created the perfect context for the codification of abduction as trauma to be ventilated, diagnosed, and treated, and for the consequent classification of alleged abductees as victims in need of therapeutic treatment.

While the practice of hypnosis was kept alive by a burgeoning New Age movement during the 1970s and 1980s, it was widespread debate about the retrievability of repressed memory during the 1980s and 1990s that fueled the boom in abduction accounts and popular interest in those accounts, during those decades. Changing ideas about the nature of memory—chiefly about its ability to be "recovered" whole and intact despite having been repressed or blocked—lent credence to those claiming to come into memory of something long forgotten. During the 1960s and 1970s members of the women's movement reinvigorated the idea, somewhat dormant among mainstream psychologist professionals, that traumatic memories could remain buried in amnesia. They underscored the trauma of sexual and domestic abuse of women, while Vietnam veterans working in rap groups grappled with the trauma of war. In 1980, largely in response to these social movements, the American Psychiatric Association included Post Traumatic Stress Disorder (PTSD) in its diagnostic manual for the first time. Revived interest in trauma repopularized the idea that memories could return at unexpected moments, and that the process of remembering and forgetting was, for both men and women, in some cases beyond our control.[6] So too did it work to link men and women as victims, giving men license to see themselves as victims in response, perhaps, to social shifts that threatened to move them out of the center of power.

Allegations of a variety of types of sexual abuse, including Satanic ritual abuse, were waged throughout the 1980s. In the most typical scenario, caregivers such as parents and teachers were accused of violating children in their charge. Taken together, these widely publicized stories suggested that those places we deem most safe and sacred—our homes, schools, and churches—were in fact places of deep, pervasive peril. In several especially high-profile cases, children came to accuse day care workers of Satanic ritual abuse; adults "remembered" past abuse at the hands of allegedly Satanic parents, relatives, and neighbors. *Michelle Remembers*, published in 1980, told one such story of a woman who, under hypnosis, remembered her own abuse as part of Satanic rituals featuring her parents. The concept of mass repressed memory was brought to wider public attention by the 1983 McMartin preschool case. In this Los Angeles case, and others to follow in New Jersey and elsewhere, day care workers were accused of grizzly Satanic sexual abuse of their young charges. On the basis of the children's memories elicited by social workers and psychological counselors, a number of day care workers were convicted and sent to jail. So too was Richard Ingram, a chief civil deputy of a sheriff's department in Washington state whose daughters accused him and his wife of including them in Satanic and non-Satanic group sex activities throughout their childhood. In 1989 Eileen Franklin's recovered memory of seeing her father rape and murder her friend as a child was heard as evidence toward his conviction.[7]

George Franklin's trial initiated a public conversation about whether or not recovered memory could stand as evidence in a court of law. Experts were brought in to argue both sides of the case. Psychologist Lenore Terr testified for the prosecution, arguing that in the face of protracted abuse subjects could indeed become dissociative and repress traumatic memory.[8] Psychologist Elizabeth Loftus, testifying for the defense, argued that memory is malleable and therefore ultimately unreliable as evidence.[9] Largely on the basis of Terr's testimony, Franklin was found guilty in 1991. In that same year, high-profile disclosures of child sex abuse by celebrities such as Marilyn Van Derber (Miss America 1958) and actress/comedienne Roseanne Barr made claims of recovered memories ever more horrifying in their ubiquity. It was within this maelstrom of accusations, revelations, and debate that Hopkins and other abduction traumatists published their case studies of abductees' coming into memory of traumatic abuse by extraterrestrials. They did so with increasing zeal and media visibility, and with decreasing concern about the vicissitudes of memory.

It Is Better to Ventilate

The cultural climate in which such accounts circulated helped reinvigorate the notion set forth in early accounts of abduction by aliens that experience of unwilling contact with extraterrestrials lay just beneath the surface of consciousness for vast numbers of Americans and was only in need of unlocking. Indeed, in his first book, *Missing Time*, (1981), Budd Hopkins characterized alien abduction as an "epidemic" that he believed might "be almost entirely invisible."[10] As accounts of abduction by aliens proliferated during the 1980s and 1990s, the phenomenon came increasingly to be talked about in the therapeutic language of trauma, diagnosis, and treatment. A diagnosis of abduction by aliens could explain away a wide range of feelings and occurrences. In *Missing Time*, Hopkins draws focus to the invisibility of the trauma that unfolds under hypnosis, and the deeply disconcerting notion that things may have happened to us—may continue to happen now—that we do not remember. His fascination is coupled with a seeming inability to accept uncertainty about his subjects' pasts. He laments that, "very often the witness senses that something odd happened to him in the period of missing time and he simply doesn't want to find out what it was."[11] By Hopkins's logic, a vague sense of uneasiness ought to be enough to drive one to recover memories of abduction, for equally compelling to him is the prospect that abduction often leaves no traces: "no signs or clues may necessarily have remained."[12] He is palpably gleeful about the case of a young man who "was abducted in his early twenties, but who, like the others, had absolutely no conscious memory of a sighting; all that he had to go on was the 'feeling' that 'something may have happened' to him one night in 1973, on a particular road in Maryland, as he drove home from his girlfriend's house." Hopkins's rendering of the story reveals his rather voyeuristic pleasure in reporting that "hypnosis revealed a classic abduction."[13]

The idea that we are all potential sources of fascinating, if shocking information is intriguing, and experts like Hopkins seek to cultivate the sense in readers that they ought to unearth hidden facets of themselves and their pasts. *Missing Time* takes up Raymond Fowler's speculative proposition that untold numbers of us may be potential, or latent, abductees and it is the book that seems in particular to have opened the flood gates of memory about alien abduction.[14] Hopkins seems to view Fowler's notion that such memories might "burst into the conscious mind of thousands of people" as a sort of personal challenge. He describes how he and the psychologists work hand in hand to help those who report "lost time":

> The investigator begins his interrogation of the witness . . . very subtly, so as not to alarm them, the investigator inquires into the specifics of the time problem. He then asks if they experienced any unusual physical sensations, of heat or cold, or whatever. . . . The investigator then asks the witness if they would like to undergo hypnosis with a professional psychologist to help them recall the details of their encounter that they cannot remember.[15]

Hopkins opens *Missing Time* with an acknowledgment of the debt UFO investigators owe to "psychiatrists and psychologists who practice hypnosis" who, he suggests, by "relying upon regressive hypnosis as the most efficient method of unlocking the forgotten period of time" have "become our most powerful allies."[16] Indeed, Hopkins has, over the course of his career, moved from being an investigator who works *with* therapists to fashioning himself *as* a therapist. In response to the influx of letters he received in response to *Missing Time*, he began in 1983 to hypnotize patients himself. In his second book, *Intruders* (1987), Hopkins writes that his belief that "many people who have undergone consciously unremembered yet traumatic UFO abduction experiences" has led him to "shift the emphasis in [his] investigations from simple information gathering to therapeutic considerations—helping the abductee deal with fear and uncertainty and an inevitable sense of isolation from those who have not had to suffer through this unearthly experience."[17]

Hopkins also focuses single-mindedly on convincing people—abductees and readers—that abduction memories are of real traumatic events, possessed by untold numbers of people currently struggling under the weight of repression and denial. At the very beginning of his book he states that missing time masks "some kind of systematic research program, with the human species as subject," or "human sample taking."[18] Beginning with Hopkins, any tentativeness about the reality of what "happens" to abductees "inside the space ship" has dropped out of accounts of abduction.

Hopkins and other widely published abduction experts, including David Jacobs and John Mack, use the language and concepts of psychotherapy to authorize the "retrieval" of abduction accounts. The concept of ventilation is especially instrumental in gathering such accounts; emboldened by therapeutic rhetoric, Hopkins encourages potential abductees to "ventilate" rather than repress. He asserts to the mother who thinks her daughter may have been abducted that "it is better to ventilate a traumatic experience that might otherwise, if it is kept buried, cause difficulties."[19] Later he quotes a psychotherapist friend as saying, "Think of all the energy a person in a situation like that wastes, just trying to keep something unknown and disturbing out of his thoughts. It would be so much better to explore the experience and undergo whatever temporary pain there might be, just to not have to waste all that energy keeping the memory buried."[20] Hopkins concludes that, "ventilation of the experience is, I believe, therapeutically helpful for almost everyone."[21]

UFO investigator David Jacobs has also trained himself to perform hypnosis in order to access the trauma of alien abduction in his subjects. Jacobs is a tenured professor of American history at Temple University and author of *Secret Life: Firsthand Documented Accounts of UFO Abductions* (1992). Jacobs explains in the introduction to his book that he has been involved in UFO organizations since the 1970s. In 1973 he wrote his dissertation on the history of "the UFO controversy" in America, and in 1975 Indiana University Press published it as *The UFO Controversy in America*. Faced with the mystery of alien abduction, Jacobs decided that "if I were to make sense of what was happening, I would have to do abduction research myself. This meant that I would have to learn hypnosis." In order to do so he "discussed hypnotic techniques with [Hopkins] and other researchers. I read books on hypnosis. I attended a hypnosis conference. I learned about the dangers and pitfalls of hypnosis."[22] Learning hypnosis enabled him to glean "testimony of some sixty individuals," and to overcome "the memory problem: of alien enforced amnesia." With memory "problems" so persistent and visible in the culture at large, abduction traumatists stepped in to redefine that which already seemed problematic about memory; they argued strenuously that memory is troubled not by virtue of its instability, but by virtue of its vulnerability to control by external, alien agents.

Alien abduction investigators such as Jacobs have increasingly worked PTSD, and related ideas about traumatic memory, into their accounts of the abduction phenomenon. Jacobs has done so most explicitly, suggesting that, "While similar to PTSD, Post Abduction Syndrome (PAS) differs in that the external forces compel the abductee to repress the memories of traumatic events, even though the abductee may want to remember them" and that "PAS is generated not only by past experiences but by on-going events as well."[23] Jacobs's definition of the nature of alien trauma, shared by other experts and abductees, is telling. First, control over the process of remembering and forgetting is displaced onto the alien: repression is believed to be enforced, not a function of the human subconscious. Second, and more critical to understanding how abduction traumatists depart from others, is the notion that, unlike other sorts of abuse and trauma, abduction is not relegated to the past. Not only memories of events, but events themselves burst into the present, haunting abductees. Nonetheless, the PAS acronym worked to legitimize the notion of abduction by aliens, at least for those who felt they might themselves have been abducted. Though PAS was not listed in the American Psychiatric Association's *Diagnostic and Statistical Manual of Mental Disorders,* it seemed closely aligned with PTSD, which was. Abduction by aliens could thus be understood not as far-out belief but as a diagnosis demanding treatment. Finally, broadening acceptance of other narratives of repressed memory and victimization in the culture at large during this same period contributed what is perhaps best characterized as an increased willingness on the part of the public to entertain the notion that alien abduction might be real, if not to wholesale legitimization of the alien abduction phenomenon.

The Signs of Abduction

Since the publication of his book *Abduction: Human Encounters with Aliens* (1994), John Mack has headed up the Program for Extraordinary Experience Research (PEER), which is affiliated with Harvard Medical School. When people who feel they may have been abducted contact PEER, they are sent, among other things, a document called "An Experiencer's Guide to Therapy," which offers a quite thorough and useful overview of different sorts of therapeutic practices and what can be expected from them. Among them is hypnotherapy, and the guide warns that "some of the images recovered under hypnosis are memories of past experience, while others are symbolic representations of important personal matters, and it may be quite difficult to distinguish between the two. Thus, hypnosis as a means to recover the 'real truth' may prove to be quite disappointing." This consumer warning echoes Dr. Simon's warning given thirty years earlier against the charisma of hypnosis: "real truth" is thrown into quotation marks, suggesting that it is open to interpretation. Mack nonetheless continues to use hypnosis to treat abductees, and his book is surprisingly free, given his credentials, of the sort of caution about hypnosis and memory included in the PEER publication. He explains that, "the type of hypnosis or nonordinary state I employ has been modified by my training and experience in the holotropic breathwork method developed by Stanislav and Christina Grof. Grof breathwork utilizes deep, rapid breathing, evocative music, a form of bodywork and mandala drawing, for the investigation of the unconscious and for therapeutic growth."[24] His justification for using hypnosis is that "it is my impression that the reports provided under hypnosis are generally more accurate than those consciously recalled."[25]

The case study with which Mack opens his book is called, "You Will Remember When You Need to Know" and features Ed, a married technician in his forties. In it Mack explains that Ed's case was chosen among others for inclusion in the book precisely because it was "more plausible than the account he could provide from conscious memory" and thus "supports the argument for the power of hypnosis to recover memories of abduction."[26] Mack chose it because of its accuracy and plausability, because it represents hypnosis as a "clarifying" rather than "distorting tool." Among the things Mack seeks to clarify is the role his subjects' extraterrestrial victimization may play in challenging "the Western scientific worldview" and "Western scientific ideology" and in demonstrating that "our consensus framework of reality is too limited."[27] Clearly Mack seeks to critique rather than embrace the sort of rationalism that Hopkins espouses. Despite his scholarly, traditional credentials, his work is much more rooted in the New Age movement concerned as it is with "personal growth and positive living." The push to diagnose alien abduction, to quantify the sense of trauma it suggests and to treat it through therapeutic methods, seems common to all the experts I discuss here.

In the alien abduction scenario, while there is faith in the process of bringing to light, no cure *can* result. For although Hopkins promises to help abductees "move on," or in Jacobs's words, "come to terms successfully with the predicament that she [sic] finds herself in," the definition of this progress is unclear, for the source of trauma—believed to be both real and present—cannot be treated.[28] Perhaps as a result the focus shifts somewhat compulsively to the identification of clues, signs, and symptoms, to the imposition of order onto what is essentially a chaotic experience. Indeed, in the face of what is characterized as a "plague of uncertainty," Hopkins and others have made it their job to define abduction "clues:" By the end of *Missing Time* he assures his reader that "by now the reader is familiar with many clues, both obvious and subtle, which indicate the possibility of a buried abduction." In his presentation on "Recognizing the Signs of Abduction," which I attended at the Whole Life Expo, Hopkins included "body marks," "vivid dreams" (those including smells or pain), and "fears and phobias."

Other abduction therapists have provided similar lists: Edith Fiore's limited distribution, (and now out of print) book *Encounters* features one as its back cover copy. Her checklist of abduction symptoms includes "Inability to account for periods of time," "sleep disorders," "waking up with unusual bodily sensations," "appearance of mysterious marks on your body," "feeling monitored, watched, and/or communicated with," "vague recollections of a close encounter," and "unexplained healing of ailments or afflictions." Likewise a survey on the Alien Abduction Experience and Research (AAER) website offers an "informal survey" including the following questions:

Do you take more vitamins than most people?
Have you seriously considered [installing] a security system for your home even if there was no justification?
Have you had nosebleeds or found blood stains on your pillow for unexplainable reasons?[29]

Fiore insists, "If you've experienced one or more of these phenomena, chances are good that deep within your subconscious mind lie the buried memories of a Close Encounter of the Fourth Kind—an abduction by alien beings." *Encounters*, she promises, "will show you that you are not alone."

Of course, in the context of alien abduction, not being alone takes on complex meaning. On the one hand, it suggests the terrifying but exciting prospect that we may coexist with extraterrestrial entities. At the same time, it indicates that by coming into memory of abduction we become members of a community of people who have shared similar—and similarly vexing—experiences, or at the very least the same "truth as it is felt." Abductees too have cultivated this sense of what could be by appealing to other abductees to come forward. *Missing Time* abductee Steve, for example, is quoted as saying, "If anything happened to me, it could happen to you."[30] *Missing Time* ends with Hopkins's appeal to the reader that "if someone should strongly suspect such an encounter, the final page of the book provides information on how to go about reporting it."[31] Taken together these act as strong inducements to "remember." Indeed, Hopkins reports that he has received thousands of responses to his initial query.

They've Used Me! Believing the Victim

The social dramas surrounding accounts of repressed memory during the 1980s and 1990s demonstrated the ways in which ambiguity over the nature of truth and memory can be readily manipulated to different ends. The panic over Satanic ritual abuse (SRA), for example, resulted in the baseless incarceration of alleged nursery school Satanists and, more broadly, fueled an anti-feminist backlash against women who worked outside of the home and left their children in day care. In the case of alien abduction, experts—still mostly men, many of them uncredentialled—have found a means for shoring up their own power and authority by exploiting popular anxiety about the unstable and contested definitions of reality. They have done so, paradoxically, through an appropriation of feminist rhetoric about claiming one's own personal history as a means to empowerment.

Writing alien abduction narratives as stories of repressed trauma—a project in which I hope I have demonstrated many abduction experts are engaged—works to cast abductees as victims. Hopkins makes this equation more explicit in *Intruders*, written well within the trauma and recovery culture of the 1980s. Hopkins writes that the "sort of free-floating, apparently unreasonable dread" experienced by abductees is like that experienced by rape victims, for "on some level UFO abduction is a species of rape."[32] Alleged abductee and horror writer Whitley Strieber takes this analogy even further in his best-selling book *Communion: A True Story* (1987), published the same year as *Intruders*. He asserts that "there has been a lot of scoffing directed at people who have been taken by the visitors. It has been falsely claimed that their memories are a side effect of hypnosis. This is not true. Most of them started with memories and undertook hypnosis to attempt greater recall." He insists that "scoffing at them is as ugly as laughing at rape victims."[33] Likewise Jacobs, writing in 1992, contends that,

> No matter how they handle the experience, all abductees have one thing in common: they are victims. Just as surely as women who are raped

are victims of sexual abuse or soldiers can be victims of PTSD, abductees are victims who require sensitivity and, if needed, help in understanding what has happened to them and the possible consequences that abductions have had for their lives.[34]

In equating the experience of male and female abductees with victimized women, abduction traumatists register the history of trauma since the 1960s. The authorities who sought to legitimize inquiry into the Hill case in the early 1960s did so by comparing them to shell-shocked veterans—a mostly male population. In the context of the 1980s and 1990s, abductees were repeatedly equated with the typically female victims of rape and sexual abuse.[35] Abduction traumatists capitalize on the visibility victims of sex abuse have gained through the efforts of some feminists to end women's silence; to testify to the everyday realities of domestic and sex abuse. Many of the rhetorical moves made by abduction traumatists are drawn, specifically, from the feminist-originated incest survivor movement (ISM). *The Courage to Heal* by Ellen Bass and Laura Davis (1988) is held up by both defenders and detractors as the Bible of this movement. Like the alien-related sources I discussed earlier, it features an array of possible symptoms that allegedly point to the hidden truth, or repressed trauma, of childhood incest. The checklist asks, "Are you prone to depression?" "Do you find yourself clinging to the people you care about?" "Are you satisfied with your family relationships? Are you overprotective of your children?"[36] Those who have disputed the vagueness of Bass and Davis's incest survivor symptoms point to the near universality of these conditions: who among us is never depressed, is fully satisfied in familial relationships, and does not feel protectiveness (too much?) for their children? Bass and Davis nonetheless argue strongly that if you think you have been victimized, you have.

Both abduction traumatists and the ISM from whom they take a page, are motivated by an impulse to quantify a felt sense of pain, the source of which is either invisible, missing, or through some trick of memory, no longer fully present. In both cases, efforts are being made to name, know, and treat—to diagnose—psychic pain. What seems important to take away, however, is that such symptoms indeed speak to a general felt sense of pain and emotional suffering. In each case, details, clues and "evidence" are ultimately stand-ins for a larger emotional pain that subjects are otherwise unable to name and locate. Surely it can be argued that the impulse to speak one's pain is often a good one: the

ISM sought to underscore the victimization and oppression of women, to undo a historical power imbalance between men and women, locating that imbalance not only in the public, but also in the private, domestic sphere.

But to what end do we believe the victims of alien abduction, a crime whose alleged perpetrator is not even human? It is not as clear what power imbalance is redressed when we believe the victims of alien abduction. Certainly "ventilation" of alien abuse does not disrupt, but rather perpetuates an existing power imbalance between "victims" and "experts," for the more hidden truths and traumas are revealed, the more validated the expert becomes. One cannot dismiss the fact that experts with prior academic status may stand to lose that; certainly Mack and Jacobs have met their share of criticism from outside of the community of alien abduction believers. At the same time, while losing academic credibility, each has gained a certain subcultural popular celebrity and, along with that, book royalties and lecture fees. While I'm not suggesting alien abduction experts have become rich this way, constituting alleged abductees as victims does allow those who treat them to be perceived by many as healers, heroes, and truth-tellers. And believing the victims of alien abduction in the guise of both scientific evidence gathering and correct and sensitive politics sanctions the elicitation and publication of story after story of extraterrestrial dominance and submission.[37]

Not surprisingly, accounts of abduction produced in the 1980s and 1990s offer increasingly explicit accounts of sexual encounter between alien and human. In these accounts of sex with aliens, the experts present themselves as those faced with the difficult but scientifically important task of bringing the truth—including forced arousal—to light. Jacobs warns his reader in the introduction to *Secret Life* that, "this trip may be shocking to some, especially the descriptions of sexual procedures, but it is a journey that has to be made. If not, we may be playing ostrich in relation to an event of such fundamental importance that our failure to recognize it will be the subject of amazement for future generations."[38] Jacobs insists, "It must be emphasized that this is not a sexual fantasy situation, and most men and women feel that it is an uncontrollable and traumatic event."[39] John Mack likewise includes the story of a patient named Catherine that includes, he warns the reader, "the most difficult few minutes of my work with her." Mack continues, "as she sobbed and panted at times crying hysterically or expressing rage, I needed to assure her repeatedly of my presence and to express my sorrow over what she had been through as I asked for details. My sense was that she was determined to follow through to the end despite the fact that she was reliving a powerfully traumatic experience." During the session Catherine remembered that, "the tall being inserted 'a big metal thing' in her vagina, which was intensely upsetting. Then he took a longer and thinner 'version' of this and 'put it up inside me.' "[40] Catherine "became increasingly distressed, panting and crying, as she described how one of the beings spread her legs apart on the table and the examiner stared at her face and genitals."[41] Mack determines that he must continue, based on his sense that it is ultimately healthier, in Hopkins's words, to ventilate.

Hopkins argues that, "in none of these cases involving either men or women do we have what can be called a basically erotic experience . . . even if some of them result in a more or less involuntary ejaculation."[42] Despite the repeated denial (or overly narrow definition) of eroticism made by abduction hypnotherapists, published accounts of what occurs during abduction almost always include such accounts of arousal, penetration, and seduction, all "involuntary," forced upon the submissive abductee. Jacobs adds a description of portions of a "psychological procedure" he calls "Mindscan":

> From time to time the aliens will induce rapid, intense, sexual arousal and even orgasm in a woman. . . . A few abductees report that arousal occurs through manual, genital manipulation during Mindscan. Others think that it is a combination of physical and Mindscan procedures that quite suddenly creates sexual feelings. . . . In spite of their attempts to fight it, sexual arousal builds to a peak in a few minutes and then subsides.[43]

Mack's patient Peter remembers his feelings of violation as "a cup was placed over his penis, ejaculation was forced, and sperm taken from him." Scott reports a similar device and exclaims "they've used me!"[44]

Ultimately believing the victim of alien abduction allows top-selling abduction traumatists to offer up a type of sci fi porn, and in the last decades of the twentieth century there was an ample audience eager to consume it. The accounts of alien-human dominance and submission found in such books offer narratives of sexual encounter that need not be hidden behind plain brown wrappers; their presence in readers' homes may be authorized by the more socially acceptable pursuit of scientific, or paranormal, inquiry. And if Hopkins, Jacobs, Mack, and others are voyeurs, so too are their readers, who, through abduction narratives can watch *them* watch. While the various kinds of pleasure readers of abduction narratives take from their reading is not of primary concern to me, I am left wondering whether this is what abductees intend when they enter into a therapeutic relationship with an abduction expert. What is at stake for them in becoming players in these semipornographic dramas, cast as submissives, or terrestrial "bottoms" for the popular entertainment of thousands of readers? I turn to this set of questions in my next chapter.

3

Good Subjects
Submitting to the Alien

Jean is one of the hundreds of alien abductees who have turned to Budd Hopkins for help in making herself "whole again."[1] She is a sixty-five-year-old divorced psychotherapist who shares an apartment on West Fourteenth Street, in Greenwich Village, with a colorful cockatoo that flies around us, perching occasionally on Jean, or on the rims of our drinking glasses, as we talk. Of the New York area abductees whom I interviewed, Jean veers toward the New Age end of the interpretive spectrum. What Jean shares with almost all of the abductees with whom I have spoken is a sense that trying to remember and understand her abduction has taken her on a quest into her past, and into herself, to discover truths that lie hidden there.

Like many abductees, Jean's journey began with a conscious experience of seeing a UFO, in her case on Fire Island about twenty-five years ago. She recalls feeling "frozen" in bed by a bright light, but could not remember what happened next. She and a friend tried calling the Air Force but "they laughed at us." Jean did not think much more about the experience until the early 1980s when she read Hopkins's book *Missing Time*, which includes the stories of a number of people who, under hypnotic regression, recalled their own abduction by aliens. All of these abductees decided on hypnotic regression because they, like Jean, had memory lapses following what they describe as conscious sightings of UFOs. After reading *Missing Time*, Jean too decided to undergo hypnotic regression with Hopkins himself. Under hypnosis with Hopkins, Jean comments, "whoosh—it all came out." She now knows that she has been abducted since she was five years old, and continues to be abducted today.

I asked Jean how she felt upon recalling her abduction experiences. She explained that *before* her regression she had a general feeling of "victimization." "As a psychologist," she added, "I couldn't understand this and tried to come to terms with it." Reflecting on possible causes for such feelings, she noted that she had problems with her parents, "but nothing severe." She wondered, "what am I not understanding?" Hypnosis revealed many of the "classic," or typical, features of abduction including forced capture and physical experimentation and manipulation, as well as visions or messages about the fate of the planet. So although hypnosis was frightening, for Jean it was also validating and in her words "relieving." In fact "it was a big relief." She recalls thinking to herself "Holy shit—there's something real here."

Jean's experience typifies that of almost all of the alleged alien abductees with whom I have spoken and about whom I have read. Time and again people burdened with bad feelings for which they cannot account read a book on alien abduction, or see a television show or movie, that acts as a "trigger" that sometimes unleashes conscious memories of abduction. This often propels the person, if the resources are available, to seek the help of an abduction expert like Budd Hopkins. Such experts can be readily located through information in their own books, by contacting one of a number of UFO investigation agencies, such as the Mutual UFO Network (MUFON), and more recently through the ample resources available on the Internet. The accounts abductees offer about their abductions, accounts based largely on material "accessed" with the help of the therapist during hypnosis, are also accounts of coming into memory itself, of the process of piecing together their own pasts and creating a narrative that accounts for present feelings of unease. Remembering abduction is, for almost all alien abductees, part of a therapeutic process.

Within this process, many abductees come to identify themselves as victims. This chapter seeks to understand what may be at stake for them in this self-definition, for while it may be obvious why experts seek to treat abductees as victims, it is a more vexing problem to try to understand why abductees have come to view themselves in the same light. A host of conservative critiques of a so-called "culture of complaint" that emerged in the 1990s (mostly after the apex of popular interest in alien abduction phenomena) would suggest that abductees are just one more group of "crybabies," jumping on the proverbial bandwagon of complaint and blame-placing rather than pulling themselves up by their bootstraps and getting on with their lives.[2] Busy worrying aloud about the "fraying" and "decaying" of American moral character, these conservative critics at best overlook, at worst direct us to look away from, what may be real social causes of suffering or alienation that might produce such widespread feelings of victimization. They also fail to consider how it is that in the late twentieth century so many Americans have come to believe, paradoxically, that victimization is the most viable mode of empowerment available to them.

Jesus, Is That Your Penis? Techno-sexual Violation

In contrast to the vagueness of, the lack of referent for, uncomfortable feelings such as those expressed by Jean, contemporary accounts of abduction by aliens offer excruciating detail about the who, what, when, and where of remembered abuse. Alleged abductees offer very specific renderings (both in word and image) of the extraterrestrials they believe have taken them, the brightly lit, clinical spaces in which alleged abuse occurs, even of particular smells encountered on board the spaceship (including burnt match and wet cardboard). And nowhere is the sense of power struggle that seems to be at the heart of abduction accounts—the drama of dominance and submission—more reduced to its essence than in the repeated scenarios of sexual violation at the hands of the alien captors. Both male and female abductees report having been raped by technology-wielding extraterrestrials, sometimes seemingly ad infinitum. Jerry, for example, remembers something being implanted or removed from her vagina by the aliens fifty times.[3] John Mack's patient James remarks that, "I feel like a lab animal, just sort of lying there and taking it."[4] While aliens themselves are typically described as sexless, or at least without visible genitals, they wield numerous phallic gadgets that do the work of penetration for them. Hopkins reports that one of his female clients, for example, remembers "two small clips being attached to her labia, spreading them apart, and then a thin probe moving into her. She could not move, but she could sense the probe at or in her cervix, apparently snipping or cutting."[5] Inside the UFO Kathie describes lying down with her legs elevated while something "finger-thick" was punched into her vagina and on, it seems into her uterus. Andrea, another of Hopkins subjects, felt that the probe penetrating her was "long and hard and obviously of a diameter thin enough not to tear her hymen."[6]

Men too report the technical violation and penetration by aliens. In his best-selling *Communion* (1987), Whitley Strieber offers this graphic rendering of his forced anal penetration in the alien "operating theater":

Two of the stocky ones drew my legs apart. The next thing I knew I was being shown an enormous and extremely ugly object, gray and scaly, with a sort of network of wires on the end. It was at least a foot long, narrow, and triangular in structure. They inserted this thing into my rectum. It seemed to swarm into me as if it had a life of its own. Apparently its purpose was to take samples, possibly of fecal matter, but at the time I had the impression I was being raped, and for the first time I felt anger.[7]

When abductee Ed tells Mack he's been raped by aliens, Mack notes that, "I still wasn't sure if by 'rape' he meant a mechanical procedure of the type I had encountered in other abduction cases, or an actual act of intercourse."[8] Of course distinctions between the two blur for abductees as aliens both induce orgasm, often through the simulation of a hand and/or vagina, in order to collect sperm for the interspecies breeding project, and forcibly penetrate their male victims. Ed, for example, remembers "her" using "a very smooth, handlike thing."[9] In Strieber's account, as in other male accounts of abduction, there is sometimes the vague sense that the violating alien is in some way female, or at least female enough for abductees to justify their own sexual arousal (heterosexuality is evidently assumed, in all accounts I have read, to be the norm). Strieber thus remembers his shock and horror when, "She drew something up from below."[10] He reacts by asking "Jesus, is that your penis?" He feels deceived by the alien: "I thought it was a woman," but instead, "that goes right in me . . . punching it in me, punching it in me. I'm gonna throw up on them."[11]

Other abductees recall less clinical sorts of sex with aliens such as Mack's subject Ed, who reports one incident that occurred during his adolescence which certainly seems in keeping with the fantasy life of a heterosexual male teenager. Under hypnosis he reports to Mack that in 1961 he was transported in a "pod" wherein a female alien "sensed my horniness." They had sex, including "fondling of breasts, insertion of the penis in the vagina, and active participation by both individuals." He nonetheless recalls falling victim to "forced arousal."[12] Jacobs has also found "evidence" in hypnosis of aliens mentally forcing humans to have sex with others humans during captivity. In a telling displacement of those sexual desires deemed dangerous or kinky onto the alien, Jacobs adds that, "sometimes the aliens display a great interest in promoting human sexual activity, especially for young girls."[13]

The extent to which this procedure is sexually arousing, to which female or male abductees are desired or desiring, is a source of confusion for many abductees. On the one hand such procedures are described as strictly technical, used by the dispassionate aliens in their ongoing research project. Will nonetheless observes that, "it looks like a piece of machinery no good mistress of domination would be without, something rather kinky."[14] Ed expresses mild concern when he recognizes the desire of "the two guys," who he remembers "looking at me all over. . . . They look at my genitals. . . . They look at my back. They look at my rectum."[15] Ed, in contrast, assumes an utterly passive role in the proceedings: "somehow they made me erect and she mounted me. It was very perfunctory." He notes that, "She rode me and she was on top of me until I orgasmed, and then she got off and left the room and the two guys, they took little spoons and scraped the leftover semen off my penis and took it in a sample in a bottle and kept it. I never could move. She or they came and just took what they wanted." Ed subsequently, and somewhat indignantly, concludes that "they had more than a reasonable interest in my genitals."[16] Male abductees typically claim to resist desire for the advances of the alien and desire for their own submission, however, by emphasizing their own feelings of disempowerment.

To a certain extent, of course, such accounts resemble and seem indeed to be informed by dominatrix fantasies, fantasies of dominance and submission, typical to heterosexual pornography. But by attributing the desiring sexual gaze, and tendency toward kinkiness, to the alien, these male abductees can play outside of the boundaries of procreative heterosexual sex, without implication or censure.[17] So too can they play at transgressive desire and kinkiness, and assume the passive role fairly common in hetsex fantasy, shamelessly, guiltlessly, suggesting that this role, like their arousal, is quite literally thrust upon them.

I Wanted to Please the Leader

Yet within the larger context of coming into memory of one's abduction experiences, passivity and submissiveness are often framed as enviable qualities. This is especially true in the course of the therapeutic process. Since the Hills, abductees, while claiming forced loss of control to the alien, have in fact relinquished control to a host of experts offering to help them. Reflecting on the experience of undergoing hypnosis, the Hills note their utter submission to the trance, to Simon's commands, but seem untroubled by it. Barney notes,

> I began to realize that there were two things that could happen here: One, I could be hypnotized and made to forget that I had been hypnotized so that I would awaken and would assume that I hadn't been hypnotized at all; two, I could be hypnotized and if I was told I could remember, I would retain a knowledge of all that had taken place under hypnosis.[18]

Betty, recalling a session during which she fell into an unintended trance, recalls that, "I continued to feel that if it became too distressing, the doctor would be able to control it."[19]

Barney could not describe the spaceship he claims to have entered because, as he reports, his eyes were closed. When Simon asks why, Barney says "I did not dare open my eyes. I had been told to keep my eyes closed." When Simon asks who told him that he says somewhat vaguely "the man." When asked what man, he does not answer but rather adds that "it was comfortable to keep them closed."[20] When Betty is pressed to say why she would want to keep what she had learned secret she adds, "Because I wanted to please the leader, and because he told me to forget about it."[21] The Hills' comments suggest the ease with which abductees authorize the doctor to control remembering and forgetting. In a broader sense, they underscore how complicated the abduction scenario is in its symbolic enactment of power relations. While it is standard for abductees to report feelings of terror as they lose control over their bodies, minds, memories, and identity, so too do they at the same time register a certain pleasure in submitting. Surrendering control to the aliens, like surrendering control to the therapist, is something of a relief. What's more, obedient submission to alien and/or therapist is rewarded with praise for being a "good subject." Hypnotist authors of abduction accounts frequently characterize those who fall in and out of trance easily, such as Betty Andreasson, as "good subjects." And abductees, eager to "please the leader," desire themselves to be recognized as "good"—that is, easily tranceable, and by extension, willing to submit, to cede control to dominating external forces.

This mixture of fear and fascination with loss of control, and the desire to please "the leader" is especially evident in Strieber's *Communion*.

58 | *Good Subjects*

In it Strieber describes the process he went through in deciding to seek the help of a hypnotist. He notes with ambiguity,

> I had never been hypnotized before and I was apprehensive about it. . . . I was afraid of relinquishing control over myself, which seemed deeply disturbing. . . . I found, though, that I trusted Don Klein when he told me that even under hypnosis people cannot be readily compelled to say things they do not want to say. I would not be out of control, not really.[22]

Under hypnosis, Strieber remembers and details his rape and violation by aliens including forced ejaculation and anal penetration. And despite his insistence that "the hypnotized subject does have a will of his own," Strieber experiences "fear so raw, profound and large that [he] would not have thought it possible that such an emotion could exist."[23] This episode is so intense that it results in illness, including "lowered body temperature, weakness, an unpleasant sense of being somehow separated from the world around [him]."[24] Nonetheless, one of the first questions he asks upon coming out of his trance is "Was I a good hypnotic subject?" He is assured, to his relief, "You were excellent."[25]

An Interest in Woundedness

As the book unfolds, Strieber speculates that his abduction may be a sort of forced therapeutic confrontation with his past. After touching "a wand" to his forehead and inducing images that evoke emotions, such as a painful image of his dying father, he comments, "That is the last thing I would have thought would have come out of me."[26] He wonders what to make of this experience at once "strange and yet somehow or another so productive."[27] His hypnotherapist presses him to say in what way it was "productive" and Strieber answers, "Well, in two ways. One is, they learned a lot about me. . . . This afternoon I just learned a lot about myself. I learned a lot. Things I didn't have any idea worried me. About my dad and mother." Fairly early on, then, in his coming into memory of abduction, Strieber is able to reconcile his own feelings of having been a rape victim with speculation that perhaps his rape, and the larger alien project of human experimentation, had "a hidden and tremendously therapeutic potential which, if correctly marshaled, could be of great value."

Strieber concludes that the aliens were "trying to figure out how [he] ticked," and one wonders if the pleasure of being the object of such attention is not at least as valuable as its therapeutic potential for Strieber.[28] In addition to the relief/release of submission, abductees often express pleasure in feeling that they are the focus of the therapeutic gaze; that what makes them tick is important enough for sustained attention and analysis, not only by investigators and psychologists and hypnotists, but also by aliens. Some abductees, including several of those whom I interviewed, think that the aliens are most interested in human emotion and psychology, or at least in *their* emotion and psychology.

Henry, a Brooklyn abductee whom I interviewed in 1999 (and whom I discuss in more detail in chapter 9) went to Dr. Jean Mundy in New York City for help understanding what he thought might be memories of an alien abduction. He was surprised that under hypnosis "nothing came through about being experimented on."[29] Rather, "it seemed" (Henry went out of his way to emphasize the "it seemed" acknowledging that he does not know in what sense these memories refer to actual events) "I was taken aboard a ship . . . and I was examined psychologically." When Dr. Mundy asked Henry why he thought they had come for him, he conjectured, under hypnosis "because of the car accident." When pressed further, he explained, "The car accident I had the week before in Union, New Jersey. I survived, didn't get hurt or anything but I had been driving the Volkswagen turning from Route 22 onto the parkway, turned over several times, had my seatbelt on. The car was totaled, no one was in it but I was really shaken up by it. There was a psychological exam to see my state of mind, how I was handling a trauma like that." Both Strieber and Henry posit that the aliens are interested in them *because* they have suffered. Their victimization is, in the end, what they have to offer; their emotional and physical suffering is made over as the object of alien desire.

As players in this drama of dominance and submission, abductees are paid attention to. As victims of some special form of Post Traumatic Stress Disorder they warrant attention, and they do so because their alien abduction experiences are extraordinary. Indeed the renewed credibility given ideas about trauma and its after-effects seems predicated on the definition of trauma as out of the ordinary or, in the language of the American Psychiatric Association's diagnostic manual, "outside the range of usual human experience."[30] Judith Herman takes exception to this definition in *Trauma and Recovery,* making the excellent point that sexual abuse and domestic abuse are not in the least extraordinary; rather, they are endemic in a culture in which existing systems of power keep women and children disempowered. And yet emphasizing the extraordinariness of trauma—at least in the case of alien abduction—serves the dual purpose of gleaning sensational narratives, and of authorizing alleged abductees, experts, and readers to ignore those frustratingly intractable sources of terror and suffering that plague subjects in their everyday lives. Mundane and ordinary sources of terror and suffering are, by virtue of their ordinariness, submerged in the subtexts and margins of alien abduction accounts. Abduction traumatists play a major role in overlooking those terrestrial sources of anxiety that plague their subjects in favor of the more fantastic scenarios of extraterrestrial brutalization that unfold under hypnosis.

There is a lot to be learned from reading between the lines of alien abduction stories for how abductees talk about the conditions of their lives outside of their alleged experiences with aliens. Whatever forces have traumatized them, ordinary or extraordinary, they can talk about them—or at least about the truth of their suffering as it is felt—in the context of their abduction therapy. The therapeutic process, while in many senses ineffective in "treating" alien abduction, does help locate a culprit in what might otherwise be a depressingly protracted reality of inequality, social abuse, and individual and social suffering. Abductees talk indirectly, through their accounts of alien abduction, about the strains of life in the present day—from racism, single-motherhood, and economic instability, to chronic illness, anxiety, and insomnia.

Though Fuller does not explore the pressures that the Hills felt as an interracial couple in the early 1960s, those pressures were great enough to have sent Barney to therapy in the first place, and Dr. Simon indeed concluded that whatever had happened to them may have been the result of the related pressures they experienced.[31] Fowler mentions the everyday burdens that Betty Andreasson dealt with as incidental evidence of her pluck at sticking with the painful process of retrieving "the truth" about her abduction. These burdens included the following: In 1966 her husband was in a head-on collision and spent months in traction, whereupon her parents moved in temporarily to help her with her children. In 1975, the year leading up to her hypnosis, Betty divorced her husband and began to "shoulder the responsibility of raising her remaining family single-handedly."[32] This family included seven children, ranging from three to eleven years old, all of whom she decided to move from Massachusetts to Florida in order to get permanent help from her parents. This was at the same time that she was undergoing hypnosis. Just before Betty left for Florida her father died; she moved to Florida anyway and got work as a waitress. And in 1977 two of her sons, aged twenty-three and seventeen, were killed in an automobile accident.[33] Fowler marvels at Betty's spirit, and her ability to stay focused on extraterrestrial events:

> The round trip to Dr. Edelstein's office was over four hours. The long hypnosis and debriefing sessions, coupled with the burden of remembering the unnatural experience, left Betty mentally and physically exhausted. But packing, leasing her house and managing everyday household affairs had not dissuaded her from cheerfully attending each hypnosis/debriefing session. We marveled at the tenacity of this woman. In spite of the pressures of a busy schedule, it was obvious that she was determined to find out what had happened to her.[34]

It never once occurred to any of the seven investigators in attendance that Betty's experiences may have been connected psychologically to the staggering conditions under which she was functioning. No wonder that, in the midst of her "busy schedule," Betty A. showed up for her "debriefing" sessions: she was being listened to, intently, by a roomful of people, all focused solely on her, her past, her present, her mind, her body.

Kathie Davis, characterized by Hopkins as a "fine hypnotic subject," is the central subject of *Intruders*.[35] During her numerous regressions Davis "remembers" a detailed array of experiments to which she has been subject by her alien captors. It is Davis's account that serves as the centerpiece for Hopkins's theory, explored in detail in my next chapter, that humans are abducted by aliens as part of an interspecies breeding project. Hopkins also includes information about the terrestrial realities with which Davis was dealing at the time:

> Since her birth in 1959 poor Kathie had suffered just about every medical anomaly I had ever heard of. Her overweight condition seems to be the result of hormonal imbalance. She began menstruating regularly at

the age of 7, the beginning of her pubescence. By the age of 10 she had grown to her present height, 5'3" and was under treatment for high blood pressure. At the age of 14 she was operated on for gall stones, and her gallbladder was removed. She has suffered from hepatitis, and almost died during a severe bout with pneumonia which presented all the symptoms of what is now known as Legionnaires' disease. She had her appendix removed and once spent two weeks in traction because the two extra vertebrae in her spine somehow fused. Very early in 1983 she was hospitalized with what seemed to be an asthmatic attack. A lung collapsed and she was treated with an intravenous bronchial dilator; she suffered an apparent allergic reaction to the medication and spent the following two weeks in the hospital.[36]

Elsewhere in the text Hopkins speculates that Davis has "had a long struggle with several chronic, possibly psychosomatic illnesses—colitis, irregular heartbeat, acute anxiety, insomnia and so forth."[37] Yet these conditions—a lifetime of hospitalization and illness—are not in and of themselves worthy of Hopkins's attention. Rather, they corroborate his foregone conclusion that she has been abducted by aliens. Her health problems, she and he agree, are the result of long-term alien tampering.[38] As in the stories of incest survivors discussed in my last chapter, anomalies in one's personal history can only make sense in light of recovered memories, of incest or, in this case, alien abuse.

In some cases accounts of sexual abuse at the hands of aliens seem to stand in for what may be real sexual abuse at the hands of humans. Among the seven abductees John Mack considers in *Abduction,* almost all grapple with a history of sex abuse in the family. We learn, for example, that Sheila is coping, in the wake of her mother's death, with grief compounded by the knowledge that her mother was an incest survivor. Before entering hypnotherapy with Mack, Sheila suffered severe depression and made an unsuccessful attempt at suicide. Lee suffers from fear of sexual intimacy that she feels must be attributable to childhood sex abuse; her brother Scott, also an abductee struggles with a lifelong seizure disorder. Jerry's parents were divorced when she was eight. She has no contact with her father. A high school dropout, she married at nineteen and then divorced after learning that her husband was "playing sexual games with the children involving oral sex."[39] She continues to struggle with alcohol abuse. Catherine too has lost contact with her father, a disabled alcoholic prone to "impulsive angry outbursts."[40] Mack underplays these facets of the personal histories he has collected by confining them to case study prefaces. He sees these details as relatively insignificant, except perhaps as evidence in support of his theory that perhaps abducting aliens, "may play some sort of healing or restorative role."[41]

Believing the alien-related details of abduction allows and authorizes abductees and abduction experts to ignore, minimize, or elide other facets of abductee experience. Mack, who opens his book with an anecdote about a thirty-five-year-old woman who "remembered consciously being sexually abused by her father at age four and weeping in the cellar afterwards. Several familiar alien beings—she recalled encounters from fourteen months old—'checked me to see if I was hurt, cause I did hurt,' found underwear for her . . . and 'did up my sandals.' "[42] For Mack, this experience, "led them to intervene in a protective or healing manner." Mack's inability, or unwillingness, to even consider this as the fantasy of a child who has just been abused by her father is unsettling, perhaps especially because of the authority his credentials and institutional affiliation confer. Mack engages, but skirts, the question of whether some alien abductees are in fact sex abuse victims who "remember" abduction rather than their actual human sexual abuse.[43] He will only allow that abductees may *also* be sex abuse victims, and that that is why aliens may be drawn to them. He arrives at the disturbing conclusion that "the alien beings seem interested in human woundedness."[44]

To a certain extent Mack epitomizes the cultural climate in which abduction accounts have flourished, a climate in which victims, trauma, and woundedness are items of widespread popular fascination. It is, then, perhaps especially critical to consider his assertion—and the alien abduction phenomenon—closely in order to understand who, if anyone, is served by the idea that it is through pain, and perhaps only through pain, that we may be transformed. If one indeed believes in the actual existence of abducting aliens, I suppose that the notion of working with, rather than seeking to eradicate, the source of one's felt pain may be productive. If, however, one reads the abducting alien as symbol, metaphor, or symptom of even more difficult and inchoate individual and collective feelings of anxiety and disempowerment, as I do, then the decision to accept and embrace one's victimization is deeply troubling in its passivity. It perversely glamorizes extraordinary types of suffering while directing us to look away from those more common problems that produce human misery and suggests, finally, the futility of seeking to combat such misery on a social or collective level.

Eradicating Peculiar Dread

Among the abductees I have read about and spoken with, most, like the experts who treat them, want to minimize problems they have had beyond or outside of their abductions. It has become an article of faith for many abductees that all present feelings of anxiety, traumatization, and suffering can be traced back only to the alien, as in Jean's assessment, with which I opened this chapter, that the alien is something "real" on which to fix blame for otherwise unattributable bad feelings. Jean notes that as a child she "rebelled" against her parents, that she had "problems" with them but "nothing severe." So too does Queens abductee Mike minimalize any terrestrial strains he may feel, insisting instead on the actuality of alien abduction. Mike is of Puerto Rican descent, and grew up in Washington Heights. He is in his early fifties, married, and has two teenaged children. When I met with Mike in his home in Ozone Park, he recounted his first conscious memory that something was amiss. He was coming home from a bar—he insists he was not drunk—and saw a "huge football shaped light hovering over a building."[45] He did not consciously think it was a UFO, but experienced "raging paranoia and fear" and was "scared to death." Mike woke up the next morning bloodied, with a swollen eye and nose. He did not know how he had gotten into bed, but thought he must have been mugged. At the Emergency Room he claims the doctors wanted to know about his nasal surgery, about which he knew nothing. Some time later he had an anxiety attack when he saw floating before him what he now realizes were alien eyes. Once he began to explore these strange occurrences through hypnotic regression with Hopkins, he "got confirmation after confirmation of the real." Yet again, as in Jean's case, the "real" is defined as the most extraordinary scenario of alien control and manipulation.

I asked Mike if there were not other factors in his life that might have caused an anxiety attack or nervous breakdown during this period. He had told me earlier about a sporadic employment record, difficult always with two children to support. He had worked as a crisis intervention counselor at a rehabilitation center, then as a graphic artist until 1989 when "the printing industry died." He then opened a music store that closed in 1991 because of an economy in which "no one was buying anything." He now makes a go of it as a freelance computer graphic artist. He nonetheless insists that nothing in his background would justify such extreme emotional upset. He rather offhandedly notes that the mere fact that his father chased him with a belt occasionally cannot have warranted a midlife anxiety attack.

I do not mean to suggest that all abductees are victims of some sort of well-defined, nameable form of abuse that gets projected onto the alien. Rather, I want to read closely those facets of alleged abduction experience that those in the abduction community—as well as conservative detractors of a "culture of complaint"—dismiss, for while memories of aliens get "ventilated," other forms of personal and social suffering remain repressed and ignored, deemed unworthy of attention. Taken together, we see that such ordinary stresses and strains are, perhaps by virtue of their ordinariness and intractability, enough to strain us to the breaking point. For some, perhaps abuse by aliens constitutes an extraordinary trauma more palatable than money problems, chronic ill-health, or belt-wielding parents. So too is alien abuse perhaps more palatable—even pleasurable in the ways I have suggested above—than personal and social neglect. And submitting to the hypnotist and/or the alien, proffering, if unconsciously, a quasi-pornographic narrative, is perhaps a small price to pay for the attention abductees gain.

Once abductees "remember" the "reality" of abduction, relief soon follows; or, in Jean's words, whoosh, it all comes out, like the simultaneous pleasure and pain of involuntary orgasm or ejaculation. For Mike, coming to recall all of these violent and traumatic experiences of alien abduction "helped him understand everything." The "memory" of his experiences threw things into focus for Mike, as he retrospectively realized that every "weird thing" that had happened to him was "abduction related." The revelation of his victimization by aliens "fit like a glove." Steven, the *Missing Time* abductee discussed earlier who had the feeling that "something may have happened" to him on a Maryland road in 1973, was, like Jean and Mike relieved to know "that there had been a cause, after all, for his peculiar dread of that specific stretch of Maryland highway."[46] While experts cultivate identification of abduction "reality," so to do victims take comfort in being able to name what ails them, and to place it "out there" beyond their control.

Resisting Abduction?

Within the alien abduction scenario, most abductees find both a source for feelings of victimization, and a means for expressing their own passivity and submissiveness. And yet, at the same time, increasing numbers of them reject the victim label, attempting to resist fixed interpretations of their experiences, or of themselves as inherently wounded and traumatized. Such folks often point the finger at Budd Hopkins who, they believe cuts off other, more positive or enlightening interpretations of their otherwise puzzling experiences. While most abductees have arrived at some theory of their own about what "really" happened during abduction, they are generally wary of any interpretation that is too neat or fixed, insisting on the complexity and opacity of the abduction experience. There is also a growing sense among alleged abductees since the mid-1990s that the truth of what is retrieved during hypnosis is open to interpretation, that experts are to be taken with a grain of salt, and that abduction should only be talked about and interpreted by those who have experienced abduction. Accordingly, abductees increasingly ask to be called "experiencers" rather than abductees.

For some, this wariness stems from a distrust of hypnosis specifically: even Betty Hill is now adamantly opposed to the use of hypnosis to treat abductees. In her recent correspondence with the Center for UFO Studies she states, referring to the growing number of abduction experts, that, "I am alarmed at the harm they are doing to innocent people with their brainwashing to make money for themselves." People who think they may have been abducted continue to write to Hill for help, and, as she notes, "if one had hypnosis, I refuse to see them. They are brainwashed. I am interested in real abductions, and always advise the person against hypnosis."[47] In the intervening years since the Hills first met Dr. Simon, it seems that her suspicion that the doctor was in some sense the controlling and manipulating alien force has, for her, been realized.

Hill's loss of faith in retrieved accounts of long-forgotten experiences coincides with a larger cultural shift away from the sorts of "believe the victims" sentiments that fueled the social panic discussed in my last chapter. Members of the False Memory Syndrome Foundation (FMSF), founded in 1992, have worked hard since then to discredit the use of retrieved memories as evidence of child sex or Satanic ritual abuse.[48]

Composed mostly by parents who had been accused of such abuse, the FMSF have argued that,

> False Memory Syndrome is especially destructive because the person assiduously avoids confrontation with any evidence that might challenge the memory. Thus it takes on a life of its own, encapsulated and resistant to correction. The person may become so focused on memory that he or she may be effectively distracted from coping with the real problems in his or her life.[49]

In 1994 the FMSF, particularly critical of the use of techniques such as hypnosis in eliciting "memories," succeeded in lobbying the American Medical Association to make an official statement against the use of retrieved memories as evidence. The statement reads, "The AMA considers recovered memories of childhood sexual abuse to be of uncertain authenticity, which should be subject to external verification. The use of recovered memories is fraught with problems of potential misapplication." Partly as a result of pressure exerted by FMSF, George Franklin's conviction, discussed in my last chapter, was overturned in 1996: evidence emerged that Eileen Franklin had indeed been hypnotized before testifying, and her memories bore closer resemblance to (incorrect) details of the case reported in the mass media than to the actual facts of the case.

An alien abductee self-help movement also emerged during the 1980s and 1990s and abductee Katharina Wilson has been at the forefront of this movement. Wilson has kept a detailed diary of her abduction experiences since 1983, some of which she shares through her newsletter, "Puzzle Pieces: A Self-Help Guide for Abductees." According to Sean Casteel, the UFO investigator who interviewed Wilson for the *Mutual UFO Network UFO Journal*, she is notable for her "determined rebellion against the authority of 'the typical abduction scenario' as laid out by major abduction researchers like Budd Hopkins and David Jacobs."[50] She emphasizes her own authority, which is based not in expertise, but in experience, arguing that she is more able to relate to abductees because, "on a very basic level, Budd is a researcher and I'm an abductee."

Wilson's rejection of expert authority has not, however, resulted in a rejection of the belief that she has been abducted by aliens. Like Strieber

68 | *Good Subjects*

and Henry, she asserts in an online interview with UFO investigator Michelle LaVigne (published on Wilson's website) that,

> My experiences have shown me that the aliens are interested in human psychology. This is evident in my encounters that involve theatrical concepts. . . . Stimuli have been presented to me through a variety of methods and the aliens have observed and probably recorded my reactions. They have also studied my psychological reactions and thought processes involving different emotions, but they seem most interested in my ability to feel empathy.[51]

Wilson hopes to empower other abductees by advocating forms of resistance to abduction, and by challenging a rigid concept of abductee victimization set forth by traumatists.

Her suggested modes of resistance, however, do not include a rejection of the belief that one has been and will continue to be abducted. Wilson notes that "In 1994 I was becoming tired of the same old thing and I silently told the aliens that if they 'had' to interact with me, it was going to be on my terms. . . . I was angry and frustrated with the aliens for using me so long in their psychological experiments." She says that by 1995, "my experiences definitely changed. . . . I wasn't used as much in a psychological and physical sense." UFO researcher Ann Druffel, though not an abductee herself, devotes an entire book to the title subject in *How to Defend Yourself against Alien Abduction*. Her book features "alien abduction resistance techniques" including "mental struggle," "physical struggle," "righteous anger," "protective rage," "intuition," and "appeal to spiritual personages."[52] Such strategies seek to move abductees beyond the feeling that they must continue to be victims. While they do offer "coping strategies," they once again fall short of attempting to "cure" abduction: of moving abductees beyond the belief that are being abducted. They redefine abductees as "survivors" of alien trauma, thus placing them one step beyond victim, but insuring that they remain on the same continuum of victimization, of trauma and recovery. Read this way, alien self-help is no more than the most recent plot twist in this ongoing cultural narrative of woundedness.

In *Hystories*, Elaine Showalter contends that while "epidemic hysteria" exists on "one extreme of a continuum with feminism, as a body of language of rebellion against patriarchal oppression, it is a desperate and ultimately self-destructive form of protest."[53] I tend to agree with Showalter up to a point: the sense of community and identity abductees form through their belief in having been abducted results in a compromised form of empowerment. Although they are active members of a community of believers; although they find a way to talk about suffering in the context of the abduction scenario; and although they may take a certain pleasure in identifying as submissive to external dominating forces, theirs is a belief system that is in its most basic sense about their lack of control over the world around them. Yet in the end Showalter indulges in her own form of blaming the victim: she blames abductees for blaming "external sources" such as "alien infiltration" for what she deems "psychic problems."[54] But Showalter makes too neat a distinction between internal and external, personal and social: surely "psychic problems" are themselves shaped and determined, in part, by "external sources" or forces. More useful is psychologist Janice Haaken's observation (about people with multiple personality disorder) that "the chronic demands of daily life can also be experienced as a form of captivity." Haaken adds that, "dissociation not only is a defense against trauma but also can be a defense against a world that holds one captive without providing sufficient integrative possibilities or pleasure."[55] To believe one has been abducted by aliens is to be able to transform social captivity and limited possibility into a type of pleasure, albeit bounded. If one's alternatives are living with "peculiar dread" and bearing the "burden of uncertainty," alien abduction makes a perverse sort of sense.

4

My Body Is Not My Own
The Intimate Invasion of Alien Technology

While many alleged abductees shun publicity, John Velez has been quite vocal and public with his experience. During an interview with John in his home in Ozone Park, Queens, he explained that he considers himself a survivor of alien abduction who is morally compelled to "stand up and be counted," and to let the public know that "there's something serious going on." This is why John agreed to be interviewed on a *Nova* special about alien abduction in 1996. Here is an excerpt from the transcript, available on *Nova Online*:

> *Nova*: So you've probably had experiences that might have to do with genetic experiments—have you been part of this?
> *Velez*: Yes. On several occasions I remember being subjected to a procedure that involves taking semen. Placed on an operating table, immobilized. I was induced to have an erection—Mind you there are no sexual feelings or any passion connected with this. It's a very cold procedure. I remembered feeling very stiff and sore in the groin region. And they have a cone-shaped device that's attached to a long hose, that comes from a wall. They placed that over my genitals. I experience an electrical tingling sensation, and then an orgasm. The semen is collected by this device.[1]

When asked by *Nova* why he believes aliens are here, John, after admitting his own uncertainty, concluded that, "they need us in order to reproduce themselves."

Many alleged abductees—especially those who have undergone hypnotic regressions—share John's belief that as alien abductees they have been unwilling participants in some sort of intergalactic, interspecies breeding project.[2] Velez's response also offers a glimpse into how, in the abduction scenario, an overarching sense of one's vulnerability to and violation by forces beyond our control—of power operating on us—is mapped onto the human body. As we spoke in his living room he did insist that he and his family bear "grooves, dents, and scars" from their encounters. His wife allegedly awoke with a strap mark and groove on her thigh that their doctor could not make sense of, and his son awoke once with "healed scars" on his knees. According to John (who did not share any of his own body marks with me during our interview) he is the only one in his family who wants to "deal with it" even though it is "scary shit."

The sorts of techno-medical violation reported in the scenarios such as John's are the most commonly shared features of abduction accounts and so have come, to an extent, to define the phenomenon, separating it from other sorts of accounts of UFO or alien-human contact. In one sense, as I have argued in preceding chapters, abduction is a site of struggle over one's own psyche, the truth of one's memory and personal history. So too, as I explore in this chapter, is it a site of struggle over control of one's body, especially one's reproductive and sexual function, as well as what is perceived to be one's biological or genetic destiny.

It's Just a Simple Test

John, like many other alleged abductees, reports having been subjected to invasive "procedures"—during his abduction he is rendered powerless by the external force of his extraterrestrial captors and the technology they wield. The inability to control one's own body in the abduction scenario typically begins with actual physical capture and unwilling flight and culminates with a forced medical examination. During the examination the aliens allegedly take blood, scrape skin, clip hair and nails, shoot tagging devices into the cranium, and insert ocular, oral, nasal, and rectal probes. The seemingly endless variety of procedures are performed on abductees against their will while they are strapped to metal examination tables and hooked up to a tangle of wires and tubes under the blinding glare of examination lights.

Betty and Barney Hill set a precedent for the subsequent (hypno)therapeutic treatment of abduction. So too do the details of what allegedly happened during their abduction as revealed under hypnosis distinguish their story from previous accounts of sightings and contact reported during the 1940s and 1950s. Unlike those other accounts of abduction by aliens, the Hills' account featured their physical capture and clinical violation during a series of medical experiments conducted against their will. As reported in *The Interrupted Journey,* during hypnosis Betty Hill recalls having been given a "complete physical examination by intelligent, humanoid beings" during which the aliens stuck a needle into her navel:

> I see the needle, and it's bigger than any needle that I've ever seen. And I ask him what he's going to do with it . . . and he said he just wants to put it in my navel, it's just a simple test and I tell him, no, it will hurt, don't do it, don't do it. And I'm crying and I'm telling him, 'it's hurting, it's hurting take it out, take it out.' . . . I don't know why they put that needle into my navel. Because I told them they shouldn't do it.[3]

Hill objects, but to no avail. When the exam is through, she asks her captors to explain the purpose of this forced procedure and is told, to her astonishment, that it is a pregnancy test. She continues to seek information, attempting to assert some sort of control over her situation: "I asked what kind of pregnancy test he planned with the needle. He did not reply, but started to insert the needle in my navel with a sudden thrust. Suddenly I was filled with great pain, twisting and moaning."[4] Though Barney is hazier about the details of his examination, he does remember "lying on a table" and "thinking that someone was putting a cup around my groin."[5] While Barney does not explicitly interpret the uses of the cup, he does sense a need to capitulate to the aliens' agenda in order to survive: "I will be very careful and be very still and will be cooperative, and I won't be harmed."[6] In order to assuage the terror he feels, he chooses a combination of prayer and dissociation, later recalling his decision to, "just stay here and pretend that I am anywhere and think of God and think of Jesus and think that I am not afraid."[7]

To UFO buffs and investigators at the time, these reported procedures and the sense of fear and paralysis described by the Hills seemed to come out of nowhere. UFO sightings had been reported since the late 1940s, and a handful of Americans had reported seeing and having some contact—usually described as friendly—with UFO occupants. But this description of abduction, what happened during it, and the aliens themselves, was a new twist in the existing plot of supposedly real human-alien interaction. It is for this reason that UFO investigators and abduction experts continue to point to the Hill story as authentic, uncontaminated, they argue, by preexisting accounts. Preabduction accounts were, for the most part, centrally concerned with the possibilities of mass destruction or national invasion, thus reflecting the postwar, postatomic context of their telling. While the possibility of invasion by an alien army was a mainstay of science fiction dating back to H. G. Wells's *War of the Worlds* (1898), it received a shot in the arm during the Second World War and the postwar period, resulting in a glut of alien invasion films during the 1950s. These included, in chronological order, the film version of *War of the Worlds, Invaders from Mars, Zombies of the Stratosphere, Invasion USA, Killers from Space, Invasion of the Body Snatchers, Earth vs. the Flying Saucers, Invasion of the Saucer Men*, and *Teenagers from Outer Space*. Some of these alien invasion films also featured alien control of human bodies. In *Invaders from Mars* (1953), aliens implant citizens with screwlike devices in the back of the neck in order to insure a populace of docile allies who will assure the success of the Martians' inevitable takeover of Earth in their quest for a habitable planet. The "snatching" of bodies by the creeping alien menace in *Invasion of the Body Snatchers* (1956) likewise posits the body as conduit for global military and ideological domination.

As in these alien invasion movies, and in most if not all science fiction involving aliens, the Hills suggested that the abducting aliens had access to knowledge they did not, knowledge conferred by the aliens' superior intellect and technological advantage. Yet accounts of human abduction by aliens beginning with the Hills' have more in common with, for example, Aldous Huxley's *Brave New World* (1932) than with alien-themed predecessors. Huxley's novel, written between the world wars, registers the threats of Communism, Fascism, and industrial mass-production, all of which conspire in placing the needs of the state above the needs of individuals. Huxley begins his novel by walking readers through the artificial production of babies in a series of rooms —from the fertilizing room to the decanting, or birth, room. He thus underscores the complete control of individuals by the state from the time of conception. Written roughly thirty years later, and registering that intervening history in ways I will discuss below, *The Interrupted Journey* is the first allegedly true account of contact with aliens that begins to introduce a similar set of anxieties about the mass management and manipulation of human creation. This clinical facet of the abduction scenario as it emerged during the 1960s seemed to register anew a set of anxieties about the personal implications of advances in technology—specifically biotechnology and the increasing technologization of the body.

In some respects, then, abducting aliens can be read in early accounts as stand-ins for state authority on the New Frontier. More specifically, they register anxiety about state sponsorship and control of scientific authority during the Cold War, and about the growing social and moral authority of medical experts in general to manage an increasing number of spheres of human activity, including sexuality and reproduction. During the early to mid-1960s many of the sorts of reproductive technologies that Huxley prophesied were realized. Such advances were often discussed alongside optimistic assessments of American technological and scientific supremacy. In *Life* magazine's twenty-fifth anniversary issue (1960), for example, both outer space and the inner space of the human body are presented as sites for sci-tech progress, for what *Life* calls the "explosion of science." The Sputnik crisis conspicuously absent from their overview, this anniversary issue heralds "Man" as having conquered "the last of the extreme heights, deeps and wastelands of this earth" and is described as now ready "to leave it" (15). The new destination, it would seem from the articles that follow, was the human body itself. These popular accounts of scientific progress bear close analysis; in them, the stuff of science fiction is made real, and the lines between science fact and science fiction, between the present and the future, collapse with interesting consequences. This popular, and indeed often prescriptive literature about the "explosion" of certain types of knowledge and expertise during the early to mid-1960s helps elucidate one important cultural context for the Hills' modification of the story of alien-human contact.

The Human Body and/as the New Frontier

In "Explosion of Science," articles on the inner space of individual cells, on the mysterious behavior of viruses, and on the miraculous mapping functions of DNA all conspire to render the human body as a fantastic, exotic location. Likewise, an article in the June 1964 volume of *Reader's Digest* explores "The Wondrous Inner Space of Living Cells." The article begins with what must have been a startling and confounding claim: "They saw cells walking—and it was a fascinating performance."[8] It goes on to describe cells as "complex entities, each with a specific mission in life that it strives mightily to carry out."[9] Throughout, cells are rendered as actors: they "bulge," "creep," and "perform." Each cell has a surface that is its "face:" it "swallows," "gulps," and "calls" out to other cells. What's more, "DNA is the dictator of them all."[10] Human beings in their complex entirety are merely observers of this action in such accounts. In the context of the science explosion, readers of lifestyle magazines learn, to see a life form is not only to know it, but also to invest it with human qualities. At the same time, these cells, viruses, and genes exist outside of and somehow separate from "us." In such renderings of biological progress we see a blurring between "them" and "us" that results in a defamiliarization of the body; people were able to see themselves as something strangely other than, or outside of, themselves.

Five years after the anniversary issue of *Life* discussed above, another special issue of *Life* was published, devoted specifically to the explosion of biotechnology. "Control of Life" includes a series of features that together explore the possibilities of genetic engineering, fetal surgery, and what would by 1969 be called in vitro fertilization. "Control of Life" exemplifies the ways in which investigations into new scientific and medical breakthroughs were reported in such magazines in the early to mid-1960s. It tells a story of technical progress in the futuristic Space Age idiom characteristic of its historical moment, about the exploration and colonization of human bodies by science, and the implications of that project for the national/human future.

These articles also tell a story about a powerful and exclusive alliance between doctors, technology, and fetuses, now made visible through the miracles of new imaging technologies. Fantastic images accompany pieces about the magic of medicine, the miracles of doctoring, and the body as fallow terrain onto which a fantasy future is mapped. As the passive title and accompanying cover photo of an expressionless woman lying prone on an examination table suggest from the start, the human being is the object, not the subject, of control.

The penetrating entities here are doctors and clinicians; the fetoscopes and other visualization technologies that they wield; and the staring, breathing fetus itself who the pictures suggest may be quite capable of looking back. Each invasion is authorized, so it seems, by the naturalized march of "progress," and must be endured, the reader is to believe, for the good of humankind—for the future itself.

Readers of "Control of Life" meet a number of expert (male) doctors

76 | *My Body Is Not My Own*

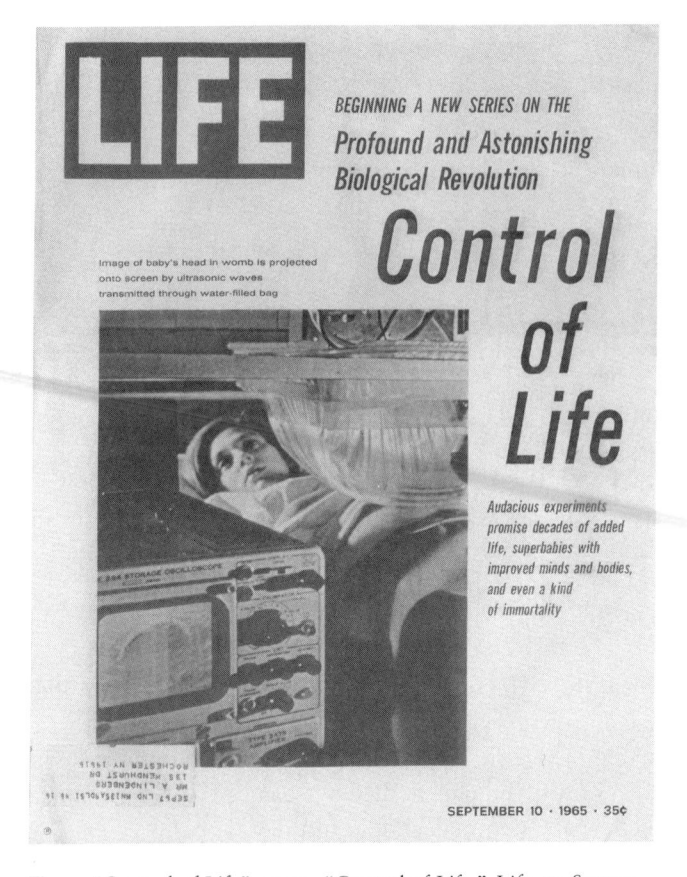

Fig. 4. "Control of Life" cover. "Control of Life," *Life*, 10 September 1965.

who, in rapturous and sensational language, forecast the possibilities of the "profound and astonishing biological revolution" announced on its cover. Readers are first introduced to a Dr. Hafez, who rhapsodizes about techniques of gestation outside the human body. Dr. Hafez reports that such techniques are particularly suitable to the Space Age as a potential means for colonizing other planets. This article is accompanied by a picture of what the reader learns are "dummy vials"—mockups of vials containing various animal embryos. The text reads,

> When you consider how much it costs in fuel to lift every pound off the launch pad . . . why send full-grown men and women aboard space-

ships? Instead why not ship tiny embryos, in the care of a competent biologist who could grow them into people, cows, pigs . . . anything we wanted—after they get there? After all, we miniaturize other spacecraft components. Why not the passengers?[11]

While the text suggests "man" as colonizer, the subtext and accompanying images suggest man—in this case most often represented by the prone body of the woman—as colonized, reduced through the intervention of technology, to the level of sheep, cattle, swine, or rhesus monkey. In the Space Age, the text suggests, human life has the equivalent value of a "spacecraft component;" distinctions between man and animal and man and machine are simultaneously collapsed. A subsequent piece in "Control of Life" continues to build the case for the scientific management of human offspring, this time through genetic engineering. Here Dr. Kermit Krantz reports with untroubled optimism that "someday . . . scientists may be able to improve the physiques, mentality and even talents of children before they are born—thus in effect creating superbabies." He adds, "if we learn enough—who knows?—maybe we can turn mediocrities into Einsteins." Later we learn that Dr. Steward, who has been working with modes of nonsexual reproduction also imagines creating duplicates of the "world's greatest geniuses." The text coyly adds that Dr. Steward, seemingly unaware of the disastrous ramifications of eugenics proposed only twenty or so years earlier in Nazi Germany, "declines to speculate upon the futuristic implications of his research." Perhaps most importantly, in each of these future scenarios, for the good of future society, it is the "competent biologist," not the human parent, who is equipped to oversee not only the reproductive process, but also the care and nurturing of the young. These experts —most often men—are depicted as clearly superior to non-experts/women, even in their ability to manage the family scientifically.[12]

Throughout "Control of Life," the identity of parents—mothers and fathers—is upstaged not only by technical experts, but also by the proposed agency of the fetus itself. Readers of *Life,* as well as of advice columns such as "Tell Me Doctor" in the *Ladies Home Journal* in the 1960s were introduced to the notion that the fetus in utero was not so much a thing as a person, an idea that has become commonplace through the pro-life rhetoric of the 1980s an 1990s. Indeed, a 1963 piece in *McCalls,* "The Secret World of the Unborn," happily reports that the fetus "is neither a quiescent vegetable nor a witless tadpole, as

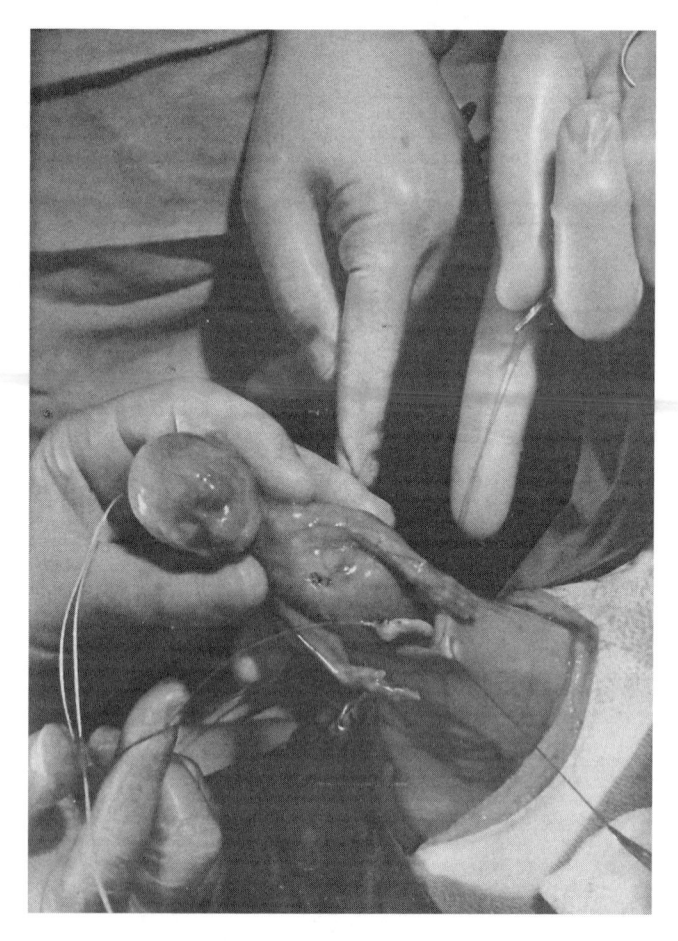

Fig. 5. Surgery on fetal monkey. From "Control of Life," *Life,,* 10 September 1965, 63.

some have in the past conceived him to be, but rather a tiny individual human being, as real and self-contained as though he were lying in a crib with a blanket, instead of his mother, wrapped around him."[13]

The notion of fetal patienthood, or personhood, pervades "Control of Life" as readers learn about doctors busy "perfecting other ingenious methods of observing and treating unborn children."[14] In the feature on fetal surgery, we witness a monkey fetus, lifted out of its mother's uterus which has in turn been lifted out of her. The accompanying text informs us that "isolated in its mother's womb, the human fetus until recently has been inaccessible to direct medical and surgical care."[15] As techniques improve we are told "fetuses will undoubtedly be removed for transfusions, medication, or correction of defects."[16] We are assured that at this point the "patient within a patient will have come into his own," not only treatable, but already socialized. This is particularly striking in contrast to the accompanying photographs, which suggest not so much socialization and therapeutic treatment as autopsy and vivisection. While the fetuses are repeatedly represented as children, people, and patients, the mother is not so much an actor in, as she is a setting for, this human drama; the human father is entirely absent from most such narratives of conception and reproduction.[17]

Feminist historians of science have investigated the historic circumstances through which the fetus has been redefined as patient, and the (pregnant) female body subjected to medical and social surveillance and management. As Rosalind Petchesky notes in *Abortion and Woman's Choice: The State, Sexuality, and Reproductive Freedom*, the post–Baby Boom fertility decline that began in 1958 and continued through 1973 drove obstetrician/gynecologists to find the "new patient population of the fetus."[18] During this period, an increasing number of women were entering college and the labor force, marrying and bearing children later in their lives, and divorcing more frequently. New technologies such as amniocentesis, in vitro fertilization, electronic fetal monitoring, ultrasound, magnetic resonance imaging, and fetoscopy all "[carved] out more and more space/time for the obstetrical management of pregnancy." What's more, as historian Dorothy Nelkin notes in *The DNA Mystique: The Gene as Cultural Icon*, while popular interest in eugenics waned in the United States after revelations of Nazi atrocities, it was insofar as "expectations of the medical and social benefits of regulating reproduction had a prominent . . . place in both infertility research and scientific human genetics" that interest in eugenics persisted through the 1950s and 1960s.[19]

Value is placed throughout "Control of Life," on the optimistic yet dispassionate management of bodies; like the aliens who operate on Betty and Barney Hill, the doctors here express only the most perfunctory concern for the well-being of people they treat. The aliens' unemotional, clinical demeanor is emphasized by both Betty and her husband Barney, who remembers being led into an examining room and told, "Don't be afraid. You don't have any reason to be afraid. We're not going to harm you, but we just want to do some tests."[20] When Betty struggles and protests against the repeated insertion of the needle into her navel, she remembers that her captors "looked very startled, and the leader bent over me and waved his hand in front of my eyes. Immediately the pain was completely gone, and I relaxed."[21] As in future accounts of abduction by aliens, the palliatives that precede the inevitable procedures may take the abductee's pain away, but they do not alter the fact that alien clinicians remain in power while their human subjects are reduced to the role of human guinea pigs. Like the women who recede into the literal and figurative background of "Control of Life," abductees have little recourse to respond to the particular vision of the future that drives the actions of those busy tinkering with their bodies.

So too for Barney Hill, and male abductees to follow. Indeed, one of the most noteworthy and striking features of abduction narratives is the extent to which the gendered model of power relations suggested in prescriptive literature of the sort discussed above has been appropriated by men.[22] In alien abduction, men too find themselves objects of the technical gaze, and are equally subject to intimate bodily violations. In *The Interrupted Journey* Barney remembers in particular the violation of the aliens' eyes, remarking, "Oh those eyes! They're in my brain!" Abductee Whitley Strieber describes them as eyes that "are asking for something, perhaps even demanding it."[23] Hill further recalls his "shoes being removed . . . I had been told not to open my eyes, and it would be over quickly. And I could feel them examining me with their hands. . . . They looked at my back, and I could feel them touching my skin right down my back. . . . And I felt something touch right at the base of my spine, like a finger pushing. A single finger."[24] By the 1980s the somewhat ambiguously techno-phallic "finger" pushing at the "base of [Barney's] spine" is fully realized by male abductees as the sodomozing alien anal probe, to which I return in subsequent chapters. The cross-gendered nature of these accounts suggests that for abductees, in the face of technical power—of the knowledge, access, and advantage conferred by it—we are all exposed, reduced, known; we are all equally likely to fall victim.[25]

In stories of abduction, the spaceship/clinic is the site of struggle between technically advanced alien clinicians and captive, immobilized human patients.[26] As Barney describes it, the room to which he and his wife were taken was filled with "different kinds of equipment, gadgets, all over the wall. . . . Everything seemed to look as if it were made of metal or plastic, but there was a white tone to everything. The surface of the table was hard and smooth and cold."[27] This story emerges as the power conferred by the doctor's expertise was augmented by a number of converging social forces in the United States, similar to those that shaped the emerging power of those psychological experts discussed in my last chapter. From the postwar period through the 1970s, a new, growing technical-professional class extended its control from the management of military and state institutions to the management of social, domestic, intellectual, and personal spheres. It often did so at the behest of—and with funding provided by—the state, and in the service of Cold War, national security imperatives.[28] The Space Age rhetoric of futurism, as seen in "Control of Life," only served to enhance the scope of medical authority: accordingly, the doctor surveys and controls not only the present but also the future space of the body. The use of human subjects in state-sponsored radioactivity experiments from the 1950s forward, which I discuss at length in chapter 6, demonstrated that the struggle for control of one's body was not just enacted between individual doctors and patients, but also on a collective level, between citizens and the state.

In the tradition of technocratic ideology in place since at least the Progressive Era, those possessed of scientific authority and technical expertise have long insisted on their own political disinterestedness and neutrality. Yet this insistence has been met with skepticism and suspicion invigorated many times over during the latter half of the twentieth century. The sheer destructive potential of technology was made manifest in the United States' use of the atom bomb; the increasing power and status of a postwar military-industrial elite became a focal point for antiwar protest during the war in Vietnam.[29] Articles such as those found in "Control of Life" dramatized the ways in which military technologies born of war were being brought to bear in the management of creation: it was the invention of SONAR for example, that enabled peering into the womb, and the impression of being peered back at. That technologies of creation and destruction may in fact be one and the same is a paradox with which many abductees grapple in their accounts of abduction by aliens.

While the audience for the sort of prescriptive literature I have discussed above is never univocal, the changing story of contact with aliens registered both the biotechnological innovations of the 1960s and public discussion of them. Through accounts of human abduction by aliens, the power/knowledge struggle between expert and nonexpert assumes a particular, if fantastic, form and location. By positing the alien as part medical technician, part bureaucrat, and part fetus, abduction narratives began during the 1960s to give shape to anxieties about the increasing power of a growing technical-professional class to control all spheres of human activity, no matter how intimate. By positing humans as prone patients/victims, they remind us that disinterestedness and neutrality in fact often serve some and disserve others. From the mid-1960s forward, abduction narratives pose and repose the question, if "technology" will bring us to a New Frontier of national, and/or human, development, where does that leave me? And more importantly, what if I am the New Frontier?

5

An Ongoing and Systematic Breeding Experiment

In 1987 Budd Hopkins's second book, *Intruders: The Incredible Visitations at Copley Woods,* as well as abductee Whitley Strieber's best-selling abduction account *Communion: A True Story,* were published. These books marked the beginning of a boom in both accounts of alleged alien abduction and in popular interest in, and media coverage of, the alien abduction phenomenon. By the mid-1990s, accounts of human reproductive violation at the hands of aliens were represented in a seemingly limitless variety of cultural sites, low and high: in self-published conspiracy literature; in tabloid newspapers; in best-selling paperbacks such as those on which I focus in this chapter; on television talk shows; on shows devoted to the investigation of paranormal phenomena such as *Sightings, Strange Universe,* and *In Search of . . . ;* in dramatic series focusing on the abduction phenomenon, most notably *Dark Skies* and *The X Files;* on television comedies including *Frasier* and *Kids in the Hall;* in advertisements for cars, airlines, and candy bars; and in documentaries produced by the Learning Channel and PBS. In this media explosion emphasis on the encroaching threat posed by aliens to human reproductivity and physical well-being has become central to the most popular, widely circulated accounts of the "truth" of alien abduction. The often explicitly gynecological/proctological alien medical examination, including the anal probe, has come to be a standard and ubiquitous feature of alien abduction, the object of parody on numerous television shows including *The Simpsons* and *South Park.*[1]

In one sense the story form set up by the Hills remained the same in the 1980s and 1990s: average people in the course of daily activities such as cleaning house, sleeping, or driving claimed to have been paralyzed, taken, examined, returned, and made to forget everything that had happened in the interim. At the same time, the story was elaborated on and expanded in critical ways by both investigators and abductees.

All continued to talk and write about forced reproductive experimentation but with increasing explicitness. These more current accounts reflect the increasing possibilities of reproductive technologies as well as fetal medicine (which boomed in the latter half of the 1970s), and genetic engineering and the attendant anxieties that emerged alongside them. So too do they increasingly reflect anxiety not only about external control and management of bodies, but also about questions of morality surrounding the creation and/or destruction of human life. Abductees continue to experience themselves—in contrast to the alien—as confused and powerless amateurs, pawns not only in the project of technological progress but also, it would seem, in the raging political debate surrounding abortion and a woman's right to choose.

I Don't Understand What They're Saying

A central facet of the interspecies breeding project remembered and reported by abductees is the forced in vitro fertilization of women. This allegedly includes, as in actual in vitro, now commonplace, the removal of an ovum from female abductees, its fertilization ex utero with human sperm, and the reinsertion of the embryo in the female body for gestation. Each step of the process—all forced and, like other traumas inflicted upon the abductee, remembered only through hypnotic regression—is painstakingly detailed in most published abduction narratives. In abduction, gestation outside of the human body *happens*: whether we want it to or not. And as Dr. Hafez playfully and speculatively predicted in 1965, it is a fantastic version of the "competent biologist," in this case the ultracompetent but unemotional alien, who controls this process, still not the male or the female human parent.

Intruders is the book first, and most centrally, concerned with proving that the purpose of abduction is an interspecies breeding project. In it, Hopkins argues strenuously, "Though it is an extremely uncomfortable issue to face, the fact remains that from the beginning, publicly reported UFO abduction accounts contain details which unmistakably point to an interest by UFO occupants in the process of human reproduction."[2] He adds that, "an on-going and systematic breeding experiment must be considered one of the central purposes of the UFO abductions."[3] Hopkins opens his exploration with a revisionist reading of the Hill narrative that points to the innovations in biotechnology in the intervening years as "evidence" of their use by aliens during the same period. Hopkins notes that, "a decade or so later" after the publication of *The Interrupted Journey*, "a device similar to the needle described by Betty is commonly used in Western medicine." He goes on to explain that,

> The laparoscope is a long, flexible tube containing fiber optics which are magnified for internal viewing. The instrument is inserted directly into the patient's navel, not for pregnancy tests per se, but for a variety of related reasons—including the removal of ova. So-called test-tube babies are produced by using laparoscopy to locate and remove ova from the female for later fertilization outside the uterus with 'the sperm of one's choice.'[4]

Hopkins's ironic tone in referring to the "so-called test tube babies" is curious; there is a sense that even when the product of in vitro is real, its definition is provisional, fictional, does not mean any one real thing: what are they really? He suggests that we can only tentatively name and know them; they are human but somehow also altered or manufactured by the intervention of technology. This rhetorical ambiguity resonates with commentary about "superbabies" in the "Control of Life" essays. "Superbabies" are entities who, upon their imminent arrival, were accorded "a kind of immortality." This is not a wholesale endorsement—doubt edges in to the most optimistic assessments of such progress. Technical interventions, Hopkins's comments suggest, continue to disrupt both our sense of what is natural, and our ability to name, to know, or to have any connection with the products of such technical intervention. At the same time, Hopkins literally sets "the sperm of one's choice" in quotation marks, suggesting that it is not only the intervention of technology, but also the intervention of choice that disrupts an assumed natural order in the 1980s.

The collective anxiety expressed by these abductees about the encroachment of technology into "natural" human functions has no doubt been occasioned by the realization since the 1960s of what were then only scientific and technological possibilities. In contemporary accounts of abduction one sees the degree to which reproductive technologies, while no longer entirely new, nonetheless remain both alienating and awesome. By the time *Intruders* was published in 1987, "so-called test-tube babies" were a reality. Serious work on human in vitro fertilization

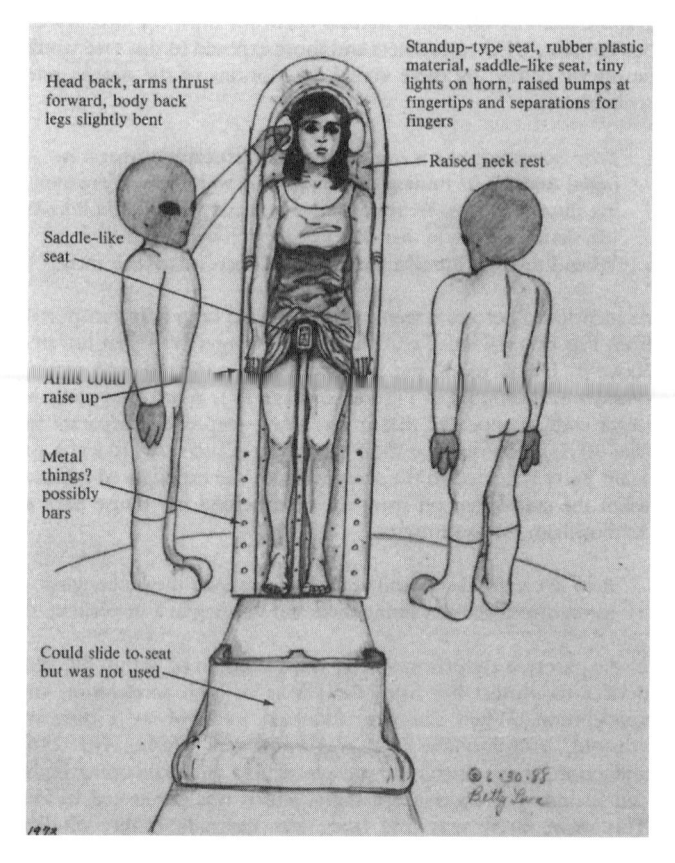

Fig. 6. Betty Andreasson's rendering of an abduction experience. Raymond Fowler, *The Watchers: The Secret Design behind UFO Abduction* New York: Bantam Books, 1990), 118.

began alongside the emerging abduction phenomenon in the mid-1960s, most notably through the work of two British doctors, Robert Edwards and Patrick Steptoe. Early results of Edwards's work on maturing eggs in vitro were published in the *Lancet, Scientific American,* and *Nature* in 1965. By 1969, Edwards and Steptoe had succeeded in fertilizing a human egg with human sperm outside of the human body.[5] In 1978 Louise Brown, the first "test-tube baby," was born to Lesley Brown, a young woman who, upon agreeing to be part of Edwards and Steptoe's experiments, did not realize that she was the first to do so, but, in fact, thought that the practice was already commonplace. In *Our Miracle*

Called Louise, Lesley Brown recalls that, "I just imagined that hundreds of children had already been born through being conceived outside of their mother's womb."[6] Lesley Brown's ignorance is important to note: it suggests the difficulty with which the nonexpert can know what is scientifically possible or actual at any given time. At the same time it points to the science-fictional nature of a process like in vitro that, while discussed extensively in mass media up through the late 1970s, was nonetheless still quite remote to the experience of most people.

Abductees take confusion about scientific possibility and its personal ramifications to its imaginative extreme. In the 1990 sequel to the *Andreasson Affair, The Watchers,* Andreasson expresses the extent to which confusion about reproductive technologies persists. In trying to make sense, fifteen years later, of what her alien/doctor captors have told her about the procedures to which they have subjected her, Andreasson is left with a sort of glossolalia, a sci-tech speaking in tongues. She reports, "They're telling me that they have to extrapolate and put their protoplasma in the nucleus of the fetus and the paragenetic. . . . I don't understand them. Something like the paragenetic will utilize the tissue and nutrients to—I don't know—transform the creature or something like that. . . . I don't understand what they're saying."[7]

Hopkins and others also step in to reinterpret specialized information. In *Secret Life: Firsthand Documented Accounts of UFO Abductions* (1992), Jacobs argues that the abducting aliens "want human sperm and eggs. . . . They want complete knowledge of the reproductive areas of human life."[8] Following Hopkins, he suggests that "egg harvesting" is a "constant feature of the abduction experience," one that is "ultimately directed to the production of offspring."[9] He describes the procedure as follows:

> With one hand he [sic] presses on the woman's abdomen in the region above the ovaries, and with the other he inserts a variety of instruments into her vagina. The first is a speculum-like instrument that creates an opening large enough to work with. Then he inserts a long, thin, flexible tube that women report goes in very far. . . . Most women in some way know that he is taking an egg.[10]

Even John Mack, who offers a somewhat more spiritual and expansive interpretation of alien abduction in his book *Abduction: Human*

Encounters with Aliens (1994) assumes assisted reproduction as a central facet of the perceived experience. Mack confirms that "it seems that some of the same women have been taken at later times during ovulation for the removal of ova from the Fallopian tubes. After the ova are retrieved by this process they are then apparently fertilized and brought to term outside the womb."[11]

Once the eggs are moved outside of the womb—outside of the space of the human body—the alien intervenes. In the abduction scenario, while ex utero, the human egg is combined with human sperm taken from male abductees by force. The sperm is taken by a variety of techniques hinted at in Barney Hill's memory of a cup over his groin. Male abductees have variously reported "a suction device of some sort," "some sort of tube or container," a "faucet thing, like a suction." Scott reports to Mack that it was the "wires that were applied to his testicles, in combination with the suction device over his penis that stimulated his erection and were 'making it happen.'" All the "stuff" the aliens were taking from him was being used, Scott knew, to "make babies."[12]

Abductees report that in abduction, the alien doctors add one extra, and critical step to this process: in creating the embryo, the aliens somehow manipulate it in order to include their own DNA, resulting in what Mack colorfully calls "the altered conceptus."[13] As Mack's patient Jerry reports, "she has been given information from the aliens that . . . after combining the male and female germ substance, the aliens alter the embryo is some way, perhaps adding a genetic principle of their own."[14] Hopkins speculates that,

> With our own current technology of genetic engineering expanding day by day, is it not conceivable that an advanced alien technology may already have the ability to remove ova and sperm from human beings, experimentally alter their genetic structure, and then replant altered and fertilized ova back into unknowing host females to be carried to term? Ova that can be removed can also be replaced, even by our own present day medical technology.[15]

Accounts of abduction produced since the 1980s increasingly register concern—as seen in John's comments to *Nova*—about the possibilities of genetic engineering and manipulation of human-alien offspring. As in

Velez's assessment, the sexualized procedure of sperm gathering is just one step in what *Nova* characterizes as "genetic experiments." The accounts I discuss here were all produced before the first complete "draft" of the Human Genome Project, and the successful cloning of Dolly the sheep. Even in the current climate of what Nelkin calls the "sacralization of DNA," wherein "spiritual imagery sets the tone for popular accounts of DNA, fuelling narratives of genetic essentialism and giving mystical powers to a molecular structure," the popular media continue to represent genetic engineering and manipulation as deeply science fictional, and in many instances horrifying in its implications.[16] Scientists remain virtually unanimous in their disapproval of human cloning; even Dr. Ian Wilmut, the embryologist responsible for Dolly, has expressed his greatest fear at "any kind of manipulation with human embryos."[17] Yet for many abductees, these science fictional possibilities have long seemed real; widely reported advances simply stand as evidence for them of what they have long known to be true.[18] The ex utero vulnerability of the embryo to forces beyond human control continues to highlight the strangeness—indeed the alienating effect—of assisted reproduction. So too does it underscore the vulnerability of what many humans believe makes them special, of what they believe to be their biological or genetic "essence." Rather, they are cast as raw material subject to the whims of scientific progress.

Once the fertilization process is completed, according to Mack, "the altered conceptus is reinserted in the uterus during a subsequent abduction, allowed to gestate for some weeks" only to be re-removed later in the pregnancy. As Hopkins describes it:

> A fertilized egg is eventually "planted" back inside the uterus; if all goes well the embryo develops normally and a healthy, normal baby is born. . . . Now all of this leads to the unwelcome speculative inference that somewhere, somehow, human beings—or possibly hybrids of some sort—are being produced by a technology obviously—yet not inconceivably—superior to ours.[19]

For Hopkins, what is technically possible becomes not only probable, but real. Female abductees, or "host females" provide a collective forum for his leaps in logic and dystopian imaginings about genetic engineering, and for the assertion of his own expert status.

They Took My Baby

According to the logic of most abductees, it stands to reason that if clinical procedures and sexual arousal are forced, so too is the production or destruction of offspring. It is in this facet of the interspecies breeding project scenario that a whole new set of anxieties gets folded into accounts of alien abduction produced since the 1980s, anxieties about parental agency and the politics of reproductive choice. Some female abductees report forced, on-board abortion procedures, and feelings of sadness and confusion at mysteriously terminated pregnancies. Kathie, as Hopkins reports, realized she was pregnant early in 1978: "Positive blood and urinalysis tests confirmed the fact. . . . Things were proceeding happily. . . . until one day in March when Kathie awoke with what seemed to be a normal menstrual flow. . . . a visit to her doctor confirmed her fear: She was no longer pregnant. Yet there had been no apparent miscarriage. . . . She just wasn't pregnant anymore."[20] Kathie remembers her confusion and distress: "I knew I'd lost the baby. . . . I went in to have the test, but I knew what it would show. . . . I kept saying they took my baby. . . . They took my baby, and I cried so hard they didn't know what to do with me. But I knew somebody took my baby."[21] As Jacobs explains it,

> the abductee with the implanted fertilized egg may not realize that she is pregnant even though she stops menstruating. The abductee may have been extremely careful in her use of birth control, or she may not have had sexual relations of any sort for many months, and therefore there would be little or no reason to believe that she was pregnant. Nevertheless . . . she may have a 'pregnant feeling.' She may take a home pregnancy test that shows positive, and then she may go to a physician for a blood test that confirms her suspicions—she is pregnant. But about six to twelve weeks later her period begins again. She is inexplicably not pregnant. She has no miscarriage, no expulsion of fetal material, no indication that something was 'wrong.' She goes to her physician who confirms that the fetus has suddenly disappeared.[22]

In such scenarios women do not have abortions or choose to terminate pregnancies. Their babies are simply aborted, taken, with the same results: the women are no longer pregnant. In some cases female abductees express a sense of reprieve when what were essentially unwanted pregnancies are "taken" by the aliens. Anita, for example, recalls for Jacobs being placed in a "birthing chair" that is "almost like the obstetrician." She is asked to bear down and "it comes right out" into a Pyrex dish held by an alien. Before they take it away, Anita observes that, "it looks like what you'd expect a very early miscarriage to look like." She twice declares that, "there's a sense of relief," noting that, "it's time to take it out so they can have it."[23]

The "relationship" between mother and fetus suggested by the rhetoric about reproductive technologies that emerged during the early sixties continues to provide ideological fuel for the notion that women should always, and under all conditions, desire to bring pregnancies to term. With the escalating circulation of photographic images of the fetus in utero since the 1960s, the fetus has increasingly been attributed human agency. The mother's body has come increasingly to be understood in contrast as abject vessel—that mass which surrounds the living, breathing "baby" inside.[24] The medical community now justifies the use of ultrasound to monitor even low risk or "normal" pregnancies on the basis

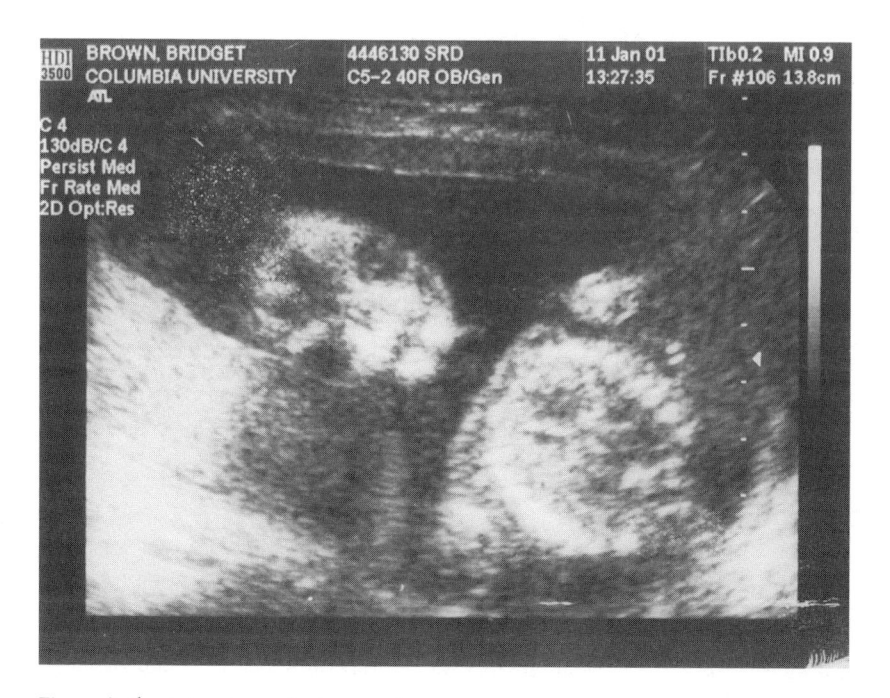

Fig. 7. Author's twenty-week ultrasound.

that visualizing the fetus enables both "reassurance" and mother-child "bonding."[25] At present, the image of the fetus in utero is domesticated—a commonplace addition to the family photo album, it provides a sort of technologically enabled prehistory of baby's life on Earth.

Perhaps a more critical ideological source for the anxiety about unwitting loss of pregnancy expressed in alien abduction narratives since the 1980s is the successful manipulation of both images of the fetus, and scientific discourse about fetal personhood by members of the religious and political right in the service of a conservative, pro-life agenda. If in the mid-1960s the images in *Life* suggested the female body as fallow terrain for the penetrating technical gaze, since the 1980s, the woman's body has become an embattled terrain in debates over reproductive rights and in the wider-ranging morality campaign that seeks to police "normal" male and female behaviors. In Anita's case, as in others, relief at termination, a fantasy increasingly proscribed by pro-life rhetoric in which women who choose to terminate unwanted pregnancies are demonized, is displaced onto the alien.

As the fetus has come to play a critical iconographic role in these political contests, so too has the fetal-looking alien come to be the central type of alien described in accounts of abduction.[26] Indeed, abductees beginning with the Hills have suggested that the abducting aliens themselves resemble fetuses; Barney and Betty described their captors as having, "rather odd-shaped heads, with a large cranium, diminishing in size as it got toward the chin. And the eyes continued around to the sides of their heads. . . . Mouth . . . like a straight line. The texture of the skin . . . was grayish. . . . I didn't notice any hair.[27] In more recent accounts abductees consistently describe their captors as fully fetal-looking, with large heads, large black eyes, necrotic skin, smooth, sexless, and hairless bodies. The fetal alien is understood by believers to be one of many species of alien: the Grey, or Zeta Reticulan. An amalgam of doctor and fetus—both creator and created—the abducting alien Grey once again elides the human parent, rendering him or her virtually useless.

This Baby Was Real

In abduction narratives produced and published since the 1980s fetuses are everywhere: abducting, operating, implanting, being implanted, be-

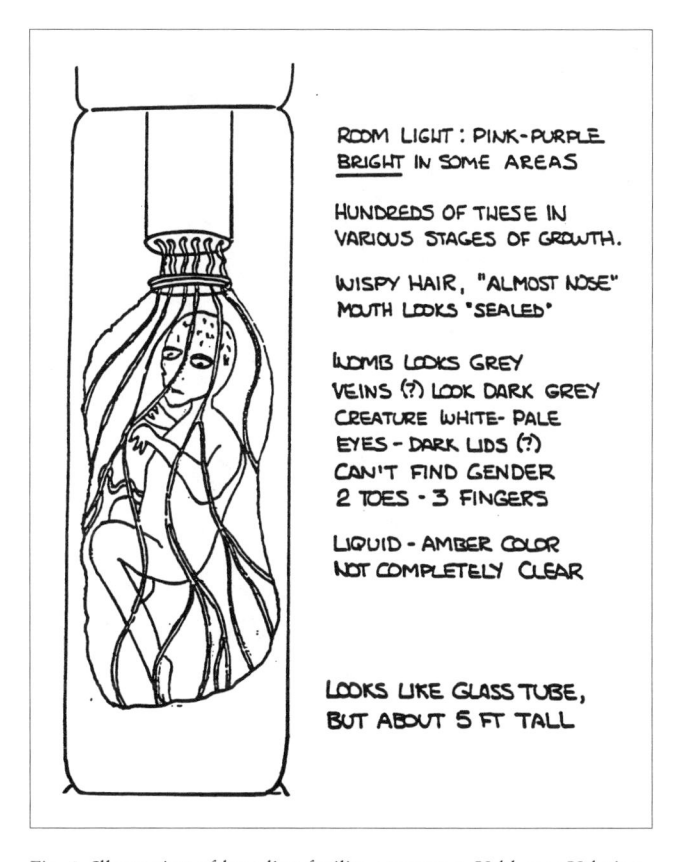

[Figure: Illustration showing a figure inside a glass tube-like container with annotations:

ROOM LIGHT : PINK-PURPLE BRIGHT IN SOME AREAS

HUNDREDS OF THESE IN VARIOUS STAGES OF GROWTH.

WISPY HAIR, "ALMOST NOSE" MOUTH LOOKS "SEALED"

WOMB LOOKS GREY
VEINS (?) LOOK DARK GREY
CREATURE WHITE- PALE
EYES - DARK LIDS (?)
CAN'T FIND GENDER
2 TOES - 3 FINGERS

LIQUID - AMBER COLOR NOT COMPLETELY CLEAR

LOOKS LIKE GLASS TUBE, BUT ABOUT 5 FT TALL]

Fig. 8. Illustration of breeding facility apparatus. Valdemar Valerian, ed., *Matrix II: The Abduction and Manipulation of Humans Using Advanced Technologies* (Yelm, WA: Leading Edge Technology, 1991), 193.

ing removed, incubated, and incubating. These fetuses suggest that while abductees cannot control loss or termination of pregnancy, neither can they control when a pregnancy is brought to term. Abductees report having witnessed the breeding project in action while on board spaceships. Jerry observes herself "naked on a table, unable to move her arms and legs" in a room lined with "lots and lots . . . of rectangular shaped containers." She remembers that, "inside of these drawers, or incubators . . . were hundreds of, I don't know if you can call it babies or not, but little just I guess fetuses."[28]

94 | *An Ongoing and Systematic Breeding Experiment*

Fig. 9. Illustration of alien-human breeding facility. Valdemar Valerian, ed., *Matrix II: The Abduction and Manipulation of Humans Using Advanced Technologies* (Yelm, WA: Leading Edge Technology, 1991), 197-C.

Jacobs describes "child presentation" as that facet of abduction during which "aliens carefully watch as women, men, and children are required either to observe or physically interact with these bizarre-looking offspring." Jacobs adds that "apparently it is absolutely essential for the child to have human contact."[29] This contact can include forced bonding and in some cases for women, forced breastfeeding. It is suggested that the abductees are, by virtue of their humanity, capable of nurturing these "phlegmatic and sickly" offspring in a way that aliens are not.[30]

Yet the guilt or anxiety about exercising one's will over reproductive choice extends into guilt and anxiety about proper, or normal, parenting. Sometimes the aliens allegedly force abductees to hold and nurture the babies, which they describe as weak and listless. Often abductees feel more repulsion than attraction to the unwanted offspring. Susan, for example, remembers,

> She's too small. The skin is very thin. . . . You know newborn babies' hands, like tissue paper? Thinner than that. . . . I see her face, now. . . . Features are concentrated down in the lower part. . . . So the skin is not robust in color. . . . It's not baby-pink at all. It's a funny . . . grayish . . . pallor. . . . It's all concentrated down. . . . The head goes down to a point.[31]

As with the superbabies and test-tube babies discussed earlier, the mixed alien-human babies are confounding: they inhabit an ill-defined border area between the real and imagined. Almost two hundred years after Mary Shelley imagined her "hideous progeny," these dubious offspring embody the ways in which the promises of technology backfire: interventions of technology in a "natural" process bear Frankenstein's monsters, for whom abductees have difficulty showing love or nurturance. At the same time, concerns about these abandoned, ailing, unlovable fetuses test what abductees understand to be a normal and natural desire to nurture. This in a culture that has, for decades if not centuries, suggested some form or another of "family values," and the assumption of traditional gender roles associated with those values, as the hallmark of normalcy and social acceptability.

While my informants did not freely offer details about their physical experimentation, they did talk freely about the possible alien-human offspring with whom they have been presented by the aliens. During a hypnosis session with Hopkins, Cassie recalls the aliens giving her a "kid" to hold with a "pointy chin and big eyes."[32] After hypnosis, Cassie believed that it was "all in my imagination." She wanted to cease hypnosis, insisting that "I'm mixing up aliens and babies and kids." For Cassie, any confusion about the realness of her presentation dream was resolved by Hopkins who pressed her to continue, insisting "no, you're having a presentation dream." Her belief that the presentation dream was "real" was corroborated by her reading of *Intruders*, and the similarities between her experience and Kathie Davis's. Davis too "remembered" meeting a hybrid baby of her own who, in her view, "looked like an angel."[33]

Of my informants, John was the only man who recalled what abduction experts have labeled "presentation dreams." After telling *Nova* about the procedures he was forced to endure during abduction, John continued to tell his interviewers about being led to a room that was full of "canisters," each containing "one of these little hybrids." John recalls being presented with one of them and being asked if he wanted to hold it. "At this point," he elaborates, "I was told that these seven—they were seven sisters . . . although there are no genitalia or sex organs that you can see. I was informed that they were my offspring." John reported being "terribly upset" at the realization that "they were going to take them away from me. That these weren't offspring I could raise, rear, or keep."[34] He believes, as noted earlier, that the aliens need humans in order to reproduce themselves. Without what we as humans have to offer biologically and perhaps emotionally, their own species will cease to exist, having become too advanced and intelligent for their own good.

While fetal aliens and alien-human fetuses are a source of anxiety and terror, during presentation scenarios, or dreams, some abductees also express feelings of connection with, and sometimes intense love for, their hybrid offspring. As some female abductees express sadness at allegedly losing pregnancies, so too do both male and female abductees report that intense sorrow often results from not being able to bond with their offspring further, because occasions for parent-child bonding are externally controlled by the aliens, as is everything in the reality of alien abduction. Jane, Maureen, and Cassie all discussed such scenarios with me, in varying amounts of detail. Jane claims to have been abducted when she was pregnant with one of her four children.[35] After being assured that they were not going to hurt her, the aliens led her "usher-like" through the ship. She recalls passing different colored rooms, including a "pink room with twenty incubators." As she describes it in a written statement that she has prepared and hands out to those who inquire,

> I was shown each incubator with what looked like an embryo in petrie dishes. Each dish seemed to have another embryo in different stages of

growth. As we approached the last incubator, it looked like a little girl, with a large head and beautiful aqua eyes shaped like the aliens'. And very sparse hair. The love I had for this child was immense. I have four children and my love was more than I felt for my own. I did not want to leave her there. I was told I would see her again very soon.[36]

Jane is not instructed, as was John, to hold the babies she sees, but she is informed that she has been "judged, tested, and passed." While Jane adds that she had "no idea what he was talking about," her story, like John's, suggests that the "appropriate" human parenting response—to desire to have and care for all possible offspring—is part of what makes us passable humans.

It is interesting to note that John and Jane are the parents of grown —teenage or adult—children. Yet a common facet of these presentation scenarios is the account that they feel more love, connection, and closeness with their alien offspring than with their own. Though she did not offer such details during our three-hour interview on the beach near her Long Island home, in an online written account of her abduction experiences Maureen describes a "disturbing dream" that she later realized was a buried abduction experience. Maureen writes that "under hypnosis, I was able to recall being presented with, and holding, a hybrid child that I knew to be mine." Maureen continues, "when I held my son Lyjor and looked into his eyes, I found myself speaking telepathically to him. And I know he understood what I was saying. I told him that there would always be a part of me in him. And he felt my sadness at knowing we would not be together except in spirit. . . . Somehow I know I WILL see him again."[37] Maureen believes that this offspring was most likely the result of her rape by a "reptilian" alien in what she believes was an underground bunker in Montauk, Long Island.[38] The dream/memory of communicating with Lyjor resulted for Maureen in what she described during our interview as "intense emotional upheaval [she] felt by way of a strong maternal urge . . . a need to 'mother' something." The urge was so strong that it "compelled [her] to go to an animal shelter the next morning to adopt a puppy."

Maureen is also the single mother of a teenaged son whom I met during my visit to her home. The son is conspicuously absent from Maureen's written narrative, and one wonders whether the maternal urges, the feelings of loss associated with Lyjor may have something to do with her changing relationship with him. I ask her about this connection and she explains that early on in her therapeutic experience she explored these possible connections with her therapist. She recalled that,

> When I first started seeing him one of my biggest fears was that they were going to come and take E. and not bring him back. I was deathly afraid of that. And we talked about it, and Dr. K. seemed to think that it was possible that because I'm a single mother and E.'s father left right after he was born that there were things about abandonment. . . . I can go with that. That sounds very plausible to me, until we uncovered an experience.[39]

"Until we uncovered an experience" is the turning point in Maureen's account. She, like other abductees, will only go so far with psychological explanations for their perceived experiences before abandoning them in favor of the assertion that what happened was real, or in this case, as Maureen insists, "this baby was real." The fear of losing her human son is understood as the symptom, not the cause of her abduction experiences. The inevitable feelings of loss attached to having one's children grow up and become alienated, uncommunicative, or simply independent are left uninterrogated by John, Jane, and Maureen.[40] So too are abductees uninterested in considering the extent to which anxieties about being sufficient, "normal" parents may be determined not by aliens but by the cultural and historical moment in which we live.

The emergence of the abduction scenario in the mid-1960s signals a pronounced and critical shift in the ways we imagine the invading alien other and the ways we imagine the notion of invasion itself. The abduction scenario suggests that humans are among the data being collected and catalogued by extraterrestrial researchers, and that the objective detachment of invading extraterrestrials is not necessarily a benign detachment. Unwilling encounters with the Greys place abductees in the position of vivisected lab animals, such as the fetal monkeys, pigs, and cows featured alongside prone women in "Control of Life." The result is account after account of human experience told from the perspective of the laboratory rat. Mack's patient Ed articulates this perspective when he argues with his captor, shouting, "I'm not just your laboratory rat, guinea pig."[41] In trying to articulate the nature of the horror his alien captors represented for him, Barney Hill struggled to find the right words. He noted that they were frightening not in a "horrible sense, like a distorted, unhuman type of creature." Rather, according to Hill, "he was more—the frightening part was the military precision of—as if he was a person who knew what to do, could do it, and was willing to carry it out."[42] Contact with abducting aliens thus comes not through cataclysmic military conflict, but through the ability of those in power —those possessed of the knowledge and technology to create and destroy—to get in, on a regular basis, to the most mundane and intimate spheres of our everyday lives: our homes, our cars, our beds, our bodies. Indeed, abduction suggests that the body itself is an object of technical conquest and colonization by entities driven less by lust for global, or intergalactic, or national dominance than by an inexplicable and overweening interest in skin, sperm, and frontal lobes—in human beings, human bodies, the very stuff of humanity itself.

I have already touched on some of the most common interpretations of the breeding program by abductees: many believe, like Maureen and John that they "need" us to sustain their species. The aliens are understood to need their eggs and sperm, their genetic material, the essence of their humanity—whether that essence is understood in biological, spiritual, or emotional terms. The narcissism of this belief is critical to acknowledge. While the terror of allegedly repeated abductions may be real to abductees, those who claim to be unwilling recruits to this project often suggest that they, and abductees as a group, are special enough to warrant sustained alien attention as research subjects.[43] Perhaps only the aliens subject abductees to the sort of self-revelatory attention that enables them to be seen and known. Only the aliens value and desire to replicate those qualities they possess. In most cases it is simply accepted by abductees that such extraordinary human qualities are genetically determined, and therefore retrievable, re-creatable; that our smallest biological parts *contain* our human essence. Like the Hills, contemporary abductees continue to speak from the position of raw data, as human guinea pigs, both terrified by their capture and at the same time affirmed as worthy of alien study, representative, perhaps, of the best the human race has to offer.

6

They Have the Secrets
Conspiracy Theory as Alternative History

Anthony is a divorced, forty-year-old child welfare worker who shares a two-family house with his grandfather in Queens. Like John, he too lives in Ozone Park, but on the more heavily trafficked, commercial thoroughfare Liberty Avenue.[1] I interviewed Anthony in his home, and he was affable and welcoming. He and I talked in his backyard, interrupted occasionally by the rumble of the elevated A train that runs parallel to the avenue. Anthony is very eager to share his thoughts and ideas about the meaning and purpose of the alien abduction phenomenon. This is in part because he has only recently come to accept—after years of what he characterizes as "denial"—what he believes is the truth about his lifelong history of abduction by aliens. More than most abductees I have met and spoken with, Anthony is convinced that an array of human elites—including but not limited to the U.S. government—participate with aliens in controlling and manipulating his and our reality. As he explains it, "We're so socially engineered we don't even know how good they are."[2] When pressed to define who precisely "they" are, he explained,

> The Illuminati, you've heard this before. I don't want to give this a conspiratorial spin to it but this is where the money goes. . . . But I think there is a group of people well aware of the ET presence here, have in fact communicated with—this is my personal feeling and the feeling among experiencers when we talk about it—they are aware of it. They are in control of not only government, because they are the secret government, and governments of the world and they do want to make a one-world government.

Despite his efforts at explanation, it was difficult to know at any given moment during our conversation which "they" Anthony was referring

British Heart Foundation
46 Union Street
Inverness
Highland
IV1 1PX

Branch No: 103
Telephone: 01463 711 918

Charity Reg. No England & Wales (225971)
Charity Reg. No Scotland (SC039426)
Vat Registration No. 626 921 824

SALE
REF 7303   1 305525   15/05/2016 15:11

Today you were served by Jim C

Non Fiction
284   2.50   1x   2.50

TOTAL   ITEMS   1   2.50

CASH   £2.50

Thank you for shopping with us today.
Through your support, you have
made a difference to the fight against
heart disease.
Please keep your receipt as proof of
purchase.

NEED TO BRING SOMETHING BACK?

Changed Your Mind?
We exchange or refund items returned in their original condition within 28 days of purchase, with the original BHF ticket attached and a valid receipt.
Items excluded from this policy:
CDs, DVDs, Videos, Computer Games, Books, Earrings, Headwear, Underwear, Swimwear.

Not Happy with Your Purchase?
If the product you purchase is not of a satisfactory quality, not as described or not fit for its purpose, we may offer an exchange or refund, in accordance with your consumer rights. Be aware that many of our items are second hand and may have imperfections.

We reserve the right to refuse a return or to require proof of identity. Your consumer rights are not affected.
Refunds will be made on the same tender type for cash or card, as the purchase.

Here to Help: customer.service@bhf.org.uk
Freephone - 0800 138 6556

to: the aliens, the U.S. government, the "secret government," the one-world government. Such confusion is, in part, a function of conspiracy theory; for conspiracy theorists such forces are always already colluding and interconnected.

Anthony's comments also suggest that who "they" are is less important than what they do; he refers intermittently to "the secret schools" which to him are, "nothing more than withholding information from the public," information in particular about "the ET presence." Anthony adds, "there's nothing honorable in it. . . . If they have the ability they will do it. I think they look at most people as not able to handle their own affairs, so you need us, so of course we entrust, so you're supposed to represent us, but when we're thinking you represent us, they're doing what they want. My personal opinion." Anthony returned repeatedly throughout our discussion to his theories about why "they" would want to withhold information and how such withholding confers power to those "in the know." In his view, withholding information is on one hand a fairly universal human tendency: "When we are in school, elementary, grammar school," he notes, "the one with the secret was the one who was important—Oh! You've got to tell me! You've got to tell me! It could have been any nonsense. That's how we operate." At the same time, he interprets information hoarding as a strategy intended to shore up the power of certain elites. He adds, "It's the same thing: they have the secrets, they have all the toys, they use our tax money to fund those toys. . . . They will do—the powers that be, whoever it is, the government is just a small component, the secret government is even more important to them—I think they will do anything to stay in power." In contrast, those without access to "the secrets"—most especially abductees who are denied information about their own role as human subjects in an ongoing alien research project—have no power.

Alien abductees express cultural anxieties about the encroachment of technology, as well as medical, therapeutic, and moral authority upon people's ability to know themselves. Conspiracy theorists add the state to the list of those external forces or authorities believed to control and manipulate human activity. In so doing, they stress not only their lack of physical and emotional agency, but also of civic agency. And unlike other abductees, conspiracy theorists offer their own historicization of alien abduction, placing their shared sense of diminishing self-control within the political historical context of the Cold War and after. In this chapter and the next I look at the accounts of these abductees, dismissed by some in the UFO community as "the paranoids": people like Anthony who believe that alien abduction is the product of a set of what one source refers to as "nested conspiracies" involving not just extraterrestrials but also a complex hierarchy of humans, most often elite groups of humans representing a monstrous cross-section of a postwar military-scientific-intelligence complex with whom the aliens are believed to be in league.[3] These abductees generally share with others the fundamental belief that they have been physically captured and experimented on by extraterrestrial entities involved in some sort of on-going research project. Conspiracy theorist abductees, however, implicate human elites for allowing, sanctioning, or participating in such human experimentation; they insist on the connection between the sort of biological engineering discussed in my last chapter and a more large-scale project in social engineering. Ultimately, they underscore the connection between the vulnerability of individual bodies and the "national body."

These alleged abductees generally share with other conspiracy theorists a belief in an unseen order, a covert power structure wherein certain elites hoard power, knowledge, and wealth. So too do they share with a smaller subset of conspiracy theorists a particular set of concerns about violation and control of American citizens by the state. But what distinguishes alleged alien abductees from other conspiracy theorists is that they experience themselves as bearing the brunt of global—even intergalactic—conspiracies personally, mentally, and physically. And so if all conspiracy theories seek to identify and reveal the puppet masters, alien abduction conspiracy theory concerns itself more centrally with the point of view and experience of the manipulated entity, the puppet itself.

Theories of Conspiracy Culture

The sort of distrust of the powers that be writ large (and of the American government in particular) that is expressed in conspiracy accounts of alien abduction is part of a much broader and longer culture of conspiracy that has taken shape in the United States in the latter half of the twentieth century, and especially since the 1970s. In his 1966 essay, "The Paranoid Style in American Politics," historian Richard Hofstadter argued that those who espoused the "paranoid style" in mid-century political culture feared a "vast and sinister conspiracy, a gigantic and yet subtle machinery of influence set in motion to undermine and destroy a way of life."[4] Hofstadter, however, suggested that such conspiratorial thinking was relegated to the fringes of political culture. Political scientist Michael Rogin later revised his thesis, arguing in 1988 that conspiratorial thinking had come to inform mainstream political culture as well, pointing in particular to the paranoid apocalypticism of President Ronald Reagan. Others have gone on to detail how, since the 1970s, this culture of conspiracy has taken shape on both the left and the right, and in both political and popular culture.

At the heart of conspiracy thinking is the sense that those institutions and social systems commonly thought to enable and protect us are actually working against us. Scholars have made the case that such conspiratorial thinking informs the literature (Thomas Pynchon, Margaret Atwood, Ralph Ellison, Joseph Heller, William Gibson, and so on), film (*The Parallax View, All the President's Men, The Stepford Wives, Safe,* and so on), and even music (the White Album, "Fear of a Black Planet," "Heard It through the Grapevine," and so on) of the last forty years. Most would agree that conspiracy theory has come to constitute its own "worldview,"[5] a "visible and widespread part of the cultural landscape."[6]

What most divides those who seek to understand conspiracy theory is the way in which they view conspiracy theorists themselves, and judge the ways in which they use conspiracy theory to understand the world around them. Until quite recently, even serious treatments of conspiracy theory have regarded its practitioners as marginal or somehow lesser. In 1988 literary critic Frederic Jameson argued, in a discussion of popular political thrillers of the 1970s, that conspiracy theory is "a poor man's cognitive mapping."[7] Conspiracy theorists struggle, that is, to make meaning of, "the multiple informational and sign systems that are made available . . . in late capitalism." Jameson says it a bit less opaquely when he suggests that conspiracy theory is "an unconscious, collective effort at trying to figure out where we are and what landscapes and forces confront us in a late 20th century whose abominations are heightened by their concealment and their bureaucratic impersonality."[8] In 1998, *Newsweek* columnist Jonathan Alter, in a widely discussed review essay of *The X Files Movie* concluded that "Communism is dead; capitalism a given. That leaves conspiricism as the civic faith of the moment—a tidy curiously comforting way to view the universe. At least someone's in control, even if he's evil."[9] Surely these two disparate cultural critics had different audiences in mind for their work, and different agendas: Jameson's to point to conspiricism as purely a symptom of late capitalism; Alter's to argue that the ineptitude of government all but precludes the actual possibility of effective cover-up. And yet they share a certain condescension toward conspiracy theory and its practitioners, Jameson dismissing such efforts at mapping as "degraded," Alter bemusedly casting conspiracy theorists as naïve rubes.[10]

A spate of more recent publications explore conspiracy theory as a way in which people make meaning of the complex world in which we live, and at the same time do a better job of taking conspiracy theory seriously as an increasingly mainstream cultural phenomenon.[11] Timothy Melley argues in *Empire of Conspiracy* (calling to mind Anthony's comment about social engineering) that conspiracy theory gives expression to what he calls "agency panic," or a sense of diminished human agency, in a society where "large governmental, corporate, or social systems appear uncannily to control individual behavior."[12] Peter Knight, argues that now, in the early part of the twenty-first century, "we're all conspiracy theorists" and that a "self-conscious and self-reflexive entertainment culture of conspiracy has become thoroughly mainstream."[13] Some go even further, viewing conspiracy theory as a utopian exercise, a liberatory quest for truth and a challenge to power.

The wild popularity of the television show *X Files* both fed and reflected burgeoning popular interest in conspiracy theory and the alien abduction phenomenon during the 1990s. *The X Files* aired from 1993–2002, nine years that overlapped with both the height and decline of popular interest in alien abduction. Conspiracy theories of alien abduction and *The X Files* existed in a sort of mutual feedback loop with one another during those years: the writers of *The X Files* clearly read the same accounts and histories of alien abduction that I read; at the same time, while abductees loudly object to the idea that *The X Files* has shaped, perhaps even "caused" their belief in their own abduction, the widespread popularity of the TV show in some sense authorized their alleged experiences as worthy of consideration by a broad populace of nonbelievers. During its nine-year run, *The X Files* explored all of the central subthemes of alien abduction. Its central characters, Agents Mulder and Scully, were seen as vulnerable victims of capture, forced psychological, medical, and reproductive procedures. Different interpretations of the abduction phenomenon were explored throughout the series, with Mulder viewing abductees as prophets for a New Age, and Scully typically viewing them as ordinary, if slightly unstable, people. Mulder espoused the "ET hypothesis" of alien abduction: that aliens are indeed extraterrestrial, and abduction by them unexplainable within a worldy, rational framework. Scully, conversely, attributed unexplained and allegedly "alien" phenomena to simple human malevolence. The central narrative arc of *The X Files*, however—also the subject of *The X Files* movie—involves conspiracy theories of the alien abduction phenomenon, in which both extraterrestrials and humans are ultimately implicated. It consistently suggests that we should be as scared of human elites—especially those with access to or control over scientific and technical know-how/progress/research—as of the aliens with whom they may create, destroy, or collaborate.[14] More broadly, the show, like abductee conspiricists, gives voice to a deep cynicism about the effects of power in our everyday lives. Each takes as a given that power operates on us whether we like it or not; it is only the form power takes that is debatable.

There also continues to be debate among those who take conspiracy theory seriously—from *X Files* fans to critical theorists—over what, precisely has "caused" conspiracy theory to become such a prevalent way of coming to understand the world in the late twentieth and early twenty-first centuries. Theorists of conspiracy culture have suggested that it is a symptom of postindustrialism, postmodernity, late capitalism, and virtuality, an outcome of the sort of confusion and disorientation those phenomena are understood to spawn. These massive social, cultural, and economic forces have surely played a role in fashioning the sort of cultural anxieties that I map throughout this book. I will argue here, however, that it is critical to look more specifically at how alien abduction conspiracy theorists revise Cold War and post–Cold War American history, and to consider how that history itself has fostered the proliferation of conspiracy culture. It is critical to attend especially to what conspiricists' historical revisions tell us about the unsettling, disorienting experience of life in the national security state.

The conspiracy accounts I will examine in this chapter and the next are concerned most often with state control and abuse of scientific and technical knowledge and information. They offer an outsider's view of the way the world works, only slightly modifying official narratives of historical events, this time from the subject position of the person denied access to specialized knowledge and information. These accounts constitute, then, a collective effort to possess what Anthony calls the "secrets," secrets to which most American citizens have come to feel they lack access.

The Invisible Government and the People's Right to Know

Conventional wisdom about the Cold War suggests that it was a clearly defined struggle between American defenders of democracy and godless foreign Communists. From this angle, the Cold War ended with the dissolution of the Soviet Union; a swell of optimism at the fall of the Berlin Wall in 1989 marked the triumph of democracy over communism, and, by extension, of good over evil. Alien abduction conspiracy theorists question the optimism and simplicity of this assessment. More specifically, they question the means of promoting the U.S. imperium and inquire into abuses of power that occurred and may continue to occur in its pursuit. Conspiracy theorists insist, more specifically, that in an ongoing struggle for global domination the state has abused and exploited its own citizens. And so if on the surface official narratives about the end of the Cold War suggest that the national body is healed and whole (or at least engaged in the sometimes painful process of healing), abduction conspiricists posit that beneath that superficial healing remains a layer of festering secrecy and corruption. The struggle between citizens and the state for ever-elusive proof and evidence of what "really happened" between the end of World War II and the beginning of the twenty-first century, the quest for truths that remain hidden by the invisible or secret government, informs and structures their lives, for as Anthony notes, to have access to the secret is to have power.

In order to understand the currency of conspiracy theory in contemporary American culture, we must consider the history it seeks to revise, especially the history of those decades since the end of World War II during which the fact of government secrecy itself has come to be common knowledge. This period in American history—escalating especially since the 1970s—has been one of a seemingly unending series of surfacings and revelations of past government wrong-doing, most often in the name of national security imperatives, and often at the expense of U.S. citizens.[15] It has been amply demonstrated that in the race with the Soviets and against Communism, the government, and most often the burgeoning postwar intelligence community, overlooked and/or violated citizen rights when deemed necessary. In several notable cases, citizens were used as guinea pigs in the process of outstripping American enemies.

The late twentieth century has been broadly characterized as one of diminishing trust in government, of escalating suspicion of the same. In the most general sense, this is viewed to be the result of social movements begun in the 1950s and 1960s: civil rights and women's rights movements protested the exclusion of many American citizens from the full benefits and rights of U.S. citizenship; the antiwar movement, and related youth movements, stressed the abuses of various types of authority—of "the system"—notably the Johnson and Nixon administrations who continued the war in Vietnam despite widespread popular protest. But concern about national secrecy in particular emerged with special force alongside growing awareness of the wages of radioactivity and atomic weapons testing. In the wake of the bombing of Hiroshima, Americans learned about the Manhattan Project and the activity at Los Alamos, the de facto location of the first massive and successful government project in techno-military secrecy. Revelations about its secret cities, and about an elite group of foreign scientists isolated in a provisional desert community were told as part of the larger narrative of U.S. victory in World War II: American lives were saved at the expense of Japanese; a war that could have gone on ad infinitum was brought to an abrupt end.

But by the mid-1950s, in the wake of the Bikini Atoll atomic tests, Americans began to question the wisdom of atomic testing, noting its peacetime killing effects. Evidence of radioactive damage in the Bikini Atoll prompted concern about the Trinity site tests in the United States, and about the bombs that continued to be tested in Nevada sites throughout the 1950s and into the early 1960s. In 1954 inquiries into the effects of radioactivity in nuclear tests in the South Pacific were met with government silence. This silence prompted the American Civil Liberties Union push for the declassification of information about nuclear weapons testing. In 1966 the ACLU published a report, "The People's Right to Know: A Report on Government News Suppression," urging the government to grant citizens access to government records. The ACLU's push resulted in the passage of the Freedom of Information Act in 1966. Through this public struggle over classified information came an increased awareness that citizens were systematically denied access to information that might directly affect them.

A widespread sense of the institutionalization of government secrecy in intelligence organizations such as the Federal Bureau of Investigation (FBI), the CIA, and the National Security Agency (NSA) was helped along by the publication in 1964 of *The Invisible Government* by journalists David Wise and Thomas Ross. This best-selling book was the first exposé of the "secret world of intelligence and national security."[16] Wise and Ross gave the American public reason to believe that there were certain hidden forces at work within government: not Communists or foreign subversives, but a vast "interlocking, hidden machinery that carries out the policies of the United States in the Cold War."[17]

Certainly the Watergate scandal stands as a watershed moment in the forging of national anxiety about government dishonesty and secrecy. With Senate hearings broadcast daily on national television, the American viewing public learned that intelligence agencies had been deemed above the law and authorized by the government to spy on American citizens under the aegis of "counterintelligence"; lies had been told and cover-up orchestrated at the highest levels of government. But Watergate was in fact just the tip of the proverbial iceberg of government cover-up around intelligence abuses, and in 1975 alone, a presidential commission, a select committee from the Senate and a select committee from the House of Representatives all investigated the intelligence community. The result was an unprecedentedly thorough, and public, examination of the inner workings of the "secret government." This series of investigations and hearings looked into burgeoning allegations that the CIA had repeatedly violated its own charter and had in fact not just spied on, but also experimented on, U.S. citizens. The Rockefeller Commission, as well as the Church Committee, found that the CIA had an extensive domestic operation with files on hundreds of thousands of Americans.

Disturbed by both the way in which CIA operatives had been depicted during related hearings as inept buffoons, and the relative lack of attention paid to statements made by CIA spokesmen during the hearings about an ongoing project in behavior modification, journalist John Marks filed a Freedom of Information request with the CIA. This led to the discovery of yet another cache of related documents that neither the Rockefeller nor Church investigations had unearthed. They detailed one of the more disturbing projects to come to light, MKUltra. MKUltra was a program of research in behavioral modification carried out from 1953–1964. A Cold War initiative undertaken to combat what was perceived to be Soviet success at brainwashing and mind control, it included "research and development of chemical, biological and radiological materials capable of employment in clandestine operations to control human behavior."[18] In one facet of MKUltra, from 1955–1959 the Army Chemical Corps administered LSD to more than a thousand American soldiers at Edgewood, Maryland. The goal of these tests was to see how the drug influenced the effectiveness of soldiers, and then later to see its effect on interrogation. Subsequent field tests involved eleven separate interrogations of ten subjects. None of these subjects were volunteers, and none were aware that they were to receive LSD. Marks was the first to explore the possibility, supported in these newly uncovered documents, that the government had in fact tried to fashion "Manchurian Candidates," or assassins responsive to remote commands, programmed through mind control experiments.[19]

Though many records about programs in behavior modification and social control had been destroyed in 1973 at the instruction of then CIA director Richard Helms, the ones that survived offered startling details about the intelligence community's use of citizens as unwitting test subjects, and revealed the names of researchers and over thirty universities and institutions that participated.[20] Senator Edward M. Kennedy, member of the Senate subcommittee that addressed the MKUltra revelations in 1977, chastised the intelligence community, observing that "a 'volunteer' program in which subjects are not fully informed of potential hazards to their persons is 'volunteer' in name only." The most profoundly disturbing facet of the project was, as Senator Kennedy summarized it, that "individual rights were also subordinated to national security considerations," and, it seems, the prurient interests of certain operatives. Kennedy placed responsibility firmly on the shoulders of the "invisible government," arguing that "the intelligence community of this Nation, which requires a shroud of secrecy in order to operate, has a very sacred trust from the American people. The CIA's program of human experimentation of the fifties and sixties violated that trust." In the late 1970s the government was faced with the challenge of restoring that trust.

Kennedy concluded that, "The best safeguard against abuses in the future is a complete public accounting of the abuses of the past."[21] In this assertion the senator revealed a certain optimism that a "public accounting" of the past would preclude further public ill health and secrecy. His comments showed faith in the process of bringing to light, as well as a desire to place such abuses firmly in the past, to make them dead and gone. History is, of course, not nearly so neat, and rather than putting violations and secrets to rest, the investigations of the 1970s led to further Freedom of Information Act revision and more stringent shows of policing intelligence by Congress. These inquiries have revealed a host of abuses that continue to be exposed. Kennedy's recommendations advocate a sort of public, overtly political version of the "talking cure" espoused by abduction traumatists discussed in earlier chapters. The suggestion that revealing secrets—ventilating, if you will, on a grand scale—somehow enables "closure" has become a cliché in contemporary political discourse. Abduction conspiracy theorists intuit the disingenuousness of this suggestion, viewing the move toward any form of closure as just another strategy for keeping secrets.

Stop the Cosmic Watergate! UFO Activists and the Call for Declassification

The debate over the existence of UFOs has been a time-honored if marginal site for American popular struggle to learn the "truth" about government dealings, and for suspicion of the truth as presented by the state.[22] The UFO community has been convinced since the late 1940s that the government was at best turning a blind eye to the truth. Accounts of government techno-secrecy produced by UFO believers have sometimes converged with, sometimes diverged from more dominant and overtly political accounts of reality. As many layers of Cold War–sanctioned secrecy have in fact come to light—in particular the role of the CIA in domestic surveillance—UFO believers have stepped up their demands for truth telling, declassification, and all around coming clean. Since the early 1950s there has been a cohort of ufologists who believe that under Project Sign, the first Air Force–CIA–sponsored inquiry into UFOs (1947), the Air Technical Intelligence Center (ATIC) concluded that UFOs were of extraterrestrial origin. For these early conspiracy theorists, knowledge of the existence of classified information drove the belief that government reports were just smoke screens hiding the real UFO investigation. Those "real" records were believed to have dematerialized into the nonrealm of classified information, the bugaboo of all conspiracy theory. During these years numerous civilian organizations formed to investigate UFOs, including the International Flying Saucer Bureau (IFSB), the Aerial Phenomenon Research Organization

(APRO), and the National Investigative Committee for Aerial Phenomena (NICAP). Countering one bureaucracy with another, such groups are driven by the belief that there must be more and better information that has been left out of official accountings.[23] In 1969, with the publication of the Condon Report, the government decided to discontinue twenty-two years of investigation, concluding that UFOs were not of extraterrestrial origin. Again, this conclusion did not end popular inquiry into the existence of UFOs, but rather fanned the flames of conspiracy theory, as do all official denials.

It is the position of Citizens Against UFO Secrecy (CAUS), founded in the late 1970s, that the problem of government cover-up must be dealt with judicially. In the early 1980s CAUS was plaintiff in two actions under the Freedom of Information Act, one against the CIA and one against the NSA, for the release of classified documents. As Peter Gersten, current attorney for and director of CAUS, notes in one position paper, "CAUS is against all secrecy, whether it be by the government, the military, the civilian population or the alleged alien presence. CAUS believes the public has an absolute right to know about . . . contact from a different, possibly extraterrestrial, intelligence and technology." He concludes his paper, "where there is secrecy there is no truth. Without truth there can be no justice. And without justice there can be no freedom. It's time to set ourselves free."[24] As Gersten noted in a recent email update to members, he is particularly adamant about alien abduction, which he argues, "by definition, includes nonconsensual intrusions and violations of human rights." Gersten offers pro bono legal assistance to anyone who possesses eyewitness testimony, physical evidence, government documents, or other "genuine evidence" of UFO/alien contact.

Others believe that UFO secrecy and cover-up call not for adjudication but for self-described activism. In 1992 and 1993 a small group of believers calling themselves "Operation Right to Know" gathered in Washington, DC, and marched in front of the White House in an effort to persuade government to release thousands of pages of documents. Protestors carried signs reading "Stop the Cosmic Watergate" and chanted "hey hey UFOs, people have the right to know."[25] An organization representative stated that "the US government has orchestrated the most spectacular deception of a people in the history of the world." Many UFO truth-seekers believe in working within the system; they share with the Right to Know protestors and CAUS a certain hopefulness about democratic process, and a seeming belief that by working together toward a common cause, citizens really can make a difference. Furthermore, ufology has always been the province of amateur investigators seeking the truth, and their actions also exhibit great faith in the ability of the determined individual to take on the system. The fact that it was a citizen's Freedom of Information Act request that led to the release of the MKUltra documents has become part of UFO conspiracy lore. Investigators persist in believing that they can and will find the one evidential key that will unlock the alien-government conspiracy.

In some cases when information is not revealed or discovered, ufologists have been known—in the spirit of self-fulfilling prophecy, or entrepreneurship, or perhaps some compelling combination of the two that characterizes UFO conspiracy theory—to create their own. One such case involves the "discovery" of documents revealing a postwar project to study and conceal knowledge of UFOs. During the late 1970s and early 1980s, Charles Berlitz (best-selling author of several books on the Bermuda Triangle) and ufologist William Moore set to work to reopen a long-dormant case about a 1947 flying saucer crash near Roswell, New Mexico. It was their hope that, as stated in their 1980 book, *The Roswell Incident*, with "the discovery of new information and the eventual help of the Freedom of Information Act . . . the consequences" of the crash would come to light.[26] They allowed, however, that the "mystery" of the Roswell crash would "probably be revealed only when governmental authorities release the mountains of UFO information they have been collecting throughout the years."[27] Despite a civil action against the CIA by CAUS in the early 1980s, "mountains of information" were not forthcoming. But in 1984 the documents that Berlitz and Moore so desired appeared on the doorstep of Jaime Shandera, a film producer of Time-Life documentaries living in Los Angeles, in the form of 35 mm film. Developed, the film supposedly revealed seven pages of typed documents, each marked "TOP SECRETMAJIC/EYES ONLY." Shandera, it turns out, had his own investment in theories of UFO cover-up: he was already discussing a fictional film based on Roswell with Moore.

These found documents revealed the supposed existence of a top secret, elite group called the Majestic 12 whose job it was to study the Roswell material in the aftermath of the alleged crash and to cover up the government's knowledge of the UFO phenomenon. Immediately dismissed by some in the UFO community as a hoax, embraced by many others with enthusiasm as the "smoking gun" in the emerging story of Roswell, the Majestic 12 documents finger a particularly powerful elite composed not of elected officials but of military, scientific, and technical experts. The list of members reads like a Who's Who of the national security state. It includes Dr. Vannevar Bush, Truman's Science Advisor and Manhattan Project architect; James V. Forrestal, the first Secretary of Defense; Admiral Roscoe Hillenkoetter, the first Director of the CIA; and Dr. Detlev Bronk, Chairman of the National Research Council, and member of the Atomic Energy Commission. While early versions of the revived Roswell story suggest a government trying to keep the lid on an event that even they could not explain, the revised version of events suggested a more coordinated effort to keep the truth about the "alien problem" from citizens. Powers outside of, above, and beyond the purview of democratic process—personified in an increasingly demonized military-scientific-technical elite—are rendered the puppet masters in the changing national and international order.

The "discovery" of the Majestic 12 documents fueled the growing popular fascination with Roswell through the 1980s and the 1990s, sending increasing numbers of investigators to Roswell, propelling a flurry of publications. In an ironic twist, this led to the Air Force's admission that it had covered up the truth about the 1947 crash. In 1994, in response to growing public inquiry into the crash, and to the spate of recent publications, the Air Force issued a report revising its original weather balloon claim, and asserting that "the wreckage . . . was part of an airborne system for atomic-age spying" called Project Mogul.[28] This admission only fanned the flames of conspiracy theory, and investigators felt unsatisfied that information about alien bodies "witnessed" in the desert crash remained hidden. This in turn prompted the Air Force to publish yet another report, this one 231 pages long and optimistically titled "Case Closed." It revealed that the bodies seen were crash test dummies used in parachuting experiments over the desert in the 1950s. It suggested that witnesses were confusing the debris from Mogul, and the dummies from these parachute tests, and in effect collapsing them into one event. Whoever named the report clearly had no insight into the cultural logic of conspiracy theory, in which to announce things closed—to seek to bury the past—is always read as an invitation to disinter.

Awareness that the truth about what happened in the past, and continues to happen in the present, is often controlled and circumscribed by those in positions of power, does not deter UFO investigators or conspiracy theorists from seeking it. On the contrary, many UFO conspiricists share a sort of optimistic sense of mission about locating definitive evidence or proof of "the big secret"—government coverup of the existence of UFOs and aliens. Their mission is invigorated by the endless possibilities of secrecy: it stands to reason that if the government has and does keep secrets about weapons testing or counterintelligence, it must be keeping secrets about the existence of UFOs and their occupants. The knowledge that classified information exists, and the possibility of attaining "new information" drive the process of citizen investigation undertaken by scores of ufologists. It suggests that truth, or more precisely proof—the Holy Grail of conspiracy theory—must indeed be "out there": not so much out there in the heavens or locked in the psyches of abductees, as mired in government bureaucracy, shored up in real and imaged halls of power.

Bearing Witness: Abductees as Living Proof

Published accounts of alien abduction most often emphasize individual, personal, and psychological trauma and recovery: they are generally framed as ordinary people's efforts to come to terms with extraordinary events in their lives. Early treatments such as *The Interrupted Journey* (1966) and *The Andreasson Affair* (1979) do not even entertain the question of government involvement or cover-up. Emphasis is placed instead on solving the puzzles of lost time and individual repressed memory; or understanding the purpose of on-board medical experiments performed on abductees; or with decoding alien messages and their meanings. Despite the resistance to conspiracy theory by many of the experts who have come to shape the discourse about alien abduction, and by many abductees themselves, some high-profile abductees, such as Whitley Strieber have thrown themselves headlong into this process of historical inquiry and revision. Those abductees who embrace conspiracy theory hold themselves up as proof of government wrong-doing. They believe themselves to be, in Strieber's words, "on the front line" and so while they continue to be marginalized by some within the community of believers, they are treated by others with a certain awe and respect, as heroes or martyrs to the cause of truth seeking. In structuring his own multivolume account of what may have happened to him, Strieber explores the full range of explanatory frameworks, but seems increasingly to be drawn to ruminations on conspiracy theory. He seeks not to separate abduction from, but rather to try to understand it in terms of, other stories being generated within the UFO community, such as stories about the Majestic 12 and the alleged Roswell cover-up. In so doing he, like my informants, engages in the eclectic practice of being an alien abductee, which revolves around gathering, combining, and recirculating accounts and interpretations of the abduction phenomenon.[29]

In his first book, *Communion: A True Story* (1987), Strieber praises several then recently published books about Roswell and the Majestic 12. He refers specifically to *Clear Intent* by Lawrence Fawcett and Barry Greenwood in which the authors, according to Strieber, "prove that some extraordinarily strange things have happened, and that the government has kept these things secret."[30] With this vague yet irrefutable truism, Strieber connects with conspiracy theorists and a world of possibility opens up, of which he himself is the center. The "strange things" have not just happened, they have happened to *him*. Abductees such as Strieber thus come to offer what can be taken as the ultimate form of proof to conspiracy theorists: the eyewitness account. In *Transformation: The Breakthrough* (1988), Strieber's second book, he immerses himself in the world of missing documents and ex-military informants as the chimerical sources of secret knowledge.[31] In it, as in other conspiracy theory accounts of alien abduction, alien-human contact is occasionally upstaged by repeated Deep Throat–like encounters between members of the military intelligence community and civilian abductees. While Strieber's books are filled with reports of typical abduction atrocities, such as sexual violation and sperm harvesting (and in Strieber's case the repeated injection of long needles into his head) he also reports episodes of contact with human informants. In these scenarios, human informants—intelligence insiders and possessors of "the secrets"—are themselves construed as alien; they are at once threatening and enlightening, bearers of sacred information to those of us who do not otherwise have access. In these scenarios, declassification is promised, promises of declassification are broken, and contactees are left to reconstruct "proof" from memory. As in all conspiracy theory, proof remains elusive.

Strieber, like the UFO activists discussed earlier, concludes *Transformation* with a call for the end of secrecy in government and with a quite reasonable call for a more democratic approach to intelligence, based on "a complete restructuring of the intelligence community." He argues, echoing the sort of ACLU activism discussed earlier:

> The Freedom of Information Act should be greatly strengthened and attempts to evade it . . . should be criminalized. . . . The Air Force should be put out of the business of presenting public 'studies' such as the Blue Book and Project Mogul rubbish. All federal intelligence activities should be overseen in detail by a civilian review board with absolute powers to declassify, and fully answerable both to Congress and the executive. The clearly stated objective of this board should be to minimize classification.[32]

As someone who believes himself to be bearing the brunt of such historical abuses quite personally, even physically, Strieber manages to marry the abduction genre with the conspiracy story: he blends the emphasis on individual trauma and domestic or psychic disturbance that characterizes abduction from other UFO stories—the invasion of self—with the global historical grand narrative of conspiracy. He and other abductees bring to the discourse of UFO investigation the personal motive: not only do they act as individuals against the system, but as victims bearing witness. They claim to be in the pursuit of both collective justice and a sort of personal vengeance. While other investigators must wait for documents, or fabricate them, abductees claim their experience, and their allegedly violated bodies, as evidence.

The Folly of National Healing

In 1994 President Clinton created an advisory committee to investigate mounting reports of human radiation experiments (HRE) conducted during the Cold War. He order a CIA-conducted agency-wide search for information about such experiments. This search, spearheaded by Secretary of Energy Hazel O'Leary, resulted in the declassification of millions of pages of documents, revealing that Cold War experiments exposed thousands of Americans to radiation. The panel found that CIA officers participated in the discussion and planning of human radiation experiments, including those involving the placement of troops at atmospheric weapons tests. Experiments included injecting critically ill people with plutonium, and using semicomatose brain-tumor patients to find out how much uranium it took to induce kidney damage.[33] It also revealed that soldiers and sailors had been exposed to radiation during atomic bomb tests in the Pacific and later at a secret military Nevada test site, sixty-five miles north of Las Vegas. The panel found that while "the great majority of cases were conducted to advance biomedical science," many were conducted to "advance national interests in defense or space exploration." Those experiments—whether radiological, psychological, or biological—were originally sanctioned by the same wartime mentality that sanctioned the MKUltra experiments, wherein ethics, legality, and individual rights were temporarily waived in the name of the Cold War imperative of competing with Soviet counterparts.

In his remarks upon accepting the report, the president applauded O'Leary's "ongoing commitment to finish the end of the Cold War."[34] He viewed the investigation as a deliberate effort to "restore the confidence of the American people in the integrity of their government."[35] In an effort to do so, the president first called for compensation to those subjected to experiments. It was not the first time the U.S. government had offered monetary compensation for abuse of citizens, with the hopes, undoubtedly, of laying the past to rest. In 1973 the government paid ten thousand dollars to more than six thousand survivors of the Tuskegee study and their families. In the Tuskegee study the U.S. Public Health Service withheld treatment from roughly four hundred black men from Macon County, Alabama, who had been promised free medical treatment and were then denied treatment for syphilis, which they did not know they had. The purpose of the study was to study how syphilis spread and how it killed. The Tuskegee study went on for forty years (1932–1972), during which time 28 men died of syphilis, roughly 100 died of syphilis-related complications, 40 wives were infected, and 19 children contracted the disease at birth.[36] Also in 1973, Congress directed the Department of Veterans Affairs to provide disability benefits to atomic veterans of Nevada nuclear test sites. In 1989 seventy-eight million dollars was awarded to those harmed near a uranium processing plant in Ohio. In 1990 President George H. W. Bush signed the Radiation Exposure Compensation Act establishing a trust fund for the injured.[37] In 1996 Secretary O'Leary announced that the government had agreed to pay $4.8 million to twelve people as compensation for injecting them with radioactive materials in secret experiments.[38] And in 1996 James Stanley, a former soldier given LSD during the 1950s by the

CIA in one of the experiments detailed in the MKUltra papers, won four hundred thousand dollars in a suit against the government. One of the Edgewood "volunteers," Stanley had believed he was participating in a test of equipment and clothing.[39]

After the decision was announced, Stanley expressed his feelings of victory and added that now, "I would like somebody in Washington to give me an apology."[40] In the 1990s the public apology became something of a commonplace—a sort of twelve-step response to historical abuses, a public coming clean.[41] Indeed the historical apology has become part of a collective, national narrative of retrieved memory. After calling for compensation for the victims of radiation experiments, Clinton added just such an apology, stating that, "today, on behalf of another generation of American leaders and another generation of American citizens, the USA offers a sincere apology to those of our citizens who were subjected to these experiments, to their families, and to their communities."[42] In response to the widespread and ongoing project of revising history, official apologies have been offered for historical actions and oversights, including the wartime internment of Japanese Americans, and U.S. participation in the slave trade.[43] In 1997, twenty-four years after the Tuskeegee victims received monetary compensation, Clinton offered an apology to the eight survivors of the study, to their families and to all African Americans.

The Clinton administration championed this therapeutic rhetoric of moving beyond official "denial" and into the process of national "healing." In a carefully worded statement in October 1994, Dr. Ruth Faden, a biomedical ethicist on the advisory committee, assured Americans that the official act of remembering and restructuring the unseemly slice of history uncovered in the HRE investigation was now under way. Faden declared that "We are now piecing together the story of the past, an unsuspected past, to help inform the future on these questions." Faden's rhetoric echoes Senator Kennedy's, suggesting that to confess, to confront and attempt to piece together a past trauma through narrative is to step toward "treating" or overcoming it. This rhetoric suggests that public traumas, like private ones, can be "treated" by a sort of talking cure. It suggests that once the original trauma is faced and confronted, the "symptom"—in this case widespread public distrust of government, anxiety about the lengths to which it will go in the name of its own advancement, and the lengths to which it will go to conceal indiscretions and crimes—will disappear. I make the case in earlier chapters that abductees underscore the shortcomings of overly simplistic notions about the healing properties of "ventilation" on the personal level. In the context of alien abduction narratives such an approach seems in many instances only to compound pain; abductees are forced to "relive" trauma vividly and, at the same time, to endure the fresh trauma of alleged continued forced abductions which no amount of talking can cure.

As applied to history, the notion that apologies necessarily bring closure makes even less sense. Past actions cannot be reversed through apology, and power imbalances remain in place despite knowledge of past abuses of power. As Clinton himself pointed out in his apology, it was "those citizens who count most on the government for its help—the destitute and the gravely ill" who have most often been subject to such violation, and who will most likely continue to be. Certainly, for conspiracy theorists, including the alleged abductees whom I discuss further in the next chapter, official apologies for historical abuses lead not to public healing, but to confusion over to what extent abuses of power are pathologies that can be treated, or structurally determined features of various social and political hierarchies. Official apologies have also resulted in a deep and intractable cynicism and suspicion of the powers that be, and a Stephen King–like sense that dead things cannot and will not stay buried. This is only augmented by the unfortunate fact that similar abuses seem to continue into the present, often at the expense of members of the military who have committed to serve the country. Since the first Gulf War over one hundred thousand veterans have complained of a wide array of health disorders referred to as Gulf War Syndrome. The CIA adamantly denied any knowledge of soldier exposure to chemicals or toxins. Two Pentagon reports ruled out radioactivity and uranium as the culprits. Even scholar Elaine Showalter weighed in on the origins of this elusive syndrome, characterizing it as one among several modern hysterias, psychological in origin (and in fact to be read alongside alien abduction). But in October 1999 a third Pentagon study was released that reveals that an experimental drug used on troops may indeed have been the cause of their symptoms. A variety of subsequent studies offer conflicting conclusions about the correlation between service in the Gulf War and the variety of symptoms that constitute Gulf War Syndrome.[44]

Since September 11, 2001, and the wars in Afghanistan and Iraq that quickly followed, the time span between abuses of power in the name of national security, revelation of said abuses, and official apology seems to have collapsed in on itself. In September 2001, for example, New Yorkers were told to return to downtown workspaces and residences deemed environmentally safe; less than two years later it was revealed that the Environmental Protection Agency had been told to minimize the environmental danger of the collapse of the World Trade Center towers. President George W. Bush began to argue for war in Iraq during late 2002. He declared his intention to attack Iraq in January 2003, building his case for war largely on the assertion that Iraq was in possession of weapons of mass destruction and had links to Al Qaeda. Only a little over a year later, in February 2004, Bush called for an independent investigation to study intelligence failures regarding Iraq's arms. By June 2004 both the 9/11 Commission and the Senate Intelligence Commission established that no link existed between Iraq and Al Qaeda, and that Iraq did not, in fact, possess weapons of mass destruction. In May 2003 Bush declared an end to major combat operations in Iraq; four years later the war continues and the death toll steadily rises.

The performance of national contrition has come to seem almost comical, contributing for many only to a wearying sense of the inevitability of state secrecy and deceitfulness. In the end, conspiracy theorists reflect a deeply cynical, shared belief that knowing what happened doesn't bring us any closer to knowing what's happening—no closer to admission to the secret schools. It makes conspiracy theorists of us all, for in the face of this dizzying barrage of information and disinformation, we are all left to cobble together versions of reality that square with our experiences of the world. Objectivity having come to seem as chimerical as extraterrestrials, we are left only with subjectivity which, when taken to the extreme, can indeed take the form of narcissism. Perhaps it's this sense of the seemingly bottomless nature of government secrecy, the sense that the project of declassification is an infinite one, that both haunts and compels the popular imagination of investigators, conspiricists, and abductees, who believe they are onto the biggest secret yet. Unable to control the course of this particular history, or the manner in which or pace at which buried information comes to light, conspiracy theorists can at least become actors in their own dramas of declassification.

7

This Is Worse Than Friggin' Aliens
Conspiracy Theory and the War against Citizens

> We fear humans a great deal; not that aliens are so great.
> —Anthony[1]

Maureen, an alleged alien abductee who lives on Long Island, is a self-described skeptic who comes across as funny and down-to-earth. She is divorced, currently employed part time in a local shop, and shares a modest home with her elderly father and teenage son in a sleepy beach community that I visited in August 1999. Maureen made us egg-salad sandwiches, which we packed up in an Igloo and took to the beach. As we walked out of her house, I admired her collection of books on alien abduction, all of which were housed above her computer in the kitchen. They included several books on what is known among UFO/alien abduction believers as the Montauk Project.

According to proponents of the Montauk Project conspiracy theory, military abductees, or MILABs, are citizens who are abducted not by aliens but by top-secret intelligence operatives. While some MILABs report seeing extraterrestrials during their captivity, they are thought to be apparitions—screen memories implanted by their human captors to keep them from remembering what really happened to them. Accounts of such military abduction have flourished not only in the Southwest—a not surprising site for acting out national atomic age/Cold War trauma and anxiety, given its proximity to Los Alamos and top secret military bases such as Area 51—but also and most recently in Montauk, Long Island.

I asked Maureen what she thought of the Montauk Project books and she responded, "Do I believe all the stuff in the Montauk books? No. Believe it or not I'm a skeptic. . . . I don't believe this stuff. I'm a real nuts and bolts kind of person. You practically have to hit me over the head with something for me to see it, so I take everything with a grain of salt because even I find this hard to believe."[2] It came as some surprise to me, then, to learn that Maureen believes that she herself may be a MILAB, and has produced extensive online accounts of her abduction by aliens and humans. Like so many other abductees, she drew her conclusions based on the logic that anomalies are only anomalies until patterns begin to emerge. In Maureen's words, "there are certain things that happened that—how many times do you have to see coincidences before they're no longer coincidences?"

For Maureen, ill-defined snippets of memory and bad feelings transformed into a full-blown and semicoherent narrative under hypnosis. Maureen claims, "I'll be honest with you, what I remember under hypnosis, a lot of it, I don't just take it unquestionably as truth." "Stuff came out," she notes, "that I never in my wildest dreams thought possible." During one hypnotic regression,

> What came out was that I was taken back in 1970 to an underground bunker in Montauk. . . . I remembered everything, I remembered details, I couldn't believe it. I remembered being brought into this bunker, now when we were out at Montauk, we went to this campsite called Ditch Plains, but where I was taken was up by the lighthouse, we were never there, we never went that far. . . . We stayed in Ditch Plains. I described this . . . what I called a door in the hill, and the door moved and . . . then I described what it looked like in the bunker and then we went through there into this bright hallway and I was taken in this elevator down, I don't know how many levels.

Maureen's memory, as retrieved during hypnosis, did indeed include extraterrestrial aliens. However, she remembers encountering not the typical abducting alien Greys who are thought to experiment on people inside of spaceships, but a "reptilian," another sinister type of alien reported to have been seen by some abductees. According to Maureen, when she first began to remember her experience at the Montauk facility, she "saw a reptilian while I was there. And when I came out of hypnosis I was like jeez this is far out. . . . Then I talked to my uncle, that's who we'd gone out to visit that day and he remembered I'd been missing, I was missing for about three hours they were out looking for me." During a subsequent hypnosis, Maureen came to remember that "while I was down there they brought me into this room and what I saw was this reptilian, and this reptilian sexually assaulted me."

Maureen had difficulty believing that what she "remembered" had actually taken place. And she was more upset, ultimately, not by her presumed sexual assault by a reptilian alien, but by the presence and involvement of human beings. As we sat on the beach eating the brownies Maureen had packed us for dessert, she said, "I know it sounds so crazy when you tell it, but as I'm telling it I'm still seeing it in my head. After the hypnosis I said this is just too nuts, I can't, I mean it just can't possibly . . . First of all it would mean that, I remember seeing military people, humans, and if that's the case I just . . . This is worse than friggin' aliens."

Before her hypnosis, Maureen had already decided that her anomalous experiences (including multiple bedroom intrusions and levitation) were most likely caused by aliens. She had turned to the Internet to find out more about alien abduction and that is how she found her hypnotherapist (this after rejecting a traditional psychotherapist who suggested that her belief in aliens was fabricated). In order to investigate her memories, she contacted an acquaintance she had made from the Mutual UFO Network, named Bill. She told Bill that, "I don't know what to think about it. I don't know whether to believe it or not, but I gotta find out now." In order to do so, they decided, in an interesting enactment of a psychotherapeutic commonplace, to return to the scene of the original trauma to see if it would trigger any conscious memories. Bill "said 'Let's go out to Montauk and see if you can find this place you described.' I said all right—if I can find that door in the hill that'll give me some validation." As she describes it,

> We went out there to Montauk, September of '95, and we walked into this parking area and I said it looks familiar but not what I remembered, but I remembered being on a cliff overlooking the water. So there was a cliff area there, I walked out to it . . . and I started walking back towards the lighthouse away from them. I'd only gone about five hundred feet and there it was right in front of me just the way I described it. It was an abandoned bunker on the outer perimeter of the camp. And I called them over and said I don't believe this, that's it, and it was

exactly how I described it. . . . It was concreted over so we couldn't see what the inside looked like.

Like the scores of investigators and conspiracy theorists who find confirmation of their worst suspicions in government admissions of previously denied activities, Maureen finds confirmation, or validation, seeing it "just the way [she] described it." The fact that the portal to her nightmare had been sealed off—and that what lay behind the door in the hill remained inaccessible to her—did not deter Maureen. Rather, it propelled her in her quest to find out more about her own experience and the experiences of others who claimed to have been taken and violated by the very people and institutions meant to protect and defend us. Like the classified document, the "concreted over" door does not deter abduction conspiracy theorists, but rather stands as evidence of continuing cover-up and abuse. These abductees draw on newly revealed information, on the fact of continuous revelation, to construct related stories of continuous violation. They claim that such traumas, rather than buried in the past, continue into the present; and that they are regularly acted out on their bodies.

The Dark Side Hypothesis

We abductees are the human sacrifices of our times. This would probably be acceptable to the vast majority of us if we could believe that it was for the good of the whole. If asked and treated decently and with dignity, a lot of people would go out of their way to assist any species. Humans have been sold out. . . . But our blood has bought you nothing . . . and it has not saved you or your children from the aliens. It has served only to line the pockets of the select few in the central power group, be they government, financial, religious, and/or alien leaders.
—From *Matrix II: The Abduction and Manipulation of Humans Using Advanced Technologies*[3]

Accounts of UFO/alien abduction exist on a sort of spectrum of acceptability. Abduction narratives as best-selling "true stories" often attempt to steer clear of conspiracy theory, or, as in the case of *Communion* author Whitley Strieber, remain somewhat modest in conspiratorial claims made, presumably to avoid accusations of paranoia and to strengthen claims at "normalcy." Strieber, for example, remains restrained in his judgment about government knowledge of, or involvement in, the alien abduction phenomenon. He agrees with many abductees that the U.S. government has long known about but denied the "alien presence" here on Earth. In *Transformation,* he reflects that,

> When the policy of denial was instituted, I doubt if anybody ever dreamed that the visitors would one day start marching into the homes of America in the middle of the night. But it appears this may be happening. If so, then the public has ended up on the front line. And the visitors are not only entering our homes, they are entering our brains. And we do not know what they are doing to us.[4]

Strieber lets the government off the hook by allowing that they never would have dreamed of the outcome of their cover-up of the existence of extraterrestrials.

Other conspiracy theorists, including MILABs like Maureen, work in the freer mediums of self-published literature, such as the Valerian volume cited above, and on the Internet. They are much less generous in their assessments of government intentions than Strieber. These versions of alien abduction conspiracy theory are sometimes called the Dark Side Hypothesis. According to the Dark Side Hypothesis, the U.S. government did not just turn a blind eye to the abduction of humans by aliens, it at best sanctioned, and at worst engineered, the use of American citizens in an array of scientific experiments. This hypothesis extrapolates from the Majestic 12 story discussed in my last chapter, further fleshing it out in a way that accounts quite specifically not just for crashed flying saucers and sightings, but also for the alleged abduction of humans. It is the Dark Side conspiracy theorists who hammer out the details of the alleged connection between government duplicity and abductee experiences of physical and psychological violation.

Dark Side accounts are much more lurid and colorful than the comparatively dry contests over documentation and historical revision that inform the Majestic 12 debates. Indeed, the Dark Side Hypothesis offers a sort of supersized version of UFO/government cover-up, according to which not one but at least thirty-five flying saucers have crashed on American soil; not four but 131 alien bodies have been retrieved from those crashes. Championed by John Lear (son of Lear Jet inventor William P. Lear) this theory is laid out in spectacular detail in the 450-page

Matrix II.[5] Published by the Leading Edge Research Group, and edited by one Valdemar Valerian, *Matrix II* consists of all variety of types of documents in camera-ready copy—many of which have been Xeroxed to the point of unreadability—including first-person accounts of those claiming to have been abducted and manipulated by the infinite range of "advanced technologies" referred to in the title.

Lear reports in *Matrix* that after years of frustration over unregulated alien activity within U.S. borders, on 25 April 1964 at Holloman Air Force Base, "a meeting was held between elements of the U.S. government and the species known as the Greys."[6] According to Lear, the terms of that treaty are as follows: first, the United States would allow the aliens to maintain underground bases. The Atomic Energy Commission's underground facilities were offered, and larger facilities were built around the Southwest." Second, "the United States would allow the aliens to abduct its citizens on a periodic and limited basis for medical examination, providing that the people were returned unharmed and without memory of the interaction." And third, in exchange for access to human bodies the aliens would provide the United States with technology in "beam weaponry, gravitational propulsion, stealth technology, mind control and implant technology."[7]

According to abductee Cynthia Crowell (also in *Matrix II*), such a treaty was not difficult in the United States, "for the people had assigned the power to make such treaties in their behalf to a small group of elected officials."[8] As she understands it, "the aliens would share technology with the Earthlings, and in exchange, all they requested was the right to collect biological samples, conduct experiments, and live in peace. Our technocrats found this offer to be irresistible—a small price to pay for advanced technology." In Crowell's account, as in those of Mario and others, the powers that be blur into one another, and are understood to be interconnected and colluding against "regular citizens."[9] Here Crowell blurs elected officials with technocrats, an interesting slippage in terms of the set of forces thought to be conspiring against regular folks during this period, one that suggests the perceived power of those with scientific and technical knowledge above those without. Yet at the same time, in these less mainstream versions of alien cover-up, the entire purpose of the Cold War is revised, as in other abduction scenarios, narcissistically placing the citizen-abductee-victim front and center.[10]

The Dark Side Hypothesis locates the abuse of citizens by aliens and

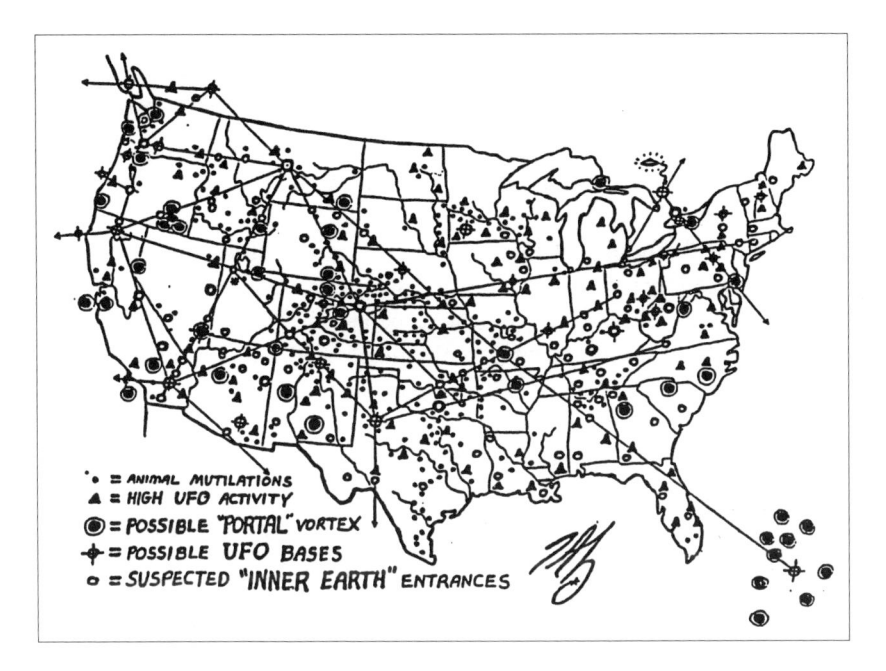

Fig. 10. Sighting frequency map from *The Matrix*.

human cohorts not only on spaceships, but also within American borders, inside an intricate web of top-secret or abandoned military bases and underground tunnels. These Underground Bases are sites in which citizens are purportedly experimented on, mutilated, sacrificed—treated like guinea pigs for the advancement of alien races and other complicit terrestrial elites. Demonized human scientists and technicians are rendered working alongside aliens in these luridly reanimated underground laboratories.

Some of the hottest spots on this fantastic dystopian map of the United States include Groom Lake/Area 51 near Nellis Air Force Base in Nevada, and Hangar 19 in Wright Patterson Air Force Base in Ohio, where alien technology and bodies are believed to be stored. Existing on the literal and figurative fringes of the military intelligence landscape of the southwestern United States, one anonymous *Matrix* "historian" locates the ongoing, underground project as an extension of what began in Los Alamos. The author writes, "Data indicates that there are many other bases with similar function, and that many of the early underground facilities belonging to the Atomic Energy Commission in the

1950s were eventually turned over to projects relating to alien technology. Most apparently were added on to by forces that occupied them."[11] The more restricted the site, the more ardent the investigation of human-alien-related wrong-doing and scientific/technical atrocities. Among the underground facilities discussed in *Matrix II* are, a "laboratory-type facility" in Arizona and a Nevada Facility "geared towards genetic work." Abductee Christa Tilton reports six in the Mexico Area, seven in Oklahoma, five in Arkansas, and several in Kansas. As *Matrix II* notes, "many of the bases appear to be run by entities, nonhuman or otherwise, that are totalitarian, domination-based, military and elitist in nature."[12]

The most infamous of these facilities, according to believers, is the alleged Dulce Facility in New Mexico. It is worth noting that descriptions of Underground Bases such as Dulce differ from spaceships in key ways. Rather than the cold and clinical terror that descriptions of UFOs suggest, underground facilities are more like Dante's hell: crowded, bustling, multilayered spaces through which "witnesses" descend in dismay. Each level of Dulce supposedly houses more deeply horrifying misuses of science and technology. According to one anonymous "witness," "There are at least 7 levels. We know . . . that the first two or three levels are primarily U.S. government personnel. We know that senators and astronauts have been brought to the facility and have been shown the first several levels. The facility appears to be a state of the art cryogenetics facility and lab."[13] As he continues, and the reader descends, the use to which each space and the technologies it houses are put becomes increasingly gruesome: "Research at the 4th level includes research on the human aura, research on telepathy, dreams and hypnosis —all geared toward control and manipulation of other beings." Level 5 is purportedly alien quarters, while Level 6 "has been referred to as the 'nightmare hall' by employees." The author writes, "Many limbed humans and other creations . . . reside there. It is an attempt to breed slave beings suited for specific tasks." Finally, "Level 7 is where human children and adults are stored as a source of biological materials." On this level "Humans have been seen stored in clear cylindrical containers over 6 feet in height, suspended in a yellow or amber fluid—alive and conscious but unable to scream or say a word. . . . In the same area are . . . the vats containing animal and humanoid body parts." As the witness descends into Dulce, humanity is literally taken apart, deconstructed for its parts. As in those narratives of reproductive tampering discussed in earlier chapters, humans are posited as little more than raw material for the march of progress.

The author breathes ominous life into the possible scenario of human experimentation, taking it to its imaginative extreme when he writes, "I frequently encountered humans in cages, usually dazed or drugged, but sometimes they cried and begged for help. We were told that they were hopelessly insane, and were involved in high-risk drug tests to cure insanity. We were told never to speak to them at all." Referring indirectly to the alleged "Manchurian Candidate" that the MKUltra documents suggested intelligence may have been working on creating, Valerian adds, "Technology is at a state where they can manipulate the bioplasmic body of human beings and program them through introduction of programmed reactions and images which will induce the desired result."[14] The scenarios of medical experimentation presented in *Matrix II* certainly resonate with the swirl of awe and anxiety at biotechnology expressed by so many alleged abductees. Yet the horror of conspiracy theory comes in its suggestion that such physical violation is committed in part by humans, and is inflicted on citizens by the state.

Dulce "witnesses," like other MILABs and Dark Side theorists, draw on an array of cultural narratives about the victimization and exploitation of "regular folks" in the name of national sci-tech progress. They pointedly make use of history as it is revealed through the process of declassification. So too do they draw with equal gravity on tropes and images from the science fiction, fantasy, and horror genres.[15] The Dulce scenario is perhaps most heavily indebted to the hollow earth theory popularized in the sci fi pulps of the 1920s, 1930s, and 1940s. According to Richard Shaver's theory, popularized by Ray Palmer in *Amazing Stories,* the earth's core was populated by robots left behind by an ancient civilization. The deros—or deranged robots—went bad and threatened to take over the earth and dominate humankind.[16] The author of the previous description of Dulce's alleged levels refers several times, by way of comparison, to the work of Edgar Rice Burroughs: describing Level 6, s/he writes, "it sounds like an Edgar Rice Burroughs' story, yet it exists." The author returns to Burroughs again in describing Level 7, noting, "It is like something out of the Burroughs' Martian series." Television shows and film are also referred to as the author renders Level 7: "Remember the long ships in the series 'V' where all the humans were stored? It's similar to that but it is more of a production laboratory situation." With some self-awareness about the extravagance of his or her claims, the author appeals directly to the reader, asking, "It sounds like the plot from a grade B movie doesn't it? Well, what is more comfortable for humans to handle in the guise of science fiction is actually based on fact; the main reason that this problem exists to the extent it does is that it is all literally underground and covert."[17]

While drawing on a variety of rich fictional sources, such conspiracy theorist "witnesses" argue that their claims must be true on the basis of a notion of precedence: the United States *has* engaged in mind control and physical experiments upon citizens, and so it must continue to do so. When pressed for evidence of his claims, conspiracy theorist Philip Schneider, whom I discuss further below, could only respond, "I worked in the federal government for a long time and I know exactly how they handle their business." Proponents of the Dark Side Hypothesis such as Rhonda Francis return time and again to trying to understand such accounts alongside recently revealed truths about government-funded uses of U.S. citizens,

> It's well known that for decades various military and intelligence pseudopods of the U.S. government have experimented with electromagnetically induced mind control. Many documents pertaining to our government's abiding interest in remote mind control and EM [electromagnetic] weaponry have been uncovered through the Freedom of Information Act, scholarly and medical papers have been published, researchers and victims have spoken out. There's little doubt that the technology exists, has been, and is being used. The military thinks it's quite revolutionary. They even have a special term for it: soft option kill.[18]

Helmut Lammer, a German ufologist who coined the term MILAB, reports that they were "kidnapped by a certain branch of human/military personnel, they were drugged, taken to hospital rooms and (under)ground military facilities, they saw men in white lab coats, they were examined, interrogated and sometimes implanted with military devices." Like Christa Tilton, Lammer takes as his point of departure "the documented history" of both human radioactivity experiments and MKUltra. He writes,

> Everyone who claims that secret experiments and covert operations against one's own people, including children are not occurring in Western democracies [sic] like the USA, Canada, and England should look at

the documented history of military/intelligence radiation experiments as well as mind and behavior control projects which are now known to the public.

Lammer reiterates the sentiment discussed in my last chapter that once past atrocities are unearthed, it is hard to believe they have stopped: "It's not clear when these experiments stopped, if they stopped at all."[19] For Lammer, the "invisible government" who used Americans in the race to beat the Russians are still at it; they have not stopped, but have simply and quite literally gone underground.[20] In telling stories about Underground Bases such as Dulce, these writers perform an instrumental and unapologetic blurring of dominant reality and fantasy, allowing the two sorts of accounts to bleed into one another to mutual narrative advantage. These conspiracy theorists trouble commonly accepted accounts of reality by suggesting their proximity to fiction. At the same time, they breathe life into speculative fiction by pointing again and again to its real world referents.

Victims Have Spoken Out

What most distinguishes Dark Side accounts from many of the historical and sci fi/fantasy fiction accounts on which they draw is their first-person subject position. Though certainly a variety of documents and types of proof are alleged to exist by proponents of the hypothesis (including the so-called Dulce Papers) most narratives about the mysterious facility are told by people who claim to have been there, either as employees or as victims of various types of physical and mental experimentation. As such, even those who produce the sort of baroque sci fi/speculative/horror hybrid fiction found in *Matrix II* insist on the veracity of their claims. Christa Tilton writes,

> I wish it were only a movie, but it happens to be true. It exists and is still functional today. . . . The facts are these. . . . Not only have I been abducted and taken to the underground base at Dulce, but I have met several other sane individuals that all give the same details time and time again. . . . I saw the tanks with fluid in them being stirred by something and I saw the guards and their elaborate electronic security system. I also saw clear containers with people in them! Believe me, I wish

this were only a dream, but more and more people are confirming the same visions and areas and this area cannot be taken so lightly.[21]

At the same time, in contrast to the majority of alleged alien abductees who are willing to share their stories with the public, Dulce witnesses—writing online and in publications like *Matrix II*—make only passing efforts to seem "normal" or credible. But are all proponents of the Dark Side Hypothesis and other graphic alien abduction conspiracy theories "crazy"? This question continues to confound me, and any possible answer to it remains complex and somewhat contradictory: on the one hand, some people, such as those whose stories close this chapter, come across as deeply troubled if not mentally ill. Their life stories include accounts of institutionalization, imprisonment, chronic ill health, depression, and suicide attempts. In their version of events, the unfortunate trajectory their lives has taken is rewritten as the result of a lifetime of persecution and violation by both humans and aliens seeking to control and manipulate them. When reading these accounts, it becomes clearer why legitimacy-seeking abduction experts like John Mack strive to steer clear of the so-called "Paranoids." Perhaps for the folks who inhabit this end of the spectrum of belief, abducting aliens are simply familiar and available characters—like Jesus, for example—who are available to populate the delusions of the paranoid and/or psychotic.

Others, like Maureen (whose story opens this chapter) clearly function in society and seem simply to feel less restrained about appearing "normal" to the public at large, especially when writing online, for example, to an audience that is by and large already willing to believe their claims. Such alien abductee conspiracy theorists seem to take some pleasure in story telling itself, and the truth of what they may believe happened to them only seems truer in light of other "evidence"—both from the past and unfolding daily—to support the notion of government duplicity and violation of citizen rights.[22] Finally, and somewhat paradoxically, it is those alleged abductees, including conspiracy theorists, who express awareness of the "craziness" of their own beliefs who seem most grounded in a dominant reality. Whether this is the result of their own market savvy or audience awareness, or actual evidence of their relative mental health remains impenetrable, at least to me.

Dr. Paul Bennewitz, one of the originators of the Dulce legend, is one of several Dulce investigators, or witnesses, who has come, through mental and physical breakdown, to be a sort of martyr to the cause of declassification. A "physicist, inventor, and tinkerer" who operated an electronics company in New Mexico and was also an investigator for the Aerial Phenomenon Research Organization (APRO) he witnessed one alien abductee's regression and came to believe that the aliens had implanted "some sort of communication device" in her head. Bennewitz came to believe that this communications device and her story were somehow connected to lights he had seen over Manzano Test Range, lights that flew toward the Kirtland Air Force Base area including Sandia National laboratory and Phillips laboratory. Bennewitz concluded that the aliens were engaged at Dulce in a massive mind-control experiment, "picking and cutting" at least thirty thousand people in the United States as of the late 1980s. He wrote up his conclusions in what he called the Beta Report, which was subsequently discredited by a fellow ufologist who convinced Bennowitz that he was receiving disinformation from the Air Force. Bennewitz suffered a nervous breakdown and, according to Internet conspiracy writer Rhonda Francis, "armed to the teeth and convinced that alien intruders were bombarding him with rays that disturbed his biological processes and sneaking into his home at night to alter his consciousness with drugs, was eventually hospitalized."[23]

Philip Schneider is another such conspiracy martyr who claimed to have had first-hand experience with the Dulce facility. Schneider maintains that he worked as an ex-government structural engineer who was involved in building underground military bases around the country.[24] According to a web article on "The Mysterious Life and Death of Philip Schneider," his job was to "go down the holes, check the rock samples, and recommend the explosives to deal with the particular rock." In the process of so doing, according to one account, he and his co-workers,

> accidentally opened a large artificial cavern, a secret base for the aliens known as Grays. In the panic that occurred, sixty-seven workers and military personnel were killed, with Philip Schneider being one of only three people to survive. Philip claimed that scars on his chest were caused by his being struck by an alien weapon that would later result in cancer due to the radiation.[25]

Schneider also claimed to have been a veteran of an underground battle in which he and a "small group of workers" formed a "resistance movement." He allegedly participated in an underground battle between the human, mostly military employees of the facility and the aliens, whose experiments had run too far amuck for even the government to condone. According to the legend, as many as seventy U.S. soldiers were killed in that battle. Unfortunately, according to Schneider, the aliens were victorious and remain there, "mutilating these abductees and producing androids in underground laboratories."

Schneider died in 1996, and his ex-wife is among those who claim that he was "murdered because he publicly revealed the truth about the U.S. government's involvement with UFOs."[26] To the outsider, Schneider is a particularly poignant character in this discourse. As his wife's piece details, he was plagued by physical and mental illness almost to the point of total incapacitation. In the following passage, which, for its relentlessness begins to sound almost like a joke, his wife details Schneider's physical and mental state before his death:

> He had chronic lower back pain. . . . He had multiple sclerosis which was chronic and progressive. Occasionally he had to use crutches, a body brace, leg braces, bladder bag, catheter, diapers, and a wheelchair. He often had to sleep in a hospital bed with railings, a helmet, and body braces. . . . He was taking Dilantin for seizures, and almost died three times from this medication due to an allergic reaction. . . . Philip also had Brittle Bone Syndrome and cancer in his arms. He had hundreds of shrapnel wounds, a plate in his head with a metal fragment in his brain, fingers missing from his left hand. There was a scar that ran down from the top of his throat to below his belly button, and another scar that ran from just under his ribs, side to side. . . . He had brain damage after a bomb was dropped on him while working as a civilian structural engineer for Morrison-Knudsen in Vietnam. . . . He was learning disabled.

His wife concludes that "he was a complex person—part genius and part paranoid schizophrenic." And yet despite the difficulty that must have been their everyday life—or perhaps in reaction to it—he and she believe that most of these problems were attributable to alien and/or government intervention, and that, adding insult to injury, "he had been deprogrammed so that he could not remember most of his 'past' life."[27]

Schneider's case epitomizes the ways in which the witness/abductee's body is understood to manifest the trauma of government secrecy and violation of citizen rights. Physical and psychological ailments can only be understood as the result of their victimization by outside forces. On the other hand, they also dramatize the very real ways in which individual people—individual bodies—*have* historically born the brunt of many very real state-sponsored violations, as in the cases of radioactivity, syphilis, or LSD testing.

It seems fair to say that Phillip Schneider most likely had a hard life —in exchange for his suffering, whatever its causes, he most likely got nothing. But by inserting himself into this drama, like alien abductees, he at least has a story. He stands at the center of the ever-unfolding drama of state declassification, and indeed gains a certain circumscribed status through his alleged experience, "proven" to be real and valid by the very disabilities that must have limited him to the point of paralysis in his everyday life.

The Juiciest Parts Tend to Remain Somewhat Hidden

In keeping with other lore about underground military bases, stories about the so-called Montauk Project are alleged to take place in the now-abandoned Camp Hero in Montauk, Long Island. Camp Hero was an air force station built in World War I and maintained by the state since 1984; it is open to the public on a limited basis, but has a number of off-limit areas. Local authorities state that those areas are off-limits because the many underground tunnels that lie beneath are now flooded and thus dangerous.

Conspiracy theorists, as is to be expected, see it differently, and where the official story ends the conspiracy version begins. UFO investigators Peter Moon, Stewart Swerdlow, and Preston Nicholls have written several books published within the last decade by Sky Publisher, located in Westbury, Long Island: *The Montauk Project: Experiments in Time* by Preston B. Nicholls with Peter Moon (1992); and *Montauk Revisited: Adventures in Synchronicity* (1993) and *Pyramids of Montauk: Explorations in Consciousness* (1995), by Nicholls and Moon; and *Montauk: The Alien Connection* by Stewart Swerdlow (1998). As stated on the back cover copy of the first book, the Montauk Project is, according to them,

> the most amazing and secretive research project in recorded history. Starting with the Philadelphia Experiment of 1943, invisibility experi-

ments were conducted aboard the USS Eldridge that resulted in full-scale teleportation of the ship and crew. Forty years of massive research ensued, culminating in bizarre experiments at Montauk Point that actually tapped the powers of creation and manipulated time itself.

Swerdlow, as the subtitle of his book suggests, makes the most explicit connections between the time-space experiments suggested by Nicholls and Moon, and alien abduction. An alleged alien abductee himself, Swerdlow also refers directly to MKUltra in his introduction, suggesting that,

> MkUltra was a 20th century 'modernization' of ancient techniques such as those employed by the ancient Assassins, a Middle Eastern cult during the Middle Ages who programmed subjects to kill through the use of hashish. After World War II the government began to experiment with narcosynthesis or 'truth serum' drugs. This has been documented and is not really denied by the government, however its full significance has been minimized in the extreme sense of the word.[28]

He adds, in a statement that epitomizes the conspiracy theorists' desire to uncover or expose, that "the actual research of such history is another matter, and although some of it is documented, the juiciest parts tend to remain somewhat hidden." It is the "juiciest parts"—what he elsewhere refers to as the "amazing scenario"—that inspire Swerdlow.

Swerdlow claims to have been abducted by aliens two or three times a week since childhood, sometimes physically, sometimes "astrally."[29] Like other abductees, he reports having been sexually violated and experimented upon, forced to witness violent visions of the earth's future. In contrast to Nicholls and Moon's rather wonky, gadget-obsessed rendering of the Montauk Project, Swerdlow offers, like other abductees and MILABs, a supposedly unique "eyewitness" perspective on alleged events. But unique to descriptions of the Montauk Project, and particularly disturbing, are his reports about "Montauk boys and girls"—children who have been "mentally programmed through their sexual psyche," of whom he claims there are "hundreds across Long Island" alone.[30]

This fairly new contribution to UFO-related conspiracy theory cross-hatches with accounts of Satanic ritual abuse that proliferated in the late 1980s and early 1990s. Swerdlow states that as a Montauk boy, he was trained as a "mentalist" to "manipulate other children's thought patterns, so they'd submit to mental and physical tests."[31] He adds that children who did not submit were often "terminated." Swerdlow is not the only writer to construct the Montauk Project along the lines of Satanic ritual abuse, positing children as the ultimate "guinea pigs." So too does John Quinn, a Montauk conspiricist who writes prolifically on the Internet. In aligning the Montauk Project with the Satanic ritual abuse phenomenon, Quinn underscores anxiety about the vulnerability of children to evil outside forces, or more precisely, the evil inside forces of broken families and day care. These, Quinn speculates, are implicated as "methods used by intelligence agencies like the CIA to get access to suitable youngsters in situations which require parameters of control."[32] In this light, such children make the perfect "Manchurian Candidates." Quinn writes somewhat ghoulishly that,

> Montauk Project researchers assert that the youngsters abducted for use in the experiments first had their spirits, psyches, personalities, sense of self and mental integrity completely demolished by severe, intensive carefully orchestrated psychosexual abuse until they were suitable to be reassembled and reprogrammed via supercomputers using psychotronic, EM/RF, virtual reality and "technopsychic" technologies into the desired psychological profile, to perform as needed, for use in interdimensional experimentation, as guinea pigs in the unending mind control and psychotronics work, as sleeper agents who could be activated by a variety of means—including through use of implanted transceivers, and as a "secret army" which can be called upon by the secret government in times of unusual or severe crises.[33]

Quinn contends that the Montauk base was a key site for MKUltra-type experiments dating back to World War II, and that, as a "psych base" the ongoing Montauk Project,

> dealt for the most part with psychotronic and interdimensional areas of experimentation. Electromagnetic mind-control experiments using high-powered radio-frequency transmissions were conducted continually upon visiting servicemen and women "invited" to the base for r&r; upon the population at large in surrounding communities; and most incredibly, upon numerous abducted children.

Though unable to secure hard evidence of these allegedly on-going experiments, Quinn, like other conspiracy theorists, argues that the Montauk Project is certainly plausible insofar as "the federal government intelligence agencies are responsible for an astonishing assortment of mind control experiments and projects, dating back at least fifty years."

Quinn does not claim to have experienced the Montauk Project, but Swerdlow does. He falls into the group of abductees—most of whom are also conspiricists—who I believe are, like Schneider and Bennewitz, mentally ill. His story includes details of a lifetime of delusional behaviors, a stint in jail for embezzlement that he does not remember having committed, suicide attempts, and institutionalization. His book documents his final "understanding" that all of his past ill health and unhappiness are the result of his having been subject to government/alien capture and torture, and his own co-optation into that program and activity as a self-described "Dr. Mengele." It was written, he reports, against the urging of friends and family who he notes have continually tried to steer him away from such beliefs and from the company of Moon and Nicholls. What through one lens looks like the compassion of a worried family—including three teen-aged sons—is through his lens further evidence that they are *all* out to get him.

I Was Stuck and Scared

In July 1999 I attended my first abductee support group in Manhattan. At that meeting I met Tanya, a single white woman in her twenties who lives in New Jersey with her parents. She had remained silent through the nearly three-hour meeting. When I asked Tanya if she was an abductee, she responded that she had reason to believe she was "a Montauk." As opposed to the surface "normalcy" of most abductees I meet —ones who insist on their normalcy and usually go out of their way to be engaging and rational, to talk about their lives outside of alien abduction—Tanya seemed odd. It was difficult to talk to her: thick glasses and crossed eyes made it almost impossible to make eye contact; a speech impediment made it difficult to follow her words, and she seemed to have difficulty completing a thought or sentence.

She later explained, via email correspondence, how she had come to believe she was a Montauk. First she read Nicholls's book, and thought it simply "interesting science fiction."[34] Then, she "saw a video on the truth about the Philadelphia Experiment" featuring a number of investigators, including Nicholls. She notes that "every time I watched it, I couldn't stay conscious." She felt that the voice of one of the other investigators Al Bielek, was the "trigger." This in turn prompted "an inquiry into my past in the 70s and early 80s. I found enough anomalies and things that related that I began to suspect the possibility of involvement." In the true spirit of conspiracy theory, anomalies are always invested with meaning, and are meaningful through their interconnection with other things. Tanya wrote to Nicholls, whereupon she was invited to visit Space-Time Labs (Nicholl's "facility"). Tanya then underwent tests to determine if she was indeed "a Montauk girl." She writes,

> There is a way to determine if one has the Montauk conditioning. Certain popular songs have been used to trigger the programs put into Montauk boy/girls.[35] I went into a trance state. I lost muscle tone and could not get up out of the chair that I was sitting in even though I tried. I was stuck and scared. At one point I felt as if my hands were electrified. I heard Preston call excitedly to Peter to go over and look at my hands. When the music stopped and I was brought out, Preston told me that I pretty much did what a Montauk boy/girl would do. He also said that my hands started to fade out. 'You reacted to the Montauk signature, you reacted to the Montauk chair music, you are a time traveler,' etc. on down the list. . . . Duncan casually remarked to me that he did see the Montauk colors (muddy yellow/green) in my energy field.

Like Swerdlow, Tanya believes not only that she was a victim, but also a victimizer. She writes, "Another person who allegedly was involved with the Montauk chair was terrified of me. He would just feel my energy and run away. He even apologized to me once saying that he just couldn't get near me. He even told Peter that I had hurt him real bad in Montauk." On a more mundane and poignant level that speaks to her deep sense of alienation from the everyday world of social interaction, she added, "I now wonder about other boys/men who have been unaccountably terrified of me in the past."

I asked Tanya to clarify how exactly one would define a Montauk boy or girl. She writes,

> A Montauk boy/girl is someone who usually is programmed in what is known as the Phoenix III project. They are brutalized, electrified,

tortured, drugged, altered, and programmed to be a kind of Manchurian candidate. Many are chosen for certain characteristics, such as blond, blue eyed, blood line, psychic ability, malleability, family abuse, abductee. They are programmed to run missions in time, act as couriers, be assassins, indoctrinate others, etc. . . . Boys/girls were programmed to be quite psychic. Back in the 70s and early 80s I was quite telepathic and psychokinetic in the most manipulative sense. I used to get into unwitting peoples' heads and really mess with them. This project was a lot about mind control.

Her response once again includes reference to the Manchurian Candidate, the apparent embodiment of anxieties about government engineering and regulation of citizen activity. But I am most interested in the list of reasons for why certain boys or girls are chosen to be Montauks. On the one hand, Tanya's list smacks of Aryan supremacy or eugenics, wherein children are valued for their blond hair, blue eyes, and bloodline. This is followed by the more ambiguous quality of "psychic ability," which is in turn followed by the idea that they might be chosen because they are *already* victims, either by nature (malleability), or by unfortunate circumstance (family abuse, abductee). This lumping together of "desirable" qualities is intriguing insofar as *all* of these—whether positive or negative—are construed as things that make her and others special. As in all facets of abduction, victimization is among those qualities that grant status, at least from the extraterrestrial point of view.

A recent article in the *Village Voice*, "Alien Toxins," offers new insight into the activities at one of the nation's most top-secret, or "black," military facilities, Area 51.[36] Second only to Roswell as a lightning rod for UFO belief, Area 51 is commonly held, as mentioned earlier, to house alien technology and/or bodies. The *Voice* article, however, reports on two recent cases against the government by high-profile Washington lawyer Jonathan Turley, director of the Environment Crimes Project at George Washington University's National Law Center. The cases are being fought on behalf of two recently deceased Area 51 workers, Wally Kasza and Robert Frost, both of whom were afflicted with a skin condition that other workers called fish scales, constant respiratory distress, and kidney cancer. Both have passed away since taking their case to Turley.

According to Kasza and Frost, the officers who run the facility were "taking advantage of its 'black' status to get rid of toxic waste in the most expedient and most illegal way possible" by burning it in open pits. What motivated the two sick workers to go to Turley was the facility's refusal to tell them to what toxins they had been exposed. In the article, an irate Turley insists that "two good men died at Area 51. They weren't killed by aliens. They may have been killed by the government, but through dangers that were distinctly earthbound, dangers that had nothing to do with extraterrestrial beings." He pleads, "I wish people were as concerned about Wally Kasza as they seem to be titillated by some mythic alien presence."

The material in this chapter suggests that perhaps it is, as Turley suggests, more titillating to map one's anxieties about government violation onto the alien—or at least onto a conspiracy that involves aliens and some form of technological magic, such as time travel, or telekinesis via mind control. I would add, however, that it is also perhaps *easier* to manage what seem to be in many cases very real feelings of trauma through a story that is not *simply* about how wronged some citizens have been, and continue to be, by their own government, but that is also about secret underground caves, reptilians, and Greys, and the promise of uncovering the extraterrestrial "big secret." Perhaps this is why the stories of MILABs such as Maureen and Tanya remain marginal, even within the abductee community. They are deeply disturbing for their level of sheer paranoia, and at the same time, especially when read alongside a story like the *Voice* piece, cut remarkably close to the bone. Read alongside the very real and fatal experiences of Kasza and Frost, Philip Schneider suddenly looks less clearly and markedly insane; read alongside Turley, CAUS attorney Peter Gersten seems less Quixotic in his quest for the truth about UFOs.

8

Look and See What You Have Done
Abductees and the Burden of Global Consciousness

In Budd Hopkins's most recent book, *Witnessed: The True Story of the Brooklyn Bridge UFO Abductions* (1996), he recounts the story of Linda Cortile who alleges to have been abducted from her Manhattan apartment in 1989. Cortile's story involves two "police officers," Dan and Rich, who claim to have witnessed Cortile's abduction through the window of her high-rise Manhattan apartment. What's more, Dan and Rich later recall that they too were abducted with Cortile on another occasion. In a plot twist that resonates with the conspiratorial stories of alien abduction discussed in my preceding chapters, it turns out that Dan and Rich are in fact "intelligence agents attached to the United Nations" who were in the process of transporting a "very important" third party from the United Nations to the heliport on Governor's Island. Though Hopkins never states the name of this mysterious "third party" in the book, it is widely held within the UFO belief community that it was then Secretary General of the United Nations Javier Perez de Cuellar.

Over the course of several hypnosis sessions, Hopkins determines that indeed Cortile, Dan, Rich, and de Cuellar may have been part of a highly unusual group abduction during which they were brought not to a spaceship, but to a beach. There they all allegedly learned an important lesson about the excesses of modern civilization, about the toll progress had taken not only on human bodies and minds, but also on the planet. In one critical scene recalled during hypnosis Cortile is both witness to, and agent of, an extraterrestrial message about the current environmental crisis. According to Hopkins, Cortile and the three men find themselves sitting on the beach, whereupon one of the men recalls

Cortile and several aliens walking up to them. Dan reports that "the girl held up what appeared to be a lifeless fish and said to us in a bold voice —'LOOK AND SEE WHAT YOU HAVE DONE.' "[1] Under hypnosis Cortile also remembers this event. She remembers being asked by aliens to dig on the beach to "find soil samples." She recalls,

> I see rocks. Lots of rocks. And I told them, look at that. It's a dead little fish. How did that happen? So I picked it up and I looked at it and it made me feel so sad and angry. And one of the beings beckoned to me and said, "let's sample the sand." So when we walk toward the shore with our pails, and I'm carrying this poor creature, and I'm so angry. And there are these . . . three people sitting on the sand . . . o we walk up to them, the four of us. . . . I feel this overwhelming sense of sadness and anger. Then I pick up the bluefish and it's their fault, people like them that kill our sea creatures. And one of them wants to move away from me. And I looked at them and I said, "look what you've done. Look at this creature now."[2]

Upon further reflection, the two officers claim that they "were led to believe that she is 'the Lady of the Sands,' whoever that is." Dan adds, "environmental, I suppose."[3] From this Hopkins deduces that, "on the morning of November 30, 1989, Linda Cortile was apparently a temporary and involuntary participant in an attempt to convey to a major political leader a benign alien concern with the Earth's ecology." Hopkins further claims to have received a copy of a letter from de Cuellar to Cortile attesting to the effectiveness of her message. In the letter, written "on United Nations letterhead" de Cuellar thanks Cortile for raising his consciousness. He also views the encounter as a sort of prophecy of world peace. According to Hopkins, the letter reads, "What I have seen, heard and felt on the seashore that November morning in 1989, hastened a dream that has been in a talking stage for the past four decades or so. This dream has been 'World Peace.' I can only say, it was time to make it happen. Please tell her, 'look and see what we have done in such a short time. Thank you, dear heart.' "[4] According to Hopkins, the letter ends with de Cuellar's direct address to him: "won't it be amusing to sit back in an old arm chair and watch all the nations of the world pull together. It shan't be long before the Earth becomes whole again."[5]

Since the publication of *Witnessed,* Cortile's story has been dismissed as a hoax by many members of the UFO community. Dan, Rich, and

Cortile, it seems, collaborated in producing their alleged group encounter; Hopkins claims not to have participated but allows that he was duped. De Cuellar has allegedly denied having interest in, knowledge of, or experience with UFOs or their occupants.[6] Their account nonetheless bears examination, perhaps especially because of its having been fabricated. The Cortile story can, like other conspiracy theories of alien abduction, be read as a fantastic alternative history of the Cold War and its aftermath. Several times in *Witnessed* Hopkins mentions the political context of this event. He notes that in the days preceding it, "a mood of near crisis as a result of the approaching breakdown of the once monolithic Communist bloc" prevailed; that on that same day George Bush was scheduled to meet Gorbachev in Malta, and that the motorcade's destination, Governor's Island, was the "site of the 1988 summit meeting between Presidents Reagan and Gorbachev and president elect Bush."[7] Channeling her alien captors, Cortile compels one high-profile architect of the new world order to take stock of military-industrial excesses of the last half century. In this narrative, set in the waning days of the Cold War, world peace and global unification collapse into one another; each is hastened along not by ongoing political processes but by a single interaction between a citizen and a member of a global, political elite. In this sense Cortile offers an imaginative and alternative vision of the new world order—an era of globalization—that will supposedly succeed the Cold War era. It does not foretell a new world order defined by "peace and security, freedom, and the rule of law," as posited by President George H. W. Bush in his 1991 State of the Union address. Rather, it voices concern about a shared sense of the deleterious effects of human progress—perhaps especially American expansionism and imperialism on Earth and in space—on the planet.

In this context, Cortile's story can be read as a powerful fantasy of historical and political agency: through her alleged abduction Cortile claims to have had a private audience with a very important, world-renowned political figure. When touched by aliens, Cortile and the other alleged abductees I will discuss in this chapter believe they are able to effect positive change and to unify a world seemingly controlled by external forces, including global elites such as the United Nations whose power transcends national boundaries. So too is Cortile's environmental awareness allegedly a product of alien influence. After hypnosis, Hopkins asks Cortile if she considers herself an environmentalist in waking hours. She claims, "I care for animals . . . but I'm not a fanatic about it either. I eat meat."[8] Yet as conduit for the alien message, she is transformed into the "Lady of the Sands."

Space Brothers and Missionaries from Another World: Pre-Abduction Alien Contact

When accounts of abduction by aliens first appeared in the mid-1960s, they differed from previous accounts of contact with extraterrestrials both in the hypnotic means through which they were retrieved, and in the details of what happened to abductees during forced medical and reproductive experimentation. The notion that aliens might contact humans in order to convey warnings and messages for the good of humankind, however, was already commonplace in stories of encounters with aliens published in the 1950s. In previous chapters I have offered a brief overview of the movement of UFOs and their alleged occupants from "up there" to "down here": from the flying saucer sightings of the 1940s and 1950s; to reported sightings of crashed or landed ships and their occupants along roadsides in the 1950s; to increasing crashes, visitations, and abductions beginning in the 1960s with the Hills.[9] During the 1950s an increasing number of people also began to come forward claiming to have communicated with alien visitors. Several claimed to have received messages about the state and future of humankind from these entities. The stories of two such contactees are the focus of the first part of this chapter. In them one sees traces of still somewhat subtle postwar warnings about technological excess that have come, in abduction, to be understood as what John Mack calls a "corrective initiative."[10] The accounts of these 1950s contactees gave new form to postwar anxieties about the destructive potential of human progress. More specifically they express, through a fusion of scientism and spirituality, an environmentally conscious concern about technological and military excess located specifically in fear about global destruction and its implications for the human future.[11]

Two of the most famous and widely published of the 1950s contactees were Orfeo Angelluci and George Adamski. In 1952 contactee Orfeo Angelluci reported that in May of that year UFO occupants contacted him. Born near Trenton, New Jersey, Angelluci was "an enthusiastic amateur scientist" who moved to California with his family in 1947. As he drove to his home in Burbank from work at a nearby aircraft plant, he spotted a UFO and was drawn to follow it. Two smaller balls of light descended toward him and spoke: "Don't be afraid Orfeo, we are friends!" A screen then appeared upon which were projected "images of a noble looking man and woman." As ufologist Jerome Clark writes in his *UFO Encyclopedia,* "the screen disappeared and the voice resumed speaking and gave him a spiritual message about the aliens' love of all human beings stemming from an 'ancient kinship of our planet with earth.'"[12]

The aliens who allegedly contacted George Adamski also assured him of their benevolence. Adamski, a Polish émigré who worked in a concrete factory in California, also, like Angelluci, regularly attended and presented at the UFO lecture circuit. Adamski was the first contactee to publish a book-length account of his contact, *The Flying Saucers Have Landed* (1953). Prior to the publication of his book, Adamski had already made a name for himself as something of a UFO expert and, as Clark notes, "a minor figure in the California occult scene."[13] Adamski lectured before Service Clubs in the late 1940s and early 1950s about his theories of flying saucers, and in 1949 published a science fiction novel called *Pioneers of Space*. The research done for his UFO lectures, in the meantime, culminated in an article in *Fate* magazine—a pulp specializing in reports of paranormal phenomena—in 1951.

Despite being roundly discredited and ridiculed, Adamski persisted in writing and publishing *The Flying Saucers Have Landed,* in which he claimed contact with a UFO occupant. Adamski states in his book, "It was about 12:30 in the noon hour on Thursday, 20 November 1952, that I first made personal contact with a man from another world. He came to Earth in his space craft, a flying saucer. He called it a Scout Ship. . . . This took place on the California desert 10.2 miles from Desert Center, toward Parker AZ." This "human being from another world" is described by Adamski as "beautiful" and "pleasant," about 5'6", 135 pounds, 28 years old, long-haired, and in a brown one-piece garment.[14] He sensed Adamski's surprise, extended his hand, and through a combination of telepathy and sign language, Adamski ascertained that the visitor was from Venus, and that his "coming was friendly." The angel-like "space men" described by both Angelluci and Adamski offer assurances of friendship and love and are capable of "great compassion."

From these benevolent aliens, however, Angelluci and Adamski both receive messages about the state of Earth, which is perceived to be in peril. Angelluci received his message after entering an object that looked like a "huge misty soapy bubble," which commenced flight. As Clark recounts,

> In due course a window opened, and he saw a planet of deep twilight-blue intensity. The voice told him that this lovely world was the Earth. As Angelluci wept, the voice went on "Weep, Orfeo. Let tears unblind your eyes. For at this moment we weep with you for Earth and her children. For all of its apparent beauty Earth is a purgatorial world among the planets evolving intelligent life. Hate, selfishness and cruelty rise from many parts of it like a dark mist."[15]

Angelluci went on to spread the word through magazine articles, lectures, interviews, and finally his book, *The Secret of the Saucers* (1955), warning that "a devastating war would soon come, followed by a 'New Age of Earth' and brotherhood." He was told that he was one of three people contacted on Earth, the other two, like him, "simple, humble, and presently unknown."[16]

The stories of contactees bear obvious resemblance to Judeo-Christian narratives of divine intervention. In them individuals act as visionaries or prophets, able to foresee the future of mankind. Angelluci highlights human sin—"hate, selfishness and cruelty"—as the forces deeming Earth a "purgatorial world" in need of extraterrestrial salvation and redemption. In this sense, the "devastating war" predicted by Angelluci resembles other apocalyptic scenarios that envision the culmination of life as we know it in some sort of judgment day. The message that Adamski receives from his Venusians also suggests a coming apocalypse, but one that is more pointedly the result of nuclear annihilation. Specifically, Adamski's contact was "concerned with radiations going out from the earth."[17] As Adamski recounts, "I asked him if this concern was due to the explosions of our bombs with their resultant vast radio-active clouds? He understood this readily and nodded his head in the affirmative." I quote at length here to underscore the clear atomic-age anxiety about the killing effects of radiation—and its effects not only on Earth but also on the entire universe—that informs Adamski's story of an entity descending from the heavens to put mankind on the right path:

> My next question was whether this was dangerous, and I pictured in my mind a scene of destruction. To this, too, he nodded his head in the affirmative, but on his face there was no trace of resentment or judg-

ment. His expression was one of understanding, and great compassion; as one would have toward a much-loved child who had erred through ignorance and lack of understanding. . . . I wanted to know if this was affecting outer space? Again a nod of affirmation. In this respect let me say here, it has long been known by scientists of Earth that the cosmic ray, as it is called, is more powerful in outer space than it is in the Earth's atmosphere. And if this be true, is it not just as logical to assume that the radioactive force from the bombs being tested by nations of Earth could also become more powerful in space, once leaving the Earth's atmosphere? Logical deduction supports the statement of this space man.[18] But I persisted and wanted to know if it was dangerous to us on Earth as well as affecting things in space? He made me understand—by gesturing with his hands to indicate cloud formations from explosions—that after too many such explosions. Yes! His affirmative nod of the head was very positive and he even spoke the word 'yes' in this instance. The cloud formations were easy to imply with the movement of his hands and arms, but to express the explosions he said, Boom! Boom! Then further to explain himself, he touched me, then a little weed growing close by, and next pointed to the Earth itself, and with a wide sweep of his hands and other gestures that too many 'booms!' would destroy all of this.[19]

Adamski experienced all of this only two states away from New Mexico, the home state of both Trinity Site, where the first atomic bomb had been exploded only seven years earlier, and the flying saucer crash at Roswell, which had allegedly occurred only five years earlier. In this sense his account acts as a sort of precursor to more recent conspiracy theories of alien contact discussed in chapter 7, concerned as they are with real and imagined traumas to the atomic southwest and its inhabitants. Adamski's account is, however, infinitely more optimistic in its suggestion that a literal deus ex machina came at this particular time, to this particular place, to remind us of our ecological connection to all things. It also came to warn us about the toll we take not only on Earth, but on the universe as a whole, which the Venusian's presence, as well as the story of a crashed spaceship suggests, is very much alive with entities very much like us.

Adamski fondly recalls that "the presence of this inhabitant of Venus was like the warm embrace of great love and understanding wisdom, and with his departure I felt an absence of this warmth."[20] Indeed,

Adamski feels transformed by a subsequent ride through space. *Invited* on board, he reflects that, "the very realization of the experience I was having overwhelmed me . . . No longer was I concerned with Earth alone," his transformation taking the form of heightened consciousness.[21] Through their conversation, and Adamski's ride, he is thus made aware that the earth is only part of a vaster, interconnected system. Angelluci is brought to tears by his new view of "this lovely world." As in future accounts of contact and abduction, the possibility of global destruction enables revision of our idea of ourselves and the earth by forcing us to consider the earth in context; to look at ourselves as part of the universe. Our actions affect others in the most cosmic sense. For contactees such as Adamski and Angelluci, the process of coming into global consciousness is for the most part painless, positive, and enlightening. What's more, receiving these messages distinguishes such "simple, humble, and presently unknown"[22] folks as Angelluci and Adamski, thus providing a means, albeit limited, of being heard.

Yet even in these early stories of contact and communication with aliens there is a distinct chord of warning or menace. Certainly knowledge of the "dark mist" surrounding Earth, the prospect of the earth destroyed, is not a pleasant one. In Adamski's case, through his halting but effective mode of communication the Venusian manages to equate Adamski with plant life, and both animal and vegetable with the earth itself. The visitor thus demonstrates the then-new notion that, in the face of nuclear destruction, hierarchies of the most basic order—between animal, vegetable, and mineral—collapse, leaving humans unprotected by their own assumed status as "superior" entities. The Venusians statement, as told by Adamski, makes a problem of easy notions of human domination of other species and substances, including Earth or universe, notions that in the early 1950s had thus far gone largely unchallenged as part of a potentially destructive "western materialistic worldview."[23]

As the stories of Angelluci and Adamski suggest, UFO and contactee culture was one relatively marginal outpost in which the implications of progress for the human future, the increasing proximity of humanity and technology, of Earth and space, were made sense of. From the vantage point of space, contactees began to imagine and articulate a sense of wonder about the changing world, but also the anxiety and responsibility attached to their new role as citizens of Earth. The dawn of the Space Age in the early 1960s prompted a more popular, widespread, mass-media-led inquiry into the changing relationship between human beings and the universe, as well as between human beings and the planet on which we live. Energized by President Kennedy's vision of a New Frontier, including the "uncharted areas of science and space," Space Age rhetoric offered a new, more optimistic and forward-looking paradigm for understanding the possibilities of technological progress for the human (read "national") future in the wake of the atom bomb. Speculation about humans' entering space became more widespread and was no longer confined to science fiction. The space race also offered another forum, more mainstream than contactee and occult cultures, in which the analogy between space and heaven, and by extension of space travelers with gods, was exploited, and the lines between fantasy and reality, religion and science further blurred, to varying ends.[24] Just the possibility of space flight prompted speculation about what revelations would result from the human ability to assume a previously divine perspective.

The Ecstasy of Unity

By the mid-1960s, images of Earth made available courtesy of the space race, and widely distributed through various media, fostered the notion that an outsider's view of Earth—previously possessed only by gods and alleged contactees—would heighten our own sense of its, and our, overall state.[25] The first view of Earth from "the vicinity of the moon" was taken by the unmanned spacecraft Lunar Orbiter 1 in 1966, but millions of people around the world shared the alien's-eye view of Earth transmitted via television on Christmas Eve 1968 by Apollo 8.[26] Many interpretations of the state of the planet as seen from space stressed optimism about the "loveliness" of a world otherwise understood to be in social and political unheaval.

Some, through the increasingly available views of the earth from space, came to another realization: that the earth, the universe, and humanity are all parts of a greater and interconnected whole. This revelation about our place in the universe came simultaneously from a variety of cultural locations, and worked, like Adamski's Venusian, to trouble easy notions of human superiority. In 1962 noted science fiction writer Arthur C. Clarke offered his speculative and positive perspective on the ways in which space travel would compel humankind to redefine its place in the universe. In "Space Flight and the Spirit of Man," published in *Astronautics* magazine (the publication of the American Rocket Society), Clarke speculates,

> I think man will see himself as one agent by which the whole universe of matter is slowly becoming conscious of itself. He will cease to feel an alien creature in an indifferent world, but will sense within himself the pulse of the cosmos. He'll become familiar with the marvelous and varied forms which can be assumed by matter, and he is certain to develop a feeling of reverence for the awe-inspiring whole of which he is a very small part.[27]

In Clarke's formulation, it is the astronaut who must play a central role in helping us "create the myths of the future" as a sort of intergalactic consciousness-raiser. But Clarke's piece also implies that this is true for "man" in general: that in some not-too-distant future, we will all, alive with the cosmos inside of us, learn that we are part of a greater whole, not "aliens" on our home planet, or nation, or town. In the face of this knowledge Clarke directs us to feel reverence. Clarke reiterates Adamski's notion—informed by some blend of science fiction and New Age ideology—that "man" can "no longer be concerned with earth alone," for not only are we in the cosmos, but the cosmos is in us. Such holistic ideas offer an alternative to less hierarchical and dominating models of human interaction with the world around us. Yet as the stories of alien abductees that began to appear just a few years later began to demonstrate, holistic models of the world and universe, in which humans are interchangeable with the world around us, upset and complicate commonly held notions of who and what humans are. They call into question any possible status that comes with being members of the human species, not to mention citizens of an advanced industrial nation and a major world power. The idea that "we" blur and blend with everything around us is at once both expansive and frightening.

Astronaut Edgar Mitchell, lunar module pilot of Apollo 14 and the sixth man to walk on the moon, had an epiphany during his reentry that resonates more with Clarke's speculative scenario than with the fond admiration of Earth from afar offered by other astronauts. Mitchell, writing in 1996, describes his epiphany as follows:

> Hurtling earthward at several miles per second . . . I had time to relax in weightlessness and contemplate that blue jewel-like home planet suspended in the velvety blackness from which we had come. . . . I experienced a grand epiphany accompanied by exhilaration. . . . From that moment on, my life was irrevocably altered. . . . What I experienced during that three-day trip home was nothing short of our overwhelming sense of universal *connectedness*. I actually felt what has been described as an ecstasy of unity. It occurred to me that the molecules of my body and the molecules of the spacecraft were manufactured long ago in the furnace of one of the ancient stars that burned in the heavens about me.[28]

Mitchell adds, "And there was the sense that our presence as space travelers, and the existence of the universe itself was not accidental but that there was an intelligent process at work. I perceived the universe as in some way conscious. The thought was so large it seemed at the time inexpressible, and to a large degree it still is."[29] The view of Earth from space, it seems, could at the same time reaffirm our place in existing hierarchies and call those very hierarchies and our place in them into question by suggesting that we are all reduced to our most basic atomic parts. People who reported having been abducted by aliens during this period began to express a complex combination of emotions, including pleasure in role-playing the status of those who are able to transcend earthliness, and guilt about complicity in collective corruption of the Earth. If they could see Earth from the vantage point of space, they learned, they were also responsible for confronting the truths that come with that new perspective of the planet.

The World Is Trying to Destroy Itself: Early Abduction Accounts

Alien abduction emerges, then, in a historical moment when these various ways of viewing the earth and diagnosing its value and condition were unfolding: from Space Age optimism about a New Frontier; to nostalgic and fond assessments of the earth's value and inherent good as seen from space; to holistic views underscoring the interconnectedness of human, Earth, and universe. During the 1960s and 1970s the handful of people who claimed to have been abducted by aliens continued to report receiving eye-opening messages from aliens about the place of humans in the universe. Betty and Barney Hill were, once again, the first to claim that extraterrestrial aliens forcibly took them on board a UFO, not only to perform medical experiments on them, but also to make them confront the roles they played in the universe.

In the Hills' account—marked already, as I have described, by a turn from relative benevolence to increased hostility and physical threat on the part of the aliens—the "message" imparted by the aliens is somewhat ambiguous. In between episodes of forced paralysis and medical experimentation, Betty does carry on a dialogue with several of her captors. At one point, her captors show her a map of the universe and ask if she knows anything about the universe. She recalls that, "I told him no. I knew practically nothing." The alien angrily rolls up the map and replies, "if you don't know where you are, then there isn't any point of my telling where I am from." Betty reports that "philosophically," her experience, including this exchange, "has given me a broader appreciation of the universe."[30] This exchange between Betty and her alien captor is telling: it reveals the anxieties that come along with the ability to travel through and have a more expansive view, or "broader appreciation," of the universe. With this appreciation comes the requisite concern that progress may be hurtling out of control. Betty worries that, "in the last forty years, we seem to have broken through more barriers than it has taken us all through history. We seem to be really just on the threshold of a new science and will move ahead even more rapidly than ever if man doesn't destroy himself first."[31] Published in 1966, the heyday of NASA's Project Gemini, Betty Hill seems implicitly to question the optimism of New Frontier ideology, like Adamski before her. In the process she offers a de facto criticism of and warning about progress gone out of control. And it is in this sense that concern about the terrestrial and human future coincides with the other cultural anxieties to which alien abduction narratives have since the 1960s continued to give voice. All express concern about progress, whether American national progress, or human progress; most often the two bleed tellingly into one another. All express concern that others, whether the technical professionals who control new reproductive technologies, or U.S. military expansion, are spearheading advancement that may in fact disserve the very people it is meant to serve. And in the alien abduction subplot that features anxieties about ecology, alleged abductees are made to feel both hapless, and accountable in the face of such rapid and possibly deleterious change.

In the Hill story the aliens are not as benevolent or tolerant of our foibles and shortcomings as the Venusians and space brothers of the 1950s. The aliens in the Hill story, like exasperated and long-suffering parents, are frustrated and disappointed with our limitations. The Hills' alien captors point out the egocentrism of the belief that we may in fact be alone. The aliens step in to remind us that we have done enough damage, that we would have to be foolish and remarkably narrow to believe that there is no nonhuman life in the universe, and that by extension, humans are not indisputably the dominant species in the universe.

The Andreasson Affair (1979) picks up and develops themes set in motion by Adamski, Angelluci, and the Hills about environmental crisis. In contrast to the Hill story, Andreasson's account is filled with an eclectic New Age assortment of mythical and religious symbols. In this sense her account remains more consistent with contactee accounts than does the Hills'. Andreasson's version of abduction was no doubt shaped by her "vibrant Christian faith."[32] A fundamentalist Christian, Andreasson believed it when she was allegedly told by her captor Quazgaa, that "I have chosen you to show the world."[33] Understandably Andreasson was eager to know why she had been chosen and what for but the aliens insisted that "the time is not yet"; Quazgaa urged her to release herself of fear "through my son."[34] Fowler describes Andreasson's reaction to this exchange, as reported by her while under hypnosis, as "the most moving religious experience that I have ever witnessed." She exclaims with Christian fervor, "thank you for your son!" Andreasson confirms for Fowler under hypnosis that the aliens "definitely" are connected to "the Second Coming of Christ."[35]

Andreasson's abduction experiences also included her immersion in liquid, an encounter with headless, two-eyed "lemur or monkey-like creatures," her being led through an environment that included both a pyramid and hanging clusters of crystals, as she describes them "bright bright light and clear crystals that have rainbows all in it."[36] She also witnessed a fifteen-foot eaglelike bird that was replaced by a fire, which was then reduced to ashes, out of which formed a "fat worm."[37] Fowler interprets this particular episode as Andreasson's witnessing of "the death and rebirth of the legendary phoenix . . . sacred in ancient Egypt."[38] Andreasson equates it with an Incan symbol she has seen.

Though Andreasson feels confident that she has been chosen, she is not sure what for. And while the aliens urge her simply to have faith and wait for the truth to be revealed, under repeated questioning from her hypnotist and a team of investigators, Betty begins to report that they "have come to help the world."[39] Here Andreasson's report of events still sticks close to the Christian model, according to which God so loved the world he gave his only son. But Andreasson's story shows how traditional religious narratives get modified in UFO belief by contemporary concerns about the world: for the aliens are not here, as Christ purportedly was, to redeem humankind from its sin, but rather they intervene because "the world is trying to destroy itself." The aliens claim, like the 1950s space brothers, that "we have come to help the human race, we do not want to hurt anybody, but because of great love we cannot let man continue in the footsteps he is going."[40] Contemporary abductees discussed in this chapter continue to put the most explicitly religious spin on abduction, typically believing that aliens intervene in the lives of humans not simply to study humanity for their own selfish and rational ends, but rather to save it from itself.

Unlike earlier alien contact stories, however, in abduction the aliens' love of humanity does not preclude their carrying out painful procedures on abductees. Not handsome Venusians, these aliens look "scary."[41] Andreasson is taken aboard their spaceship, placed on an operating table and forced to endure a series of medical procedures. These include a nasal probe, now standard in abduction accounts. Andreasson recalls, under hypnosis, them inserting a "long silver needle into her left nostril." She remembers, "he's taking an instrument and—ah-h-h-h! . . . ow-wow! Why do you have to put that up my nose—oh-h-h-h!"[42] For Andreasson, the news that an alien race has come to "help the human race" and prevent us from destroying ourselves comes with a price: unwilling flight and capture, and physical violation.

Our Welfare Depends upon the Earth

By the early 1970s, public awareness about environmental crises threatening the health of the planet were increasingly in clear view, thanks to the nascent environmental movement. Environmentalists acted against a range of environmental threats, including mercury in the water, PCBs, radioactive contamination, DDT, overpopulation, and scarcity of resources. In formulating their arguments, meant to catalyze political and citizen action, they drew on the emerging notions of earth as entity, and holistic ideas about the interconnectedness of the universe discussed above. In the context of the increasing awareness of such crises came the idea that the earth—possibly a living, breathing entity—was troubled, ill, and angry, struggling to survive under the burden of civilization and was, quite possibly, not happy about it.

In 1962, before environmentalism would cohere into a social movement, biologist Rachel Carson gained public attention by warning readers about the peril of chemical pesticide pollution. The focus of Carson's attack was the chemical industry and its production of pesticides and herbicides, including DDT. At the dawning of human exploration of space, she, and environmentalists to follow, would underscore humanity's continued and deleterious conquest and misuse of the earth and its resources. Though fears about the imperilment of the planet had long been established in the public mind in a more urgent way by the threat of nuclear annihilation, Carson offered an early and resoundingly popular indictment of humankind's ecological imperialism, and its possible culmination in global destruction. While her criticism was waged against chemical companies, Carson underscored that while industries make pesticides, people use them, and thus participate in global destruction. This is different from the message delivered on the desert to Adamski some years earlier. In the case of the destructive potential of atomic weapons, surely the humble contactee prophet could not be held accountable. In the case of the degradation of the planet by all manner of pollutants, many humans, at least those living in advanced, industrialized nations such as the United States, are, in fact, at least in part, responsible.

In 1970 a controversial scientific theory called the Gaia hypothesis, formulated by British atmospheric scientist James Lovelock, helped along the idea that humans were part of a more vast, interconnected global ecology composing "mother earth." Lovelock first put forth his theory at a Princeton conference about the origins of life on Earth in 1969. Lovelock's theory posited that,

> The Earth's climate and surface environment are controlled by the plants, animals, and microorganisms that inhabit it. Taken as a whole, the planet behaves not as an inanimate sphere of rock and soil, sustained by the automatic and accidental processes of geology, as tradi-

tional earth science has long maintained, but more as a biological superorganism—a planetary body—that adjusts and regulates itself.[43]

Lovelock thus proposed that "the Earth is actually a living entity and humanity a vital part of its life system."[44] Accordingly, as summarized by historian Lawrence Joseph, "our welfare depends upon the Earth."[45]

The escalating environmental crisis and the rhetoric surrounding it added guilt, shame, and fear to the mixed bag of emotions connected to changing ideas about the relationship between humans, Earth, and universe. In this emerging view, to be complicit in the earth's destruction was, by extension, to be complicit in our own. As Richard Nixon framed the dilemma in his 1970 State of the Union address, "The great question of the seventies is: Shall we surrender to our surroundings, or shall we make our peace with nature and begin reparations for the damage we have done to our air, our land, and our water?"[46] Though Nixon was conspicuously absent from the first Earth Day proceedings, in 1970, his language suggested that in confronting the environmental crisis, we were dealing with an angry Earth that was likely to fight back if not appeased. This was a logical extension of the notion popularized through environmentalist discourse, that the earth was sick—often described as coughing or suffering from a disease. A 1968 article in *Time* magazine, "Have We Reached the Limits of Pollution?" typifies the anthropomorphization of the ailing planet as angry. It suggests, focusing specifically on the peril of increasing numbers of cars, and thermal inversion, that "man, exerting too much pressure on nature, may well provoke a disastrous revenge."[47]

Collective anxieties about the earth's exacting revenge for human industrial excess also found expression in a new subgenre of science fiction film that flourished during the 1970s: revenge-of-nature movies. Anticipated by Alfred Hitchcock's *Birds* (1963), these included *Frogs* (1972), *Ants* (1973), *Dogs* (1976), *The Swarm* (1978), *Spiders* (1979), and *Squirm* (that is, worms, 1979) in which usually regular-sized members of the animal kingdom attacked man, often prompted to do so by his unthinking abuse of the environment, and of the very ecological system of which we are a part.[48] However, in the United States, at least, dependence on an overtaxed and possibly vengeful Earth was made real not by invading hordes of frogs, worms, and killer bees, but by the energy crisis, brought on by the Arab oil embargo in 1973. The everyday reality of gas lines, and the possibility of rationing, awakened people to the country's dependence on foreign oil, and also dramatized the fact that human—and more specifically American—use and control of nature and its resources is not without limits.

The notion that an angry Earth may exert revenge culminated for many in the fear that humans may ultimately lead to their own destruction and passing, like the peoples, species, and environments they have colonized and/or destroyed. Adlai Stevenson III articulated this in the conclusion of his Earth Day speech, in what is a more explicit version of Adamskis' Venusian and his rudimentary "Boom! Boom!": "We sense that our continued failure to control ourselves has placed man, himself, on the endangered species list."[10] Through the 1960s and 1970s Americans were forced to confront, on a number of levels, the wages of environmental imperialism, and citizens' possible self-destructive participation in that project.

At the same time, great environmentalist strides were made between the 1960s and the 1990s resulting from increasingly widespread support for the environmental movement, and the numerous pieces of legislation that were enacted as a result. These include the Clean Air Act (1963), the Quality Water Act (1965), the National Environmental Policy Act (1970), the Clean Water Act (1972), and the Endangered Species Act (1973). Public and private organizations have been formed to address environmental crises, including the Environmental Defense Fund (1967), Greenpeace (1969), the Environmental Protection Agency (1970), and Earth First! (1981). The United Nations conference on Human Environment was held in Stockholm in 1972 with the purpose of discussing environmental concerns on a global level; in 1972 DDT was banned; in 1973 bottle recycling, now commonplace, began in Oregon; and in 1980 the superfund was enacted to clean up Toxic Waste sites. In the early 1990s numerous state wilderness bills and the National Wilderness Preservation System added hundreds of thousands of acres of national forest.

And yet during roughly the same period, many of the catastrophic possibilities of industrialism were also realized: in 1978 Love Canal residents were evacuated after discovering that their community was built on what had been a toxic waste dump; in 1978 the Amoco Cadiz spilled 220,00 tons of oil into the sea off of the coast of Brittany, France; in 1979 an accident at the Three Mile Island nuclear reactor resulted in the worst nuclear accident in U.S. history; in 1984 a pesticide leak from a Union Carbide storage tank in Bhopal, India, killed 5,000 and seriously injured 20,000; in 1985 a hole in the ozone layer was observed over Antartica and is now believed to be contributing to the extinction of certain species of amphibians who are particularly sensitive to pollutants; in 1986 there was a meltdown of the nuclear reactor at Chernobyl, near Kiev in the Soviet Union, sending massive amounts of radiation through the northern hemisphere and affecting an estimated 75 million people; in 1989 the Exxon Valdez spilled 11 million gallons of oil into Prince William Sound; during the Persian Gulf War, an estimated 6 billion barrels of oil were released into the Persian Gulf in acts of terrorism; and most recently thousands of gallons of spilled oil threatened the delicate and diverse Galapagos Islands ecosystem. There is increasing consensus about global warming within the scientific community, suggesting that as a result of CFCs and HPFCs released into the atmosphere, primarily by air conditioners and refrigeration units, carbon dioxide is being overproduced in the atmosphere thus causing the greenhouse effect. The greenhouse effect is also thought to be exacerbated by massive deforestation of the tropical rain forests, and is thought to be hastening the death of the coral reefs, and as mentioned above, depletion of certain species that act as canaries in the proverbial coal mine of modern life.

The accounts of abduction by extraterrestrials that are the focus of my next chapter give expression to great anxiety about the vulnerable and volatile state of the earth and the incremental and sometimes ineffectual-seeming nature of environmentalist progress. So too do they express profound confusion about what role, if any, the average American citizen can be expected to play in staving off global destruction, or in effecting any type of profound social change in a world where America is increasingly the nation most responsible for industrial degradation of the earth. They further demonstrate how simultaneously rewarding and terrifying the notion of unity with the universe can be, especially when it comes unbidden. Conveying a simultaneous sense of personal chosenness and political paralysis, these accounts help elucidate how someone like Linda Cortile may be moved to refashion herself as the Lady of the Sands, hoaxing her way into a felt sense of political agency.

9

You Have a Sensitivity
The Limits of Chosenness

Jean has "always been interested in spirituality" and in fact states that she came to her understanding of alien abduction through her own varied New Age practices, including channelling, past-life regression, and participation in other consciousness-raising movements. Her move to New Age beliefs—which emphasize transformation through personal growth—was prompted by her rejection of Greek Orthodoxy, the religion in which she had been raised. As Jean remembers, she left the Greek Orthodox Church during the late 1940s because it was "too tight." It was only during the 1960s that she was able to "reconnect to her spirituality" through transcendental meditation and involvement in the Silva Mind Control Group, a meditation group that worked on what she calls "baby stuff," such as psychic diagnosis, healing, and spoon bending. Jean suggests that the counterculture that emerged during the 1960s, including the drug culture, was for many an escape, an alternative to "war and violence" but also a genuine means for exploring spirituality. For Jean, raising her political consciousness during the 1960s, through participation in civil rights and antiwar activism, was also an integral part of her personal growth and transformation.

In describing how she has arrived at her particular views about the meaning and purpose of alien abduction she notes that we have moved from national to international to cosmological views since the 1960s. She notes as of particular importance to this expansion the moonwalk and our ability to see the earth from space, which offers us "a wider view of who we are," as well as our increased awareness of human potential resulting from a variety of consciousness-raising practices such as those in which she participates. Jean concluded her brief overview of the ways in which our consciousness has been expanded since the 1960s with a statement that I hear frequently from those reacting to my project, including both alleged abductees and skeptics. She believes that ultimately it is "cosmologically egocentric" to think that we are the only living entities in the universe.[1] With a "wider view of the multiverses" available, she suggests, we would have to be blind to do so.

Of the experts to whom abductees typically refer, she identifies with John Mack who, like her, is interested in viewing abduction as a manifestation of the complex "changes in reality" detailed above. Mack's New Age interpretation of alien abduction is influenced by a combination of Western and Eastern ideas about modes of transformation and self-discovery. As such, he underscores the "important philosophical, spiritual, and social implications" of abduction, and its transformative potential. For Jean as well as for Mack and many of his patients, alien abduction serves just this purpose: to force us into consciousness of our place in the universe, as one among many species. Furthermore the heightened consciousness induced by aliens also forces us to confront our complicity in the destruction of the planet, which is viewed as the result of human hubris and species-centrism. As Mack states, "the abduction phenomenon may be seen as occurring in the context of the global ecological crisis, which is an outcome of the Western materialist/dualistic worldview."[2] In his view, this transformative, if punishing, process leads not only to personal, but also to collective transformation. What Mack characterizes as "the prevailing worldview or consensus reality" or the "Western, Newtonian/Cartesian, or materialist/dualist scientific paradigm" is disrupted. For Mack,

> What the abduction phenomenon has led me . . . to see is that we participate in a universe or universes that are filled with intelligences from which we have cut ourselves off, having lost the senses by which we might know them. It has become clear to me also that our restricted worldview or paradigm lies behind most of the major destructive patterns that threaten the human future—mindless corporate acquisitiveness that perpetuates vast differences between rich and poor and contributes to hunger and disease; ethno-national violence resulting in mass killing which could grow into a nuclear holocaust; and ecological destruction on a scale that threatens the survival of the earth's living systems.[3]

Mack's critique is all-encompassing, featuring the threat of nuclear annihilation as only one among many possible apocalyptic outcomes.

You Can Hear the Earth

As accounts of abduction proliferated in the 1980s and 1990s, alien abductees increasingly theorized that aliens seek not only to offer benevolent advice or to warn hapless humans of coming peril, but also to punish us for our crimes against nature and to shock us into recognition of our collective environmental sins. In more recent accounts of abduction, abductees continue to be warned about pending global apocalypse. While most continue to share a base-line of anxiety about nuclear annihilation, some register more general concern about environmental degradation of the planet. Such accounts, like Linda Cortile's, reflect the intervening history of environmentalism between the mid-1960s and the mid-1980s. They point the finger not only at elite members of a military-industrial-scientific elite who control nuclear weapons, but also at regular folks, including abductees, who are complicit in the pollution of the environment and the disruption of the earth's ecological balance.

Many of the apocalyptic visions reported by abductees continue, however, to cohere around scenes of nuclear destruction. Anxieties about such destruction were no doubt reinvigorated by the escalation of the arms race under Ronald Reagan, by the accompanying Cold War rhetoric about mutually assured destruction and the threats posed by the Soviet "evil empire," and by an increasingly vocal "no nukes" activist movement during the 1980s. In 1980 President Reagan unveiled plans for a $200 billion dollar military budget, along with unprecedented cutbacks in social programs. In 1982, he reopened the space nuclear power program shut down in 1973 as part of his Strategic Defense Initiative (SDI). Space nuclear reactors were looked to as sources for the production of the large electronic power levels necessary to run the space-based interceptor systems Reagan proposed would deflect missile attacks.[4] Arms escalation was met with renewed protest in which environmentalists, pacifists, scientists, and others came together to oppose nuclear policy. Thirty years after George Adamski's account, human beings still had good, and renewed, cause for alarm about "radiations," and their effects not only on Earth but throughout the universe.

Like Adamski, abductees recounting their alleged experiences during the late 1980s and early 1990s "picture in their minds" scenes of destruction. In Mack's words,

Scenes of the earth devastated by a nuclear holocaust, vast panoramas of lifeless polluted landscapes and waters, and apocalyptic images of giant earthquakes, firestorms, floods, and even fractures of the planet itself are shown by the aliens. These are powerfully disturbing to the abductees, who tend to experience them as literally predictive of the future of the planet.[5]

In *Secret Life* (1992), David Jacobs includes induced visions of ecological apocalypse—what he calls "visualization" and/or "imaging"—as lesser "secondary mental procedures" to the "Primary Physical Procedures" I have described in chapter 3. In Jacobs' estimation, the aliens have no particular interest in enlightening or raising the consciousness of their hapless human guinea pigs. According to Jacobs, the aliens induce these images not out of a love for human kind, or interest in our future, but out of a purely objective interest in what affects us, in our mental and emotional processes as one more piece of data to be collected and filed for unknowable future alien projects. In this scenario, according to Jacobs, alleged abductees "visualize scenes and objects that evoke an emotional or intellectual response. This allows the aliens to examine human emotions, abilities, thought processes, memory and perhaps even intelligence."[6] In "imaging" abductees are shown scenes "abhorrent and disturbing—death and destruction, calamity and war, atomic explosions, the end of the world, and so forth. She [the abductee] may see familiar people in it, such as her family suffering from the effects of nuclear war."[7] These images may be shown on a, "screen-like apparatus" or may be "envisioned" in the abductee's mind. As Jacobs's subject Patti remembers under hypnosis, "They keep putting images in my mind, about the destruction of the planet, and a time when people will be starving, and there won't be energy because we're using up the resources."[8]

Communion author Whitley Strieber describes a "ruler" with a "tip of silver" that when touched to his forehead induces the following vision: "I see pictures of the world just blowing up. . . . Jesus. It's a picture of a like a whole big blast, and there's a dark red fire in the middle of it and there's white smoke all around it. . . . Remembered voice: That's your home. That's your home. You know why this will happen."[9] Several pages later he continues, "The world turns into a whole red ball of fire. It just seems to burst into flames like a little ball of gasoline out in the middle of the sky."[10] When Strieber, during his abduction, is forced by the aliens to watch the images of global destruction, he assumes, as Mack notes, that they are "images of the future of our world."[11]

It is important to note that before writing *Communion*, Strieber had not only written two successful horror novels (*Wolfen* and *The Hunger*), but he had also written one speculative novel about the aftermath of nuclear war, called *Warday*, and had co-authored a nonfiction book about environmental crisis, called *Nature's End*. Strieber notes of *Nature's End* that while writing it, "I began to feel strongly that the present world situation was unsustainable. I did not think that the world was actually ending, but I could easily have been persuaded that the biosphere would soon change so catastrophically than an immense amount of human life would be lost."[12] Reflecting in *Communion* on the apocalyptic overtones of his abduction experience, Strieber notes that he had "spent the past three years working on books about nuclear war and environmental collapse. . . . Maybe the idea of visitors coming along and saving our necks was more appealing to me than I might consciously have wished to admit."[13] Strieber characterizes the experience thus: "I'm not saying that I was being threatened so much as warned. . . . There was a very stern warning . . . or maybe it wasn't. Maybe if I had not been afraid of nuclear war and perfectly happy . . . other images would have come out." Strieber is unusual among abductees in his willingness to allow that, in his words, "there was always the possibility that I was unconsciously eager to comply with an outcome that I might secretly have longed for. I might want powerful visitors to appear, to save a world that I'm pretty sure is in serious trouble."[14]

While Strieber remains preoccupied with the possibility of nuclear annihilation, Joan, a fellow abductee in Strieber's support group expresses more concern about sustained pollution and industrial corruption of the environment. During her abductions, Joan's alien captors inform her, in a more detailed version of Betty Hill and Betty Andreasson's messages, that "what we're doing now to our planet is killing it little by little, and it's going to come to a point where there's not going to be anything left. I think that they're getting ready. . . . It is ending, and they're telling us that, and they've implied that to me. What we are doing is killing ourselves. And that's scary."[15] Joan reminds her group and Strieber's readers, as Rachel Carson did twenty-five years earlier, that human beings do participate in, and are culpable for, future scenarios of ecological crisis and catastrophe.

Mack's patient Ed reports a set of induced visions not unlike those reported by Strieber of "the world just blowing up." According to Ed, the same aliens, "wired me into my emotions," whereupon the "female" alien telepathically imparted information about "the way humans are conducting themselves here in terms of international politics, our environment, our violence to each other, our food, and all that."[16] She explains things "scientifically" to Ed and elicits his "deep anxious concern over the path I could see us humans taking . . . a world trauma." This trauma is the result of the "heavily destructive path we were taking, which was also destructive to the humanoid's [alien's] planet."[17] Mack relates,

> The narrative was filled with apocalyptic images. The being communicated to him telepathically in what Ed calls 'allegorical terms' a message of 'instability on your planet, eco-spiritual, emotional instability. . . . Volcanic eruptions are a sign. . . . It's allegorical towering plumes of eruptive rage. Not ejaculations of ecstasy, but eruptions of anguish. Be careful. Pounding waves of eruption, watering, rushing, and engulfing about and around you. . . . Earth shuddering in anguish, crying weeping at the stupidity of humans losing contact with the inner soul of their being. . . . You have a sensitivity, Ed. . . . You can talk to the earth. The earth talks to you.'[18]

Finally, Ed reports that the aliens implore him to, "Listen to the earth, Ed. You can hear the earth. You can hear the anguish of the spirits. You can hear the wailing cries of the imbalances. It will save you. . . . The earth itself, the being told him, is enraged at our stupidity, and the earth's skin is going to swat some bugs off."[19]

The message here is complex and contradictory. First, the message is frightening: through some collective sin of humanity, the planet itself is offended and ready to fight back. At the same time, however, Ed the abductee "has a sensitivity." He is designated as special, or chosen, somehow above or outside of humanity; able, for better or worse, to "hear" the earth. Ed's sensitivity allows him to understand and view the world in ecstatic, almost sexual terms, and yet that very sensitivity, indeed intimacy with the state of the planet comes at a price, bound up as it is in feelings of guilt and culpability.

Strieber likewise becomes an actor in this sweeping and catastrophic global drama. As he describes his experience to his other group members, he notes,

> In the form of what can only be described as vivid bursts of information, I have received a great deal of material about the perilous condition of the Earth's atmosphere. Much of this material came in February and March of 1986 and concerned the danger of impending atmospheric deterioration. In March I called a press conference of environmental reporters in Washington, D.C. to discuss a book I wrote with James Kunetka, *Nature's End,* and to warn about the serious implications of the hole that had been detected in the ozone layer over the northern Hemisphere, with measurable crop damage from excessive ultraviolet light beginning to occur in the 1990–1993 period. . . . I had been told that the atmospheric problems will cause a reduction in immune system vitality in all animals, and the consequent resurgence of disease. As yet I have seen no scientific corroboration of this.[20]

In one sense, as a fairly well-known popular author, Strieber has some legitimacy and authority—enough, in any case, to call a press conference and expect that people will attend and maybe even take him seriously. On the other hand, without clear scientific authority, without "corroboration" of the "message," it seems that intellectual hunches, hypotheses, informed opinions, or feelings of citizen outrage do not suffice. Channeled by the alien, however, the message is understood, at least by Strieber, to be "truth," if not scientific, then divine in origin. What's more, it is a truth for which he, as mere conduit, need not claim responsibility. Like Linda Cortile, he attributes his knowledge of impending crisis to the aliens: his knowledge is not acquired, but induced, like Ed's orgasmic vision.

While Strieber receives information about a hole in the ozone layer, Betty Andreasson has learned that, as a result of chronic pollution, human reproductive ability will be impeded and "man will become sterile."[21] According to Raymond Fowler, a more detailed version of "the message" received by Betty is revealed slowly over the course of two more books that compose this trilogy: including *The Andreasson Affair, Phase 2* (1982) and *The Watchers* (1990) as well as a reprint of the original *Andreasson Affair* in 1988. In *The Watchers,* Fowler asserts that "the aliens allegedly have programmed it to be released over a period of time like the contents of a timed-release medical capsule."[22] It is interesting to consider that while in the early days of environmentalist alarm, only several years after the energy crisis, Andreasson's "message" offered no details about how the earth would be destroyed. Working still within a Christian paradigm of her chosenness, in 1979 the earth's destruction was still in large part for Andreasson a version of biblical Armageddon. By the 1990s, however, as history continues to unfold, so too do the details of her message. Andreasson and Fowler thus leave behind the more general narrative of salvation and redemption in order to talk about the perhaps scarier, and certainly more timely, issues of ecological concern that have come increasingly to be at the heart of many abduction stories.

In contrast to Jacobs, Fowler and Andreasson offer the most optimistic interpretations of alien environmental intervention. Over the course of the trilogy, as explained in *The Watchers*, Fowler learns from Betty that "they are caretakers of nature and natural forms—the Watchers. They love mankind. They love the planet earth . . . and they have been caring for it and man since man's beginning. They watch the spirit in all things. . . . Man is destroying much of nature."[23] As in all abduction accounts, however, the aliens "love" for mankind, however, resides alongside increasingly explicit violation. By 1990, Betty is not only nasally probed and "measured for procreation," but also has her eye removed and implanted with a "bb sized object," and is forced to watch another woman give birth to an alien-human fetus who has "needles put in the top of its head and its ears." She is then made to watch as it has its eyelids "circumcised."[24] As the aliens explain to Andreasson, they have to plunge needles into the heads of fetuses she is being made to observe because, "as time goes by, [humans] will not be able to produce because of the pollution of the lands and waters and the air . . . and the bacteria and the terrible things that are on earth."[25]

You Are Our Chosen One

What do abductees stand to gain by believing themselves the battered and abused conduits for such apocalyptic messages? For Strieber and Cortile, their abductee status gains them real or imagined audiences with people in power; through these channels they hope to effect change. Yet many alleged abductees explicitly disavow their own status as "chosen" by extraterrestrials. Henry, for example, insists that "no one feels good or special about this," and everyone I interviewed scoffed at the suggestion that they might be "chosen." In *Communion*, Whitley Strieber features a dialogue on this subject between himself and his alien abductor. While preparing to rape Strieber, the alien says, "You are our chosen one," to which he replies "I don't believe that for a minute. It's ridiculous. . . . Sing that song to somebody else. And also I want to go home."[26] And despite the "bursts of information" he has received about the ozone layer, Strieber insists that, "I do not have it in me to be a believer."[27] Abductee Katharina Wilson, author of *The Alien Jigsaw*, reflects on her website that "the frightening visions of the Earth's future and mankind's own powerlessness in the face of global nuclear and environmental disaster" that she receives bring with them "a burdensome sense of responsibility." Wilson says of this "enormous burden" that "rather than feeling I've been 'chosen,' I feel as if it is my duty or my assignment to help educate people about this phenomenon." She still, and at the same time, continues to feel powerless.[28]

This disavowal of chosenness seems in part motivated by fear of being labeled fanatical or crazy, a fear that is often expressed by abductees and other members of the community and on which I elaborate in my final chapter. In an ironic twist, abductees try to seem less far out and more normal by attributing what they fear may be fanatical views to the aliens they claim have abducted them. This deferral works only if they view their abduction—and the consciousness imparted through it—as forced upon them; and themselves as victims of the message of global consciousness. Perhaps most abductees sense that in contemporary culture, while saints and martyrs are easily dismissed as crazy, victims are often taken quite seriously.[29] They also seem to intuit that in a culture of rationalism, opinions and even political stances do not count as much as "truths" transmitted from on high, truths for which abductees need not claim responsibility and for which they cannot be held accountable.

And despite their vigorous protest, the fact remains that many alleged abductees do seem to feel distinctive for having been chosen to deliver painful apocalyptic messages. Many of them believe their abduction has made them special, or that they were abducted because of some special quality they possess that perhaps only the aliens can see, or both. Jane, for example, believes that aliens are responsible for her burst of creative success late in life—including both her psychic ability and her television show. She comments that, "they had a lot to do with me having my TV show. Now I go places and every one knows me."[30] Henry believes that abductees possess a "sensitivity" that predisposes them to be taken. He speculates that "maybe there's something in them, because a lot people who have this experience, the majority have some kind of so-called paranormal or psychic abilities and are more sensitive as human beings; more sensitive to others, their families. . . . Sensitivity seems to be very important."[31] While shunning many of the more "dramatic accounts" of alien abduction, George too believes that somehow abductees are more in tune with certain facets of reality, explaining that, "Whatever it is that's happening is happening so subtly, some of us are sensitive enough to pick up changes, it could be happening in the room right now, but you have to be sensitive enough to pick it up."[32]

George, like Anthony, also believes that the aliens choose people who are worthy of study because of their innate goodness, and good works:

> Some people are wrapped up with themselves, with their own little problems, they don't understand the concept that in helping others you're helping yourself. Some people spend time and energy trying to earn money . . . instead of doing something that will in turn eventually help them by helping other people. . . . To be more responsible in terms of the people around you. I think that's what it's all about. . . . I believe these beings to be far superior to us spiritually and intellectually. Like attracts like. In other words, they are attracted to those who they feel are carrying out what they're carrying out.[33]

Anthony adds, making a more explicit reference to what might be the aliens' genetic desire for such good human traits that, "I believe there is a cross-generational component to it. I think that it is extremely important, there is an investment aspect to it, as far as investing in a bloodline." When I press him to explain how the aliens choose particular bloodlines, he elaborates, "Not so much that we're so spiritual, I notice that like in my family: very humble. We make mistakes like everyone else. And we have our days, but by and large there's a subtle humbleness, a willingness to help, an unconditional kind of thing. I'll help you without asking anything in return—now would this begin to change a society that's socially engineered? Perhaps." He adds, "you have to plant the right seed everywhere."[34]

In addition to the spiritual or moral status the ability to "hear the earth" may confer, abductees also give expression through the process of forced revelation to a sort of horrified titillation at the circumstances of their own physical, or in this case, political and collective, disempowerment. Like the orgasms and ejaculations induced by clinical alien procedures, so too do visions of environmental crisis and apocalypse induced by aliens during abduction result in a mix of pleasure and pain.

The Inoculation Is for Something Positive

Abductees like Anthony believe that drastic times deserve drastic measures. Only through the forced and painful encounter with aliens, only when compelled to bear witness to the degradation of the planet, will abductees and the people to whom they spread the word wake up and realize the compromised condition of both the planet and the species. Anthony, who believes both that alien abduction is sanctioned and covered up by the government and that aliens may have benevolent intentions, tried to explain this "tough love" interpretation of the alien intervention to me by referring to a Normal Rockwell painting. He notes, "it's almost like the Norman Rockwell analogy: the kid's getting the injection, he's screaming out, he would kill the doctor if he had the opportunity but technically speaking the inoculation is for something positive." Echoing Anthony's notion of alien inoculation, Mack asserts that individual abductees are forced to take the "medicine" which "is being administered primarily where it is most needed—in the US and the other Western industrial countries."[35] This suggests that the individual is punished for collective sins, for the sins of globalization, for the sins of progress itself.

During our follow-up interview I express to Jean that I am troubled by Mack's point about the punishing aspects of abduction: why must we—or more immediately her—be administered "medicine" for the crimes of industrial society? Does she agree with this? How, I ask, does this make her feel as one who is being punished, forced to take that medicine? Her response is vague and contradictory. She believes that yes, the aliens are "waking us up to a condition." In terms of how it affects abductees, "some can handle it and some can't. Some take it as a mission. It's very individual." Jean seems to be handling it relatively well and is currently writing a book through which she will share what she has learned about the complex nature of reality that she has come to over the past thirty years of forced encounter with alien entities. In the book she "seeks a broader integrative perspective." In brief, she will argue, not unlike Mack, that "we exist on various levels, or planes, of reality and that we need all of them in order to be fully conscious: psychological, spiritual, social and political." But, Jean insists, referring to whatever the alien's agenda may be in systematically abducting human beings, "it's not being done to help us."[36] Asked whether he thinks the aliens' intentions are benevolent or malevolent, Anthony stresses the complexity of the question: they are not either/or, but both/and. The "nonhuman intelligences" with which abductees are "interfacing" want us to learn something. They need to teach us that we as a species "have to move on, we have to grow."

I remain troubled by this notion of alien "medicine" for the crimes of civilization: why, according to the alien abduction scenario, must enlightenment and raised consciousness come at such a painful cost? So too do I continue to be troubled by how this belief suggests, in the end, a New Age, or essentially personal, solution to large socio-political problems, suggesting that such problems, no matter how large, protracted, and complex, can be "treated" through what is in the end an especially punishing form of "self work." Mack epitomizes this in his suggestion that our "restricted worldview" may be responsible for "mindless corporate acquisitiveness." In no instance do abductees or those who treat them seem to point the finger at, for example, corporate culture, or even capitalism itself as the source of such acquisitiveness. "Ethno-national violence" and "ecological destruction," it is suggested, can indeed be treated through a collective version of the sort of "ventilation" espoused by abduction traumatists. This notion is at once extraordinarily narcissistic and extraordinarily demoralizing in its failure to look at the terrestrial powers that be as likely culprits.

In earlier chapters I have explored the many forces contributing, in the late twentieth and early twenty-first centuries, to a felt sense of powerlessness and alienation: some therapeutic cultures suggest that trained psychological experts have access to our own psyches, that we lack. Biotechnology and new reproductive technologies enable us to see ourselves in new and often frightening ways. Space Age rhetoric challenges a sense of place, of its meaning, and reorients us to consider ourselves not as Americans, but as citizens of Earth, or even more extremely, citizens of the universe. Yet in no instances do alleged abductees point to these forces as potential reasons for their belief in abduction by aliens.

In almost all instances, abductees draw focus away from the terrestrial powers that be as the sources of human, or indeed global, suffering and direct interested outsiders such as me back to the extraterrestrial oppressor.

Indeed despite fear about global degradation, and a mixture of anxiety and excitement about the possibility of global consciousness, none of the abductees with whom I have spoken or about whom I have read seem to register their existence in an era of globalization per se. In the broadest sense, globalization is characterized by an increased flow of people, culture, information, goods, and services across national borders. Economic globalization is, more particularly, marked by the denationalization of markets or, the "interdependence of national economies through the expansion of world trade."[37] Surely globalization in all its facets counts as a tremendous social force that may contribute to confusion about one's place—and the extent of one's power—in the world. And yet globalization, perhaps because it is so vast and all-encompassing seems to be the most invisible social force (or set of forces) of all. Indeed sociologist Manuel Castells suggests that the "placeless logic" of an internationalized economy has subverted the "structures of social and political control" threatening people's sense of control over their lives.[38] He argues that this is "more subtle and . . . potentially more destructive" than the Orwellian prophecy of Big Brother because "there is no tangible oppression, no identifiable enemy, no center of power that can be held responsible for specific social issues."[39] In a world lacking tangible oppression and identifiable enemies—first in the disappearance of the "evil empire" and then in the decentralization of power in globalization—the alleged ubiquity of aliens has increased, an extraterrestrial locus of power that can indeed be held responsible for specific social issues.

Though economic globalization is largely thought to be a project in American imperialism, not all Americans benefit from its effects.[40] As such globalization has destabilized an easy sense of the value of national identity, compelling Americans to consider themselves as just one part of a larger "global village." An ample body of work exists that considers the extent to which citizenship in the global village is, as in Marshall McLuhan's assessment, an altogether positive, communitarian experience or, in contrast, a place with "no sense of place" that results in alienation and rootlessness. Certainly the answer lies somewhere in between these poles, and the ambivalence in stories about simultaneous connectedness and flight that alleged abductees tell seems to epitomize the complexity of life in an era of globalization.

Bay Ridge and the Greater Cosmic Ecology

The paradox at the heart of the alien abduction phenomenon is that while abductees may feel personally special, chosen, even empowered by their belief in their capture by extraterrestrials, they are politically and collectively paralyzed, having come to believe social change is impossible without alien intervention. Henry is a single white man in his midforties whom I interviewed in the summer of 1999 in Bay Ridge, Brooklyn. He is a journalist for a local paper, covering community board and precinct meetings. As we spoke over a large diner breakfast, Henry offered this information about himself as biographical background: he was drafted into the army during the Vietnam War. He opposed the war when he was in service in Fort Dix, New Jersey which, as he notes, "is a difficult thing to do."[41] He was advised by lawyers to file for conscientious objector status, but was denied it because his opposition was to the current war, so his was not a purely pacifist stance. They threatened to court-martial him but, he notes, "I had the ACLU behind me, and commanding officer behind me, even had a Manhattan church behind me. . . . Eventually they let me go after six months." Henry explains that, "that's how I got involved in the Peace Movement, inside the army."

Secure in his decision, Henry adds, "they tried all sorts of things to convince me that I was doing wrong but it didn't work." After that, Henry and some friends founded a group in East Orange called the Johnny Appleseed Peace Rights group, which was active in 1971 and 1972, and involved in "the war issue, tenants rights, environmental issues." He also worked for five years as the Executive Director of the New York Metro group of the Committee for a SANE Nuclear Policy (SANE), a national organization that has worked since 1957 to act as a nuclear policy watchdog agency and to raise public awareness about the dangers posed by nuclear weapons. As is typical for abductees, it was upon reading stories of other peoples' abductions—in this case *Communion* and *Intruders* in 1987—that he realized he was an abductee and subsequently had this confirmed under hypnosis. But before reading *Communion*, Henry had already read Strieber's *War Day* and *Nature's*

End. Henry notes that in the SANE offices on Lafayette Street in New York "we had a whole bunch of copies." More recently, Henry wrote an environmental column called "EcoFrontier" for a Greenwich Village newspaper called *Downtown*. As he explains it, "I took a holistic, broad view of the environment. All sorts of topics." He adds, "I brought in the UFOs because it's all connected."

Like other abductees, Henry reacts to real environmental (and more broadly political) threats and crises but attributes them, or his knowledge of them, to aliens. Henry's perspective on how UFOs and aliens are connected to global events is shaped in part by the holistic ideas of the universe discussed in my last chapter, according to which "it" is indeed "all connected." He elaborates with the following somewhat boggling explanation:

> There's some more basic level of reality that seems to be more conscious. . . . It's all-knowing. How does one atom know another atom? . . . The apparent consciousness of the atom . . . an atom over in Switzerland knowing what an atom in New York is. . . . How do they know? So there's like a unity throughout all of the universe; the information is there; so maybe someone is picking up knowledge of them [abductees], the non-human I'll call them, being part of their family because there's some kind of connection that's interpreted in terms that they might understand, like you're part of our soul family or something and the aliens apparently are aware of these other connections about quantum physics and things like that.

In "EcoFrontier" Henry wrote a two-part piece looking at Hopkins's and Jacobs's work about the interspecies breeding project alongside "what's going on with the lower sperm count among males around the world." He adds, "Studies are going on in Scotland and Copenhagen and so forth. And the other species' depletion, like frogs and so forth, how they're being affected by pollution and try to get an overall picture." Henry believes, and concludes in the "EcoFrontier" article, that "on some level of reality there's an intelligent mechanism or beings who work on correcting that, who are attracted towards what's going on . . . what's worth saving, what's worth changing?" In that article he ponders, "How does evolution work? Is this part of evolution on a higher level, or a more advanced level, I should say." In an effort to understand this I ask, "It's almost like a physical, or literal manifestation of ecology? That things will balance themselves out?" Henry responds, "Yeah, very much so. And these beings are part of that greater cosmic ecology." In order to eludicate his position, Henry refers me to Edgar Mitchell's book, which I had not yet read at that point. As he interprets it, Mitchell realizes that "the earth and humans are all connected, all part of a living, tremendous living organism, ecosystem." Henry's theory of alien intervention is a version of the Gaia hypothesis, but one that still needs godlike entities, that needs some sort of hierarchy in place. The very inclusion of aliens in this worldview suggests that "things" *do not* balance themselves out.

Henry now runs one of several New York area alien abductee support groups, SPACE (Search Project for Aspects of Close Encounters) with approximately fifty members from the greater New York area.[42] In SPACE meetings, Henry and others take what he characterizes as a "proactive" approach to abduction: they seek to address their problems, and the aliens who abduct them, head on. I ask Henry why he no longer works for SANE (now called Peace Watch) or writes EcoFrontier. He cites personal reasons for leaving SANE, but also notes that "because of the Cold War ending, they're not as active." Henry's comments underscore how, for people who are not conspiracy theorists, the end of the Cold War precipitated a crisis of political focus: the who, what, and where of political protest and activism was thrown into question. Concern about nuclear policy loses its audience, so it seems, with the end of the arms race; pacificism and environmentalism can only be taken up—as in the Cortile story—if "provoked" by aliens.

I comment that abduction seems like a place where people continue to talk about the need for pacifism and environmentalism, while they too are perhaps "not as active" in other facets of their lives. Henry notes that peoples' passivity can be attributed to the fact that "there's more going on, more bad news kind of, issues that overload people." In the abduction community, Henry agrees, "its kept alive and focused on . . . whether it's the person's perception of what's going on with them, or something the beings provoke in them." He adds, "but it does go on."

Some months earlier I had asked Jean a similar question. My hunch was that she may displace her previous politicization into her abduction experience, so I asked if she still considered herself politically active. My question was met at first with a look of consternation and then with the question "Why do you ask that?" I explained that it seemed to me she had been something of an activist in the 1960s and I just wondered if she continued to be. She responded that while she does vote, she does not protest anymore. She suggests that this is simply, and obviously, because people generally don't protest anymore. It is a different time. Jean's palpable sense of defeat was especially striking coming as it did on the cusp of an increasingly vocal and visible antiglobalization movement. It is especially intriguing since it is not really true; and yet many of the alleged abductees with whom I spoke represent a subset of potential activists—or at least actors—whose impulse to effect social and political change have nonetheless been defused through therapeutic frameworks.

In this "different" time, people the world over are exposed to mass-media images of the Earth in crisis; many people also experience the effects of environmental decline in their everyday lives. At the same time that people may suffer from the effects of tainted soil or water or air, so may those living in advanced nations feel guilty for having created them. As the economic landscape shifts and jobs are eliminated or moved outside of the United States, increasing numbers of Americans are left to look for underpaid and often unsatisfying work in the service industries. One result of this, as Henry notes, is that many people feel overloaded. Abductees offer one especially colorful example of what can happen when one feels both responsible for the state of the world and powerless to effect change in it. In a story based on the idea that humans are not alone or indisputably superior within a vast and interconnected universe, induced images and inoculations of knowledge enable abductees to play a more effective and exciting role in the drama of environmental crisis, and in the reality of globalization, than they do in their everyday lives. Though most often denying the desire to be awakened to what Jean calls a global "condition," through the story of abduction, abductees, paradoxically, seek power through powerlessness. As participants in what Mack calls the "corrective initiative" of alien abduction, abductees can, as in all facets of the abduction phenomenon, transform their own feelings of incapacity into matters of global significance.

10

Reality Gets Exploded
Abductee Culture, Abductee Belief

Sitting at a SPACE meeting or at the Bordentown, N.J. UFO conference or at the Whole Live Expo, listening to conversations about human abduction by aliens, it becomes clear that alleged abductees both embrace and resist the opinions of the so-called expert researchers who have sought to define, and in some sense confine, the abduction phenomenon. Abductee accounts of abduction, while drawing on all available interpretations of the phenomenon, tend to exceed any single interpretation. People bring to their understanding of the alleged experience diverse worldly interests, personalities, and personal histories. And because so many abductees share stories and theories with one another—whether face to face or online—the abduction phenomenon continues to evolve, at least in New York City, energized both by newly published accounts by "experts" and by abductees themselves. By participating in the cultural practice of being an abductee, abductees become agents in the social drama of alien abduction; they discover human interaction, fellowship, support, and a means of self-expression. Whether privately or publicly, all of the people whom I interviewed for this project devote some part of their lives to the fairly enthusiastic consideration of what abduction means to them and how they think the phenomenon will affect the world at large. They also become participants in a collective project that seeks to revise mainstream notions of reality itself. As Henry states in the SPACE Explorer, "our fierce challenge . . . is to devise a new construct of reality with open minds and open hearts." The extent to which the agency they gain through abductee identity or belief in the alternate realities they suggest is empowering or enabling is a question to which I return again and again.

Immersed and Obsessed

Even those of us who are not self-professed sci fi fans or UFO buffs or conspiracy theorists are familiar with a variety of cultural narratives that inform the typical alien abduction narrative. These include, as I have argued in previous chapters, narratives about the utopian and dystopian possibilities of technological progress, and about the revelation of government secrets and industrial crimes against the planet. Despite the omnipresence of such accounts and accompanying images in contemporary culture, abductees typically want me to know that their abduction experiences are not the result of what Hopkins calls "media contamination."[1] They sometimes go out of their way to deny prior interest in UFOs or sci fi, insisting that their accounts are both authentic and pure. While it is difficult to judge the truth of such claims, it is clearly evident that once abductees "remember" or realize they have been abducted, they dive headlong—as a direct result, they argue, of their abduction—into investigation of the abduction phenomenon. And once they start talking about their alleged experiences, histories, and ideas, one sees the depth and breadth of their interest in the abduction phenomenon and the extent to which their stories are shaped, above all, by and through other accounts of abduction by aliens.

Abductees are avid consumers and producers of their own experience. They astutely navigate the various interpretations that exist of alien abduction, and craft their own positions about what alien abduction is or is not—what they believe its purpose and meaning may be. On one level, as George notes, "No one's really sure what happened."[2] Yet the process of finding out becomes for many both a private and public avocation. For most abductees the initial memory or realization that they have been abducted itself occurs through the act of reading another published account of abduction. For Mike that book was Hopkins's *Missing Time*. Mike recalls walking into B. Dalton and seeing several books on abduction, including *Communion*, *Intruders*, and *Missing Time*. He bought *Missing Time* and found that he tried to read it but could not because of an inexplicable emotional and physical reaction to it. Mike "knew nothing about the details of UFO abduction until [he] read that book." He wrote in an email to me, "it was then that I realized that my own experiences matched perfectly those that were being reported by the abductees in the book. . . . The details I encountered in the book . . . are what allowed me to 'make the connection' between my own (consciously recalled experiences) and those being reported by the abductees."[3] Raymond Fowler's *Watchers* acted as the "trigger" for Cassie, who was drawn to the book at the bookstore and bought it without thinking. She read it and had "a weird reaction"—her hands shook and she became unusually emotional.[4] Like Mike, she had difficulty finishing the book. When she began to suspect her own abduction, she wrote to Fowler, who referred her to Hopkins.

For both Henry and Maureen, Whitley Strieber's *Communion* acted as the "trigger" to memories of abduction. Like Mike, as they explain it, they had had conscious, unexplainable experiences, but reading a particular book helped them identify their experience as alien abduction. Maureen explains that in 1988 she passed *Communion* in the bookstore: "After seeing the cover of *Communion* and being both drawn and repulsed by it, 'cause it terrified me, I read the book and that's when I realized that a lot of things Whitley Strieber had written about sounded all too familiar to me."[5] When Henry decided to read *Communion*, he had already read two of Strieber's previous books about nuclear war and environmental destruction, *War Day* and *Nature's End*. Henry remembers, "When I read *Communion* it struck a chord in me about something that had happened in West Orange. And then I read [Hopkins's book] *Intruders* which came out a few months later and I wondered, because he mentioned the blue lights and paralysis, if I could have had an experience."[6] Recognition or identification, first through shopping and then through reading, led all three to seek the help of hypnotherapists who could help them remember more detail about experiences that were beginning to come into their consciousness.

As Anthony explains it, discovering and confronting one's abduction is often a "cumulative process," during which "some people will go in one direction away from the subject and then those who go immersed and obsessed with it. I was reading books like they were going out of style. I'd read books and say nah. . . . Then certain people would [in books] say certain things about their experiences that dovetailed mine."[7] Indeed, once abductees come to believe they have been abducted by aliens, most embark on research into the phenomenon, which generally begins with more reading. Abductees act as discriminating consumers and interpreters of the abduction phenomenon, wending their way through the vast popular literature that exists on the topic. Most wade through existing written accounts and the theories offered by experts such as Hopkins, Mack, and Fowler and during interviews they readily offer opinions about where these authors succeed and where they fall short of getting at the truth of the abduction phenomenon as they, the abductees, see it. A number of my informants admire Hopkins, and have sought his help, but are somewhat critical of his approach. Cassie, for example, notes that Hopkins "tries to steer you away from certain interpretations." As she understands it, he "keeps things on an emotional level." Because he "used to call himself agnostic, now humanist" he "doesn't think there's a spiritual dimension." She adds that, "you can't ignore the spiritual—he just writes it off." She has been recently drawn to the work of Zecharia Sitchin, a "multidisciplinary scholar," who has read ancient Sumerian texts and believes they contain evidence of aliens' coming to Earth for resources thousands of years ago and possibly seeding the human race on Earth.[8] George is a harsher critic of Hopkins. He believes that Hopkins's work creates "a continuous cloud of fear." He is also critical of David Jacobs, author of *Secret Life* and *The Threat*, whom he refers to as Hopkins's "clone" and who "feels a responsibility to announce to the world that there's something terribly threatening going on." Though George has not read extensively on the subject, he suggests I check out *Operation Trojan Horse* by John Keel, a Fortean who connects UFOs to other paranormal phenomena including demons and ghosts.[9] He also refers me to the work of Reverend Barry Downing, author of *The Bible and Flying Saucers*, who "may be close" to George's point of view in his assessment that "at this point we're experiencing what they experienced in Biblical times yet we're perceiving it in light of our current times."

Jean admires John Mack's approach to "changes in reality," while Maureen finds his suggestion that the aliens are responsible for heightening human consciousness somewhat off-putting. She comments, "believe it or not I'm a very spiritual person, and I don't feel that spirituality came from anywhere but from within me. So I'm not giving [the aliens] credit for that, I'm sorry." To his theory that abductees are transformed into caring more deeply about the environment and about peace, Maureen interjects, "well who the hell doesn't? . . . I can't imagine anybody who'd say I prefer war." Mike accepts Mack's theory that abduction heightens the consciousness of abductees, but only because of their traumatic nature. He adds, "Where I disagree with John is: I don't think 'raising our consciousness' is the motivation (for these beings) to intervene in our lives the way they have. I think they serve their own purposes. Whatever those 'purposes' may be. I don't pretend to know. (Unlike Mack and some others)."

When I interview people in their homes, they often show me their extensive book collections. I particularly envy Maureen's collection, which includes a number of obscure texts that I have been trying to find. Jane, whose home I have not visited, claims to have about five hundred books on UFOs, aliens, and related paranormal subjects. During interviews subjects enthusiastically suggest a variety of texts for me to read: Jean suggests Arthur David Horn, *Humanity's Extraterrestrial Origins: ET Influences on Humankind's Biological and Cultural Evolution*; J. J. Hurtack's Books of Enoch series; Zecharia Sitchin, *Genesis Revisited: Is Modern Science Catching up with Ancient Knowledge?*; and Patrick Harpur, *Daimonic Reality: A Fieldguide to the Otherworld*. Though she is not particularly interested in conspiracy theory, she is the first to refer me to books on the Philadelphia and Montauk experiments by UFO conspiracy theorists Al Bilyk and Duncan Cameron, books that led me to the literature discussed in chapter 7. Anthony, who does believe that the government is involved in the abduction phenomenon, refers me to the work of abductees Karla Turner and Kim Carlsberg as well as to the alternative science work of Brian O'Leary, who calls himself a planetary scientist. O'Leary was a U.S. astronaut appointed in 1967 to go to Mars before the manned Mars mission was canceled by NASA, and is the author of *Exploring Inner and Outer Space: A Scientist's Perspective on Personal and Planetary Transformation*. Both Anthony and Henry suggest I read a book written by another ex-astronaut, Edgar Mitchell, called *The Way of the Explorer: An Apollo Astronaut's Journey through the Material and Mystical Worlds*, a book I discussed in chapter 8. Finally Anthony also suggests I view *Forbidden Archeology*, a videotape on which "they talk about stuff they're pulling out of museums because it doesn't fit their paradigms and theories." Mike lends me a video tape that features footage of a mass UFO sighting over Mexico, and interviews with the scores of people who claim to have witnessed it. George more than once suggests that I listen to Art Bell, who hosts a nationally broadcast radio show on a variety of unexplained phenomena. He and others, through the course of my research, tip me off about magazine and newspaper articles, upcoming television shows about abduction, and people to whom they think I should talk, including both abductees and researchers. Their suggestions are quite useful as I too try to navigate the complexities of the alien abduction phenomenon. Their assumption seems generally, however, to be that by reading or viewing or talking, I too will become convinced about the actuality of alien abduction.

Everybody's Got a Theory

In contrast to the profound passivity, even paralysis, that abductees describe experiencing during their alleged abductions, the people who agreed to share their experiences with me are in most respects quite actively involved in the process of making meaning of, and producing their own stories about, alien abduction. The abductees with whom I spoke are less invested than the experts who write about them in espousing one particular theory of alien abduction, and are more likely to move back and forth between or to combine theories. Conspiracy theorists, for example, may believe that abduction involves an interspecies breeding project; those who think they have been chosen in some spiritual sense may also believe in a government cover-up; those who believe the aliens are heralding the coming of the New Age can also talk about abduction in terms of their own traumatization and recovery. Time and again abductees have warned me against overly simple or conclusive analysis. As Henry notes, "I like to keep the whole thing open, because as we go along with this I can't help but think there's a larger aspect to what's going on, a much larger picture involved in all this. It's not simply . . . abduction, hybrids, or it may not be all environmental concerns. It's more complex." As George notes, "if you focus on a certain book you miss the big picture," and Cassie echoes this when she comments that, "everybody's got a theory. It's easy to leave things out." But such calls for complexity and seeming ambiguity are often in tension with more definite statements of abduction reality that abductees are willing to put into writing. For while they may not know what the definitive truth is about alien abduction, theirs is a culture that is all about putting one's version of the truth out there: circulating and evaluating competing accounts, taking what works and discarding what does not, and throwing one's own account into the mix.

Many abductees produce and circulate their own narrative and visual accounts of alien abduction, presenting talks at conferences; writing their own books, newsletters, and websites; or organizing or attending support groups.[10] Jean is writing her book about the importance of seeking a "broader, integrative perspective," partly in response to what she observes are "divisions within the community."[11] Maureen is working on a book with her therapist, "just telling the story of the different experiences. . . . Most of the emphasis is on the use of hypnosis and support systems. It could be for abductees or for therapists." Henry too has been working on a book, a draft introduction of which appeared in the summer 1999 SPACE newsletter. According to that excerpt, the book will explore the possibility of "a cosmic ecology startlingly beyond our current conceptions and visions of contact, challenging us to expand our perceptions, intelligence, psyche, emotions and human pursuits."[12] Several of the more public abductees also maintain websites. John Velez was the webmaster and designer for Hopkins's Intruders Foundation and is currently the creator and webmaster of the Abduction Information Center.[13] Maureen's stories and related poems can be found at http://hometown.aol.com/nymush/sands or at http://www.cbjd.net/orbit/bridges. Jane has her own cable television show, an "alternative to Art Bell" called *Beyond the Unexplained*, billed (by her) as "New York's Newest Paranormal/Metaphysical Television Show."[14] She also lectures locally, as does Maureen, about her experience.

Though a number of abductees express feelings of isolation as a result of their beliefs, the cultural practice of being an alien abductee is—at least in major urban centers—not necessarily a solitary one. Reading, critiquing, and revising competing accounts of alien abduction and its meaning takes place between and among abductees. For some abductees, speaking with other abductees at venues such as conferences and support groups is a critical means for gathering information—albeit information that typically confirms their growing suspicion that they too are being abducted. As Anthony notes, it was his attendance at a free seminar on aspects of the UFO phenomenon in Jamaica, Queens, that led him "to the next stage and I became an investigator." There is a fairly extensive lecture, seminar, and conference circuit that exists both in New York City and nationwide on the topic of UFOs and all things related. UFO research organizations around the country such as the Mutual UFO Network in Seguin, Texas; Project Awareness based in Clearwater, Florida; and Seven Star Communications in Virginia Beach, Virginia, sponsor annual conferences. Recent efforts included, respectively, the "International UFO Symposium," "A Millenium of Contact," and "Planet Earth at the Crossroads." The longest running annual UFO

THIRTY-FIFTH ANNUAL
NATIONAL UFO CONFERENCE

Fig. 11. National UFO Conference Program.

conference is the National UFO Conference, which has met since 1964, usually in and around New Jersey. I was able to attend their 1999 conference, "Alien and Abduction Congress," at the Days Inn in Bordentown, New Jersey, at which Henry spoke.[15] So too do Hopkins's Intruders Foundation and Mack's Program for Extraordinary Experience Research (PEER) sponsor annual conferences. The Intruders Foundation generally meet in the New York Hall of Science in Corona, Queens, while PEER-sponsored events—such as "Star Wisdom: Exploring Contact with the Cosmos"—take place in and around their tony Harvard location. PEER also hosts a Public Education Series, as does SPACE. These organizations, as well as local New Age/self-help/adult education venues such as the Eyes of Learning Center, the Seminar Center, and the Center for Life, host lecturers on all manner of paranormal phenomena. In fact the abduction phenomenon continues to be energized in New York City, as I suspect it is not in less urban areas, by the crossover and interaction of these various groups. Hopkins, Mack, and Jacobs lecture regularly, as do somewhat less well-known figures including *Chariots of the Gods* author Erich Von Daniken, ex-CIA operative and "alien hunter" Derryl Simms, and celebrity abductees, such as Deb Kauble (featured in Hopkins's *Intruders*) and Travis Walton (upon whose story the movie *Fire in the Sky* was based.) There seems to be no end to such offerings in New York City, in the numerous spaces in which people come together to learn, share experiences, and meet other people.

Those who desire more interactivity can attend a variety of events, both nationwide and locally. Dr. Leo Sprinkle—an abduction hypnotherapist widely known within the community of believers—runs hypnotic regression workshops at his home in Laramie, Wyoming. The Center for the Search for Extraterrestrial Intelligence (CSETI) sponsors Ambassadors to the Universe training and fieldwork. Or one can choose to attend a Stargate International crisis intervention training workshop in Tucson, Arizona. Prices for such activities range from the $5 that SPACE requests per lecture, to $50 dollars for one day of lectures and activities at the Bordentown Day's Inn, to roughly $50 for three hours with John Mack at the Seminar Center. One week of CSETI ambassador training costs $600, and for $10,000 you can become a Research Founder of CSETI. There also exists a small but growing tourist industry around abduction and related phenomena. SPACE's first public lecture featured Joyce Murphy of Beyond Boundaries, a group that "leads small groups of people who are interested in the UFO phenomenon to areas of the world where sightings occur frequently." Recent packages feature expeditions to the Wiltshire England Crop Circles ($1,399 for the week, not including airfare) and to Puerto Rico for a Chupacabra safari ($1,000 including airfare for the week).[16] Power Places Tours hosted, for example, "Exploring Unseen Powers" in Bali, led by John Mack, for $3,299, including round trip airfare from Los Angeles. Those abductees who are politically inclined (and/or with tighter budgets) can join together with Operation Right to Know who intermittently organize rallies to end UFO secrecy on the Capitol steps in Washington, DC.

Finally, abductees also come together to define and debate the meaning of alien abduction in support groups, such as the SPACE meeting with which I open my introduction. For whether they are conspiracy theorists, New Agers, UFO hobbyists, or all of the above, many abductees end up seeking support in support groups, in quest not only of answers about the "truth" of what happened to them during abduction, but also for answers about their personal histories and fellowship with like-minded individuals. Some groups are led by researcher-experts, while others, such as SPACE, are abductee-led. It is difficult to know how many abductee-led groups exist in the United States, though an internet search yields a list of eleven such groups, nine of which are located on the east or west coasts.[17] As luck and location would have it, two of these groups are run by abductees whom I interviewed, Henry and Maureen. Maureen's group is called the Long Island Abductee Support Network. She was motivated to start the group by concern about abductee isolation. She explains,

> I started the group because I can remember what it was like for me—what do you do? Where do you turn? Who do you talk to? I also run an on-line support group on AOL. I talk to people all over the world, most of them have nobody else to talk to about it. The big fear is you'll be ridiculed and you're going to be isolated even more than you already are.

Maureen's group, which tries to meet every month or so, is fairly social and open-ended, sometimes meeting on the Long Island beach near Maureen's home. Concerned about the privacy of her members, she preferred that I not attend.

SPACE has been around somewhat longer and is a bit more organized. Henry sees his as providing an alternative to Hopkins's group, though it did not originate in reaction to that group. Henry explains that it is in fact an offshoot of a group that Whitley Strieber began in 1989, in response to the overwhelming response he got from his 1987 book, *Communion*. Henry explains his group's history:

> Strieber had just set up a network of support groups across the country, the Communion Foundation network, about twenty groups. He had one in the city—first meeting was May of 1989. I helped arrange that but he was head of the group. . . . Five months later he held another meeting and then he folded all the groups at the beginning of 1990 because there was a reporter out in L.A. who reported that he was a cult leader and we were following him, which is not the case, so he closed down all the groups to protect people in the group.[18]

After Strieber's group disbanded, Henry "stayed in touch with some of the people." In the early 1990s when possible abductees went to his hypnotherapist, Dr. Jean Mundy, and "couldn't get to Budd Hopkins . . . they would arrange to meet" with Henry. He recalls, they would "sit down in a coffee shop, I'd just sit and listen to them, give them support, tell them they're not alone, and that sort of thing." Henry, who is extremely soft-spoken and unassuming, at first resisted suggestions that he start a support group. He remembers, "I was reluctant to do it . . . and I did not want any publicity, didn't want it to be known that much, like a private place for people to share their experiences." Their first meeting was in March 1992.

SPACE has continued to grow through the 1990s, perhaps because it brings together the psychotherapeutic and investigative aspects of abductee practice. They have an average of twenty to twenty-five people at their meetings, every few months or so. Rather than seeking to control the "anything goes" attitude that Hopkins denigrates, Henry encourages it. In fact, as the SPACE statement of purpose suggests, SPACE is also more than a support group: "proactive interaction" occurs during outings, or what Henry refers to as "field work" during which attendees visit UFO hotspots in the region and seek sightings and contact. As Henry stresses in a recent newsletter, "As we interface, whether willingly or unwillingly, with the unknown, we can become true explorers."[19] If Hopkins emphasizes the negative aspects of abduction, Henry's group focuses on the positive facets of "experiencing."

Through researching, investigating, writing, and talking to one another abductees seek information about the abduction phenomenon, but what information they find acts as confirmation of what they already "know": that they have been abducted by extraterrestrial aliens. While the number of ways to understand the meaning and purpose of that fact are in constant discussion and contention, through other accounts of abduction, abductees receive, in Mike's words, "confirmation after confirmation of the real." In none of my interviews and reading have I encountered abductees who take nonbelieving accounts or debunking accounts seriously without quickly dismissing them. I have not encountered anyone who has moved from thinking they are an alien abductee to thinking that their alleged anomalous experiences can be understood in strictly terrestrial terms, whether psychological or otherwise.

Having a Say in the Final Cut

Through the belief in and practice of being abductees, alien abductees, I have argued, are trying to gain a sense of power over themselves, their experiences, and the world. But they are ambivalent and conflicted—both as a group and individually—about how to gain that power. Tensions and contradictions exist between abductees as a group about how to understand and respond to the perceived alien threat. The second part of this chapter explores the tensions and contradictions that exist within individual abductees: between what they say and what they do; between their indebtedness to and criticism of abduction experts; between viewing their marginal social identities as the source of isolation or viewing them as the source of status; and between the desire to convince outsiders such as me that the experience of alien abduction is real, and the desire to challenge and redefine reality itself to accommodate their beliefs.

Be Open to the Possibility That We're Telling the Truth

If one simply reads the literature about alien abduction, it is possible to conclude that abductee belief is at best a sort of sustained and willing suspension of disbelief, at worse a hoax to garner attention. My consideration of the cultural practice of abductees may also imply that people consciously choose to be abductees as a means of expressing themselves or of finding community. But while they do choose the level of involvement they will have with other abductees, and the degree to which they will embrace an identity as an abductee, to talk to alien abductees is to realize that, despite the tensions and ambivalences that exist within and among them, their belief in the actuality of their abductions is unwavering. In this they resemble religious faithful, perhaps especially converts to certain religions who exhibit the zeal of the born-again.

My informants seemed either unable or unwilling to reflect on alien abduction as a belief system, or to consider the symbolic value of their experiences. During our second interview, for example, I shared my skepticism with Jean about the various types of aliens reported in accounts of abduction and their possible roles. She corroborated these other accounts, describing good aliens (tall, fair, "Nordic") and the more sinister aliens (small and dark). I told Jean that I was struck by the very terrestrial racial typologies these descriptions seemed to draw on and reinforce. I was struck also by the rather unimaginatively science fictional, Star Trek–like sound of the pantheon of entities she was describing. There was a moment of silence, a sort of disconnect during which Jean seemed thrown off track. But the moment ended quickly as Jean returned to her narrative, conceding that of course humans do "project fears, beliefs, personalities onto what we see," but that abductees do see actual aliens. Patterns across time, Jean argued, suggest that there is another reality, and that these alien races do exist. She added that she, as an abductee, knows this "experientially." Mike took more pointed exception to my suggestion that aliens had some sort of symbolic value. When he noted that Christianity "didn't make sense" to him as a belief system, I asked how, in contrast, alien abduction made sense to him. He quickly changed the subject, but later when I asked him what he thought about the theory that abduction is an interspecies breeding project, he cut me off to insist that "it's not a theory."

For all of the abductees with whom I have spoken, their alleged experiences—many of them conscious—are both the commodity they have to offer, and the source of their conviction. Several of them now refer back to conscious UFO sightings that occurred ten to thirty years ago as the beginning of their awareness of, involvement with, or connection to extraterrestrials. Jean begins her story with a sighting twenty-four years ago on Fire Island, during which she was frozen in bed with a bright light surrounding her. Mike reports a lifetime of sightings and then the incident during which he was coming home from a bar—not drunk, he insists—and saw a huge football-shaped light hovering over a building. While he did not think, "it's a UFO" he experienced "raging paranoia and fear" and was "scared to death." He ran to his house and woke up the next morning bloodied, his eye swollen shut. At the time he could not remember how he got into bed and thought he must have been mugged. Cassie begins with the story of a close-range sighting while in college in Michigan in the early 1970s. Sitting in her kitchen talking to her roommate late at night, they noticed a fat disk-shaped craft with multicolored blinking lights hovering near the window. They stood at the window and looked, then ran downstairs and outside to watch, at which point it went straight up. She forgot about it until years later. Jane begins with her sighting in 1962 of what looked to her like "a large purple moon." When she arrived at the doctor's appointment to which she had been driving, she had "lost time." The skin on her face peeled off immediately after the sighting; she subsequently became psychic, and for the first time in her life, she claims, interested in UFOs.

Maureen has concluded that, "what I can remember consciously, I know that really happened." She adds "there are certain things that happen that you can't, when it's happening at the moment, and you know it's happening, you can't put if off as hallucination or dream." Maureen relates the following experience by way of illustration:

> The most recent one I had was really intense. I hadn't even gone to sleep yet. I was awake listening to the radio. All of a sudden I heard a roaring sound in my head and felt like a tingling that started at my head and worked its way down, almost like electricity, my body felt

paralyzed, but it also had, like a weightless feeling to it. I actually started to feel my body come off the bed . . . and when my head came back up to the headboard and I'm still awake, ya know? I'm thinking I know what this is Oh shit, do I know what this is.

Maureen tried to will it away—"I yelled in my head"—and then to grab at what looked like "long fingers and arms," and "it" was gone. She adds, "and there I was in my bed still. Now I hadn't gone to sleep yet. I was completely conscious listening to the radio when it started." The first psychologist Maureen saw suggested, as she knew he would, that she was experiencing sleep paralysis and night terrors.[20] But Maureen rejected this possibility quickly. Seeking to explain her swift dismissal of a nonextraterrestrial hypothesis, she adds, "There are certain things that happened that—how many times do you have to see coincidences before they're no longer coincidences?"

Other abductees refer to a range of unexplainable experiences, not necessarily resembling typical published accounts of abduction, that now stand for them as evidence of their repeated abductions. Anthony refers to these as "things not fitting the normal patterns of life." He includes among these his inability to remember much of his childhood, vague memories of feeling "lured" into a field behind the Aqueduct racetrack as a child, only to return with nosebleeds and no memory of what he had done there. He also includes an incident during a hunting trip in upstate New York when his car went off the road and he went into a sort of trance state, during which "there seemed to be a manipulation of time and space," and he semiconsciously discharged his weapon.

In my opening chapter I advanced the argument that belief in abduction by aliens provides alleged abductees like Anthony a narrative means for understanding inexplicable episodes from their pasts, as well as disturbing and confounding feelings in the present. Yet most of the people with whom I spoke insist repeatedly on the reality of their experience and the veracity of their stories. They anticipate skepticism and often insist that they are incapable of creating such stories. Maureen has been motivated to write her book so that therapists, in particular, will "be open to the possibility that we're telling the truth." Jane punctuated her account with such assertions, exclaiming at different points in the interview, "I don't have the imagination to make this up—why would I?" and "I couldn't make this stuff up if I wanted to!" Abductees not only insist on the veracity of their stories, but also hold up "experience" —as told through story—as the ultimate form of proof. Abductees have been telling their stories during roughly the same historical moment as feminists and other rights groups have demanded that silenced voices be heard, and that subjective experience be taken seriously as its own form of historical truth. And yet the dominant culture that alleged abductees are most specifically at odds with is a rationalist culture that continues to dismiss subjectivity in favor of objectivity and that demands more quantifiable forms of proof in order to be persuaded that, in Jean's words, there is another reality.

Pushing Evidence

Though they may have unusual ideas about the nature of reality, abductees place immense value on, and talk a lot about, evidence. They understand that it is proof in the here and now that is taken seriously. To those doubting Thomases such as me they offer first their stories of experience as evidence: it happened to them, so they at least know it is real. Henry, who is extremely open to any and all interpretations of the phenomenon, nonetheless asserts of the alleged interspecies breeding project thought by many to be the purpose of abduction that "it is going on." How does he know? "From experiences of people in the group. . . . There's just so much circumstantial evidence that this has happened." Cassie has been privy to hundreds of letters from those who think they may have been abducted. Reading these letters contributed to her own growing sense that her memories of abduction might be real because, she adds, there was "so much evidence of people having the same things happen."

Some abductees arrived at our first meetings with some sort of "evidence" in hand: pictures, photographs, reports, research studies, portfolios of drawings, and, in the case of Mike, computer images of x-rays of alien implants. George's materials include his photographs of UFOs, as well as a copy of the Sturrock report, the results of a study sponsored by UFO buff Laurence Rockefeller, which concludes that further government investigation of UFOs and their possible alien occupants is warranted. When I comment to him that many with whom I have spoken seem eager to proffer audio-visual aids, he responds, "We're just trying to share it with people. That's all. I know I can't convince people of this. All I can do is share it with you, yet some of us will try to convince by pushing evidence." Or in Mike's words, "I'll show you shit that will blow your mind."

More disturbing, and less easily explained away as misidentifications, hoaxes, or willing suspension of disbelief are the physical marks that abductees claim to bear as the result of their abductions. One of the reasons Maureen left her first psychiatrist—the one who had suggested that her experiences might be the result of sleep paralysis—was because his diagnosis could not, to her mind, explain the "nickel-sized bruises with a puncture in the middle" that she was left with. Maureen allows, in response to my own skepticism, that "everybody gets marks"—that we cannot always know the source of small bruises and cuts—but underscores that hers always appear in the same pattern, in "sets of two." At first, she recalls, "I checked what jewelry I was wearing. . . . I tore my room apart. I tried to think of every possible alternative explanation for this and I couldn't find any." Exasperated, she adds, "There's just no explanation for these marks." Anthony claims to have a number of scars of unknown origin. Jane has a scoop mark—one of the types of marks held up by Hopkins and others as definitively of alien origin—as well as what she believes is an alien implant. Her daughter, she adds, has three. A doctor who examined the area on her upper right arm diagnosed it as a calcified insect bite. She nonetheless believes that it is an implant, and when she showed it to me—a rather unremarkable bump of scar tissue, the only alleged mark of abduction I have seen in the course of my research—she added that she would not want to have it removed. Without it, the aliens would not know where to find her, which in Jane's case she openly desires.

Mike, characteristically, is less upbeat about the body marks he claims that he, his wife, and his children bear. In one of the only emotionally charged exchange I have had with a subject, Mike took issue with my "psychobabble" approach to the abduction phenomenon. He felt angry that I was not simply reporting the facts but rather might "be operating on a set of preconceived assumptions" to "make the facts fit the theory."[21] He was concerned that I was not properly objective enough in my approach. I responded, perhaps unwisely, that through this project I had only become more convinced that all accounts of reality are subjective. In the face of my frustrating relativism, Mike retorted, "I have a few 'subjective' marks on my body and the bodies of my family members you really ought to see!" For Mike, seeing Hopkins's collected pictures of such wounds confirmed the reality of what he had suspected—that he and perhaps his family had been abducted and manipulated by aliens. In the face of such "evidence," he adds, "reality gets exploded." At the 1994 Whole Life Expo at which I first encountered Budd Hopkins, I saw him present a session on recognizing the symptoms of abduction, featuring a slide presentation of the photo "evidence" of marks and wounds born on the bodies of alleged abductees. These included cuts, scars, scoop marks, and bruises. One slide of a woman's bruised inner thighs was particularly chilling. Sitting in the darkened room, watching image after image, I was disturbed and puzzled. There seemed to be no happy explanation for their existence. Either aliens really were abducting people, which I did not believe, or people had inflicted them, either on themselves or on others. The latter explanation is even more profoundly disturbing than the former, and led me to wonder what stories of terrestrial abuse may be ignored or masked in favor of the more appealing and mysterious extraterrestrial explanation.

Of course people may also, as is perhaps true in Jane's case, offer revisionist readings of their own wounds: what were insect bites may be transformed into intergallactic tracking devices. And yet when people I have interviewed talk about wounds—or worse still, wounds on their children—as I am a skeptic, my mind turns to the reality of the types of abuses that can occur in the privacy of families, many of which go unrecorded, unreported, and untold. There is also a rich history of types of self-abuse through which people, most often women, have sought power and/or recognition. In premodern times, religious martyrs bearing stigmata were listened to and taken seriously. I recall also stories I have read about people with Munchausens's disease, or Munchausen's by proxy. In the former, people make themselves ill and compulsively check into hospitals in order to be tended to and cared for in a way that they are not elsewhere. Such "caring" often includes painful invasive procedures and repeated surgeries, not unlike the injustices said to be visited upon the bodies of humans by alien abductors. In the latter, people sicken their children—often through subtle means such as poisoning—toward that same end. More common, perhaps, is the formidable number of mostly teenage girls who engage in self-starvation and self-cutting in an effort to control otherwise uncontrollable environments and emotions. Such practices, both consciously and unconsciously motivated, leave marks on real bodies.

So too, as I have argued in previous chapters, may abductees' bodies bear the traces of the various social traumas and anxieties to which their narratives give expression. Through their stories, abductees give voice to all those who have felt physically or emotionally paralyzed by the encroachment of technology in the management of daily life; so too do they express fear, anger, and distrust of those elites who understand and control those technologies. Some abductees identify quite explicitly with those citizens whose physical and mental health have been imperiled by state-sponsored science and technology experiments. In an even broader sense, abduction scenarios, with their emphasis on the violation of individual human bodies, give a remarkably precise location to the abuses of otherwise abstract and "placeless" social forces, such as globalization. In these social-cultural contexts the desire to "push evidence" makes sense in several ways at once. It is an attempt to point to and quantify even the most diffuse sorts of human suffering. It is also an attempt to reclaim authority over the meaning of one's own life in a world in which scientism and rationalism seem to be the reigning absolute truths. It is an effort to speak the language of the very dominant culture from which one may feel excluded.

But to the people I interviewed, such speculations do not hold water. They have heard numerous theories from other people and remain unconvinced that their experiences have been engineered in any manner that does not involve aliens. Thus the sort of equivocation discussed earlier resides alongside statements of utter certainty, such as Anthony's assertion that "we are interfacing with a nonhuman intelligence. No question. I can look you straight in the eye, no question in my mind about it whatsoever. On a stack of Bibles, there's no reservation whatsoever. I don't care what anybody does, if they have a shotgun to my head, that's how convinced I am with this." He adds,

> I want this on the record: I will challenge—and I'm not being belligerent—I will challenge any, and I will say any, skeptic, debunker, any place, any time, baby. And I'll tell you why: not that I'm a hero. When I speak it is unguarded. It comes from my heart. I don't have any notes in front of me. I don't have any agendas. They will probably outmaneuver me because they have higher degrees, but you know what? In the end ... you can win the battle, but whoever wins the war is the victor. And I know I would win the war.[22]

Almost Aggressively Normal

Because of the paradoxical nature of abductee belief, there is a somewhat marked—and audience-savvy—difference between how abductees talk to other abductees and believers at conferences or in groups, on websites and in books, and how they talk to me. When they speak with me, abductees seem to feel, perhaps for obvious reasons, the need not only to convince me of the actuality of their abduction by aliens, but also of their sanity and normalcy. At the beginning of our interview, for example, Mike declared, "I want you to leave knowing that this isn't an undiagnosed psychological condition. It isn't just people telling crazy stories. It's real. There's evidence." While most abductees I interviewed were not quite as evangelical as Mike, they did see the interview as, in part, an opportunity to convince me and other skeptics that they were not delusional or divorced from reality, but both sane and normal.

Perhaps because they are hyperaware of the "craziness" of their accounts, abductees sometimes work hard to convince me of their normalcy. They do so in part by noting their own uncertainty and skepticism about the abduction phenomenon. They want to underscore their own reason and good sense. In contrast to their written accounts of the same experience, they are, while talking to me, somewhat restrained about the details of their experience, somewhat reserved about sharing detailed theories and interpretations. Jean, for example, asserts that, "I read everything and am skeptical about everything." When I ask Jean about David Jacobs's theory of an alien threat she readily admits, "I don't know." Asked to elaborate on what the aliens look like, George responds, "I really can't answer that." When asked why he thinks certain people are abducted and not others, Henry admits, "I really don't know. Hard to say." Indeed, Jane exclaims, "I wish I had the answers, but I don't!"

Those abductees whom I interviewed also point to the normalcy of their daily lives, defined by a sort of middle-class respectability: many hold down jobs, are married, and have children; they are members of families and communities. Maureen lives with her father and son; she has taught religious education classes for Catholic children and volunteers in the local blood drive. Maureen indeed seems to be an accepted and loved member of her local community. As we walk through her neighborhood, it is clear that Maureen knows most everyone and everyone knows her—this is where she grew up. Jane characterizes herself as an "upstanding citizen" and "upstanding, intelligent person." She wants me to know that she worked for twenty-five years as a letter carrier, is "stable," and has four children and grandchildren. Mike stresses that he is a husband and father who is "almost aggressively normal." His phrase is apt: there is a way in which abductee efforts to establish their own normalcy seem almost forced, for they are, by virtue of what has allegedly occurred to them and the attendant set of beliefs they now hold, not "normal" in the eyes of the culture at large. While they are certainly not insane—they are not incapacitated by psychoses, unable to conduct themselves in their everyday lives, including an interview—they are at a remove from the mainstream.

They share Mike's concern that my readers and I will think they are simply, in Mike's words, telling "crazy stories." Most abductees, without prompting, bring up the question of their own sanity: they acknowledge that what they are telling me may sound crazy, they admit to at times feeling crazy, and they sometimes recall a time before they realized they had been abducted when they thought alien abductees were crazy. Those with whom I speak often punctuate their accounts with interjections about how crazy they must sound, aware that they are speaking to a different audience than they are in books, websites, and conferences. Jane follows her assurance that she "couldn't make this up" with "it's so off the wall!" And Maureen, as she recounts her sexual assault by a reptilian alien, adds, "I know it sounds so crazy when you tell it, but as I'm telling it I'm still seeing it in my head. After hypnosis I said this is just too nuts. . . . I mean it just can't possibly . . ." Several suggested that in fact they would rather be crazy in some easily definable sense: then they could be treated, their abductions would cease, and they could get on with their lives. When Maureen's physician referred her to a psychiatrist she remembers, "I said, 'no problem, if someone could tell me I'm going crazy and give me Prozac or something, and make it go away, I'll be real happy.'" Likewise Anthony, who insists that "we would accept being diagnosed as insane—that'd be easier. We would gladly—you know what? They put a straitjacket on us, give us a couple of shots, and before you know it, we're out in a wheelchair somewhere. Perfect! Good! We know what it is! We don't have that luxury."

Mike vividly recalls that before realizing he was abducted, he had heard of alien abductees and himself thought "they were delusional, with psychological problems." Jean had already believed in UFOs and aliens for years before realizing she was being abducted. Yet she remembers that when accounts of abduction by aliens began to appear and get talked about at related conferences, abductees "seemed nuts." Once people recall that they themselves have been abducted, their anxiety about their own sanity does not immediately resolve. As an informant in Hopkins's office told me, most letters to him that include accounts of abduction begin with some version of the phrase "I think I'm going crazy but . . ." Mike recalls buying *Missing Time* and, when he finished reading it, he "freaked out." He thought, "Hopkins is an opportunist. [The abductees] are crazy. Now I'm crazy too!" Reflecting back on that moment he adds, "This was devastating—I've never been crazy, like insane crazy." And yet abductees tacitly set certain boundaries for the discussion of their mental health. It is suggested that any "craziness" they may have experienced is clearly alien-induced. Belief that alien abduction is the source of self-doubt about one's sanity allows them both to explain that self-doubt away and to relegate any possible mental instability to the past. While several have referred in passing to difficult personal histories, to "nervous periods," or "difficult times," none venture into these areas, knowing perhaps that skeptical outsiders—including me—will seize upon them as further evidence of their actual insanity, as opposed to their actual abduction. As long as they present themselves as sane and normal they expect their claims to be taken seriously. As an interviewer, I do not press for details for fear of crossing some sort of line that will make them stop talking. I tacitly abide by the boundary they have drawn.

The restrained and equivocal responses alleged alien abductees provide during interviews often stand in contrast to written accounts that they produce and share elsewhere. Sometimes in interview situations, while they are skeptical, incredulous, and uncertain, they will also venture self-protective, "I'm not sure, but . . ." responses. Such was the case with John Velez's response to the *Nova* interviewer who asked, "Why do you think aliens are here?" He responded,

> All right, this is pure speculation on my part. Because I don't think anybody knows for sure. With the exception of the aliens and maybe Uncle Sam and they're not talking. What I think is going on is, I believe these creatures have always been here. I believe their role is basically a

caretaker role. I believe that their race is incapable of reproducing itself. And that these beings have lived in a symbiotic relationship with mankind throughout the ages.[23]

John concludes with a claim I discussed earlier: "They need us in order to reproduce themselves." I repeat it here to underscore a move from tentativeness to declaration that is typical in such accounts. While abductees know their beliefs sound crazy, they do believe them, and despite their efforts to seem equivocal, their basic beliefs are deeply entrenched. Maureen, for example, reminds me that she maintains a sense of doubt about the "truths" revealed under hypnosis, as well as about some written accounts of the Montauk area military abductions (discussed in chapter 7). She insists that, "believe it or not, I'm a skeptic. . . . I don't believe this stuff. I'm a real nuts and bolts type of person." The contrast between Maureen's claimed skepticism and her richly descriptive written accounts of her abduction she has posted on the Internet is particularly stark. In her piece on "Alien/Human Hybrids" she writes, "I speak from the position of one who has undergone the physical as well as emotional pain and torment associated with the Grey and reptilian alien 'hybrid program.' I contend these programs exist in order to enhance their species with the addition of human emotions." She continues by relating a dream she had wherein she was holding a "baby monkey." "Under hypnosis," she adds, "I was able to recall being presented with, and holding a hybrid child that I knew to be mine." The next paragraph shifts fully into storytelling mode as she recalls, "When I held my son, Lyjor, and looked into his eyes, I found myself speaking telepathically to him."[24]

Maureen's awareness of audience, the difference between her presentation to other "believers" and her presentation to me is worth noting. Offering accounts of one's abduction experiences in lavish detail is what most abductees do in one venue or another and through one medium or another. Yet while abductees may find a means of expression and community through their alleged abduction experiences, they must also negotiate the much larger world of nonbelievers and navigate between their own belief and a dominant view of reality that generally dismisses them out of hand. And so abductees strive to convince others of their own normalcy and respectability—indeed their own rationalism—in order to have their claims taken seriously. As Jean notes, conference attendees were "panic stricken" when abductees began to speak publicly about their alleged experiences, but as more "responsible people, reliable people" began to talk about it, the more interested she and others became. If "craziness" can be spread viruslike through language in the way that Mike fears, so too can it be met, if not with straitjackets and Prozac, then with still more language—with the testimony of normal-seeming people to profoundly abnormal-seeming events.

They'll Do Anything to Ridicule Us

Despite their best efforts to convince nonbelievers of their veracity and normalcy, abductees realize that they will be ridiculed nonetheless, that in terms of the culture at large, they are profoundly marginal and marginalized. Given the mostly hostile climate in which their beliefs will be received, abductees express ambivalence about whether or not to identify themselves as abductees, about the value of remaining discreet as opposed to the value of "coming out." Abductees express frustration at being stigmatized and lumped together with one another. Mike resents being part of a generalized "them" framed by skeptics and debunkers. He suggests that this is the same as making sweeping and biased generalizations about "all niggers." George (who is African American) also resents being stigmatized and notes that even believing experts such as Mack and Hopkins are guilty of making such assumptions. This is one of the reasons George avoids the term "abductee" altogether—it is itself stigmatizing. He recalls, "being in a conference in North Carolina, Budd Hopkins introduced me to Mack as an abductee—'and he is an abductee.' And I said, 'No, no, no, I'm not an abductee'—that's how they'll refer to you! I'm just a person who has perceived certain things. That's it. Whoever coined that word, I'd like to shoot them." At yet another conference George was introduced to Mack by a woman who said, "'Here's George. He's a member of a support group.' Rather than saying 'here's George,' she had to qualify that. That just irritates me because they lump us all in the same category."

Abductees talk passionately about being the object of ridicule from a number of sources. Anthony is especially angry about the way he and other abductees have been ridiculed by the scientific community. He believes that because "we're challenging them" and "a dominant scientific paradigm of reality," "they'll do anything to ridicule us." Adam suggests that the news media in particular have belittled abductees. He has "no respect" for them and believes they are "completely biased." Adam brings a cross-cultural perspective to bear on his analysis of the situation: having spent a lot of time in Central and South America, he believes that the U.S. news media "have probably been told by people higher up that that's the editorial policy that they have to take. And, or it could be part of the politics." He adds, "You have to realize that in the United States the government has purposefully denied, covered up, lied to its citizens about this particular event to the point . . . I mean people aren't stupid. . . . I mean, look, there are reports of this happening all over the world, not all governments are taking the same approach." He shares accounts of mass sightings in Brazil and Costa Rica that were covered in depth by their mainstream news media. Stopping short of conspiracy theory, he notes that "the *Times* doesn't want to step out on a limb. Even if they're not being told [by the government to portray abduction in a certain light], the culture of our country is 'oh, this is ridiculous; these are crackpots.'" Anthony articulates a dual sense of alien and human abuse when he explains that "we feel like we get burned twice: first having someone take us or whatever they do without our permission, then we get ridiculed. It's horrible."

John Velez is extremely sensitive to the ways in which the media skeptically portray abductees. He was one of several abductees featured on the aforementioned *Nova*, "Kidnapped by UFOs?" the airing of which constituted a watershed moment for many abductees in terms of realizing how difficult it would be to get taken seriously by the mainstream media. He agreed to appear on the show because "it was *Nova*" —he thought they would be "serious." He offered to subject himself to polygraph, psychological work-up, and x-rays; he hoped *Nova* would test his home for "magnetic traces" to substantiate his claims. Instead, experts who did not know him saw on-air testimony and analyzed it he suggests, irresponsibly. Among these experts was Elizabeth Loftus, who has made her career debunking a variety of false repressed memory syndromes. Velez is angry that Loftus never bothered to call Hopkins for background information on him. His fear and loathing of disbelieving experts extends to me, and in email conversation Velez writes angrily,

> I'm 51 years old Bridget. I wasn't born yesterday. I have had my words and meanings twisted so many times and in so many ways by so many people that I have learned to read questions that are put to me very

carefully. And to word my responses very carefully. I know exactly what you meant to say/ask. . . . I'll answer your questions, but please don't jerk me around—I find it condescending and disrespectful.[25]

John is also savvy about how possible academic ridicule of my work will inform the way I represent him and other abductees. He writes,

> You ain't going far in the academic community 'agreeing with us' that something real may be happening. Publishing a paper like that would almost guarantee—no jobs, no respect, and no recognition—in academic circles. So, knowing that one of your concerns is acceptance among your peers and the professional community I know that you will write a 'go along, get along' paper regarding this subject.

In many respects John is right—I still do not believe in aliens, and this will probably serve me better than if I did.

Abductees ultimately express a sort of ambivalence, then, about "normalcy" and its value in their lives. On the one hand, they seem to understand that some modicum of it will gain them a wider audience and more credibility than they currently have. On the other hand, it is that which makes them abnormal—their alleged forced encounters with extraterrestrials—that is at the core of the individual and group identity many are in the process of fashioning. It is what makes them interesting not only to outsiders such as me, but also perhaps even to one another. It is a wedge against isolation and, though not as common a diagnosis as mental illness, one that does offer an explanatory framework for all manner of ambient and ill-defined bad feeling.

Coming Out

When I took the train to Long Island to visit Maureen, I was surprised to be picked up at the train station by both Maureen and her sister-in-law. I was not sure whether her sister-in-law knew the purpose of my visit, so I kept quiet during the ride to the house. Soon into our trip, however, Maureen commented that she "came out of the closet" three years ago. I commented on her use of the term and its origins in the gay rights movement. Maureen reflected that she could identify with the isolation closeted homosexuals must feel. In her mind, abductees who cannot share their experiences with others experience a similar form of isolation. She noted later in our interview that her decision to come out was motivated in part by a desire to reach out to others who remain isolated. With her father's assurance that he believes that she believes, and the go-ahead from her eighteen-year-old son, she decided to come out in a more public way. Given the perils of ridicule by family, friends, the media, academia, and the culture at large, which I go on to discuss in further detail below, why then do some abductees embrace the identity while others shun it? Why do some choose to go public with their experiences while others remain silent, or at least tell only a small number of people?

> Why did I do it? I realized there are so many people who can't do it because of career choices, family situations and I was lucky enough that I had the support of my family. . . . By coming out, there was nothing that . . . It couldn't hurt me in any way, except for ridicule. And I realized . . . if people don't start coming out and talking about it, the isolation its just going to keep getting worse and worse. There's a need for people that will talk about it publicly. Eventually that will filter down and help everyone.

Maureen adds, "you feel isolated because it's been happening and then isolated because you can't share it with anybody."

John's decision to speak publicly about his experiences, despite his knowledge that he would be "dismissed and mocked," grew out of a sense of duty to his family and the public at large, informed by his belief that alien abduction is real and threatening. He notes, "I have kids. I'm a father." He "felt compelled to stand up and be counted" and to "let the world know that there's something serious going on here." He now considers himself "on a campaign to educate the public, to raise public awareness." He writes, in the same email exchange discussed earlier,

> If you had some reason to suspect that something like this was happening to you, and to your family, would you feel compelled to warn others in any way that you could? I'll bet you would. And you'd do it regardless of any ridicule or humiliation that may be directed at you. This phenomenon is major stuff and poses a potential and real threat to every living ass on the planet. That is why I do it. You can look for

all the explanations you want to, my motivations are straightforward, simple, and clear.

But not all abductees feel a sense of responsibility to other abductees, or to identifying themselves as such. Several I have interviewed feel they would rather not be part of an "abductee" or "UFO" community. George, whose wariness about being identified as an abductee I touched upon above, refrains in part out of cynicism about how his accounts will be received. When John was deciding whether or not to appear on *Nova,* George recalls John's asking him "what is my role in this?" George's advice was, from the start, "don't go to the media." Velez did, and George laments, "Well see what the media did with him? . . . I don't know why we have this tendency to think that if we run to the media we're doing . . . some kind of gesture to bring this out. I don't see how people believe that." Perhaps because George works in television production, he has some savvy about how such stories are dealt with. He adds, "once you go to the media, you've left it up to them. You have no say in the final cut. . . . You're not in the room when they do the editing, they can write the script. . . . You may have planned this in a certain way, but when it finally comes out . . . it may come out totally different." George and I spoke prior to the airing of *Confirmation,* an NBC special on abduction spearheaded by Whitley Strieber. He noted that an NBC film crew had attended Hopkins's support group meeting for that program, of which George was at the time a part. When I asked whether he was part of the segment, he responded unequivocally, "No way. They tried to get me to do it. I said uh uh. . . . I'm sitting in the back, not in the camera. 'Cause there's no point. Budd asked me, 'How do you think I should make the public more aware of this?' I said 'It's not my role!'"

George's response troubles the argument that all abductees gain a sort of status through embracing their identities as abductees. Indeed George insists on shunning the label and the expected levels of involvement in the community for a number of reasons. First and foremost, he rejects the "role" of abductee because of the way in which he believes it distracts people from attending to the world around them. He continues, "You see the condition of the world? That's my role! To try to make it better! Not to run around letting people know about the abduction phenomenon as [Hopkins] refers to it." In part because the media will not represent the experience faithfully, he adds, "That's why I feel people's energies should be put into things that will help to make this world a better place to live." George himself is an active member of his "community of fifty thousand people," Co-op City in the Bronx. He notes, "There is crime there. I'm involved in security, the elderly. . . . What you do instead of sitting on your butt, you involve yourself in things—this involves people—that's what I do. This constant focusing on ETs and trying to convey to people what's actually going on, that's a waste of energy."

And although Adam thinks support groups may be necessary and positive for many abductees, he did not even want to go that public with his experiences. He notes that, "I went through my own process to get through it. Support from family and friends."[26] His mother, who is "extremely skeptical about all those things . . . knew that something was up because of how emotional I was on the subject. . . . She said, 'Honey, whatever happened to you, I'm gonna be supportive.' . . . My dad was also very supportive." His reservation about sharing his experiences also stems out of a sense of wanting not to dwell on the experiences, and he notes, "There comes a point . . . you just want to move on and if its happening, its happening. And its gonna happen again. . . . It's sort of like you shrug your shoulders." Perhaps partially explaining the gap observed earlier between Maureen's two modes of self-presentation, she notes that she is "not as obsessive" as she once was about her experience: "you have to get on with your life." What's more, she would rather craft her own version of what it is to be an experiencer than accept Hopkins's, or Mack's. She comments, "If you're part of Budd's group, you're an abductee. Now I don't seem to need that kind of validation. I don't need Budd to tell me I'm an abductee, or John Mack. . . . I'm kinda past that point."

In addition to articulating his personal reasons for not fully identifying himself as an alien abductee through affiliation with others and extensive participation in the abductee community, Adam also points to the perils of forging one's identity around the sense of oneself as a victim, or even a survivor. He adds, "The support groups are good if it doesn't become—like I think anything that becomes your identity—that's why I have some problems with A.A. meetings too—not all—because I know they saved a lot of people's lives, but after a while if you're so dependent and you're so involved with giving yourself that identity" you lose, he suggests, other valuable parts of yourself.

In deciding whether or not to identify as alien abductees, in debating the value of claiming such an identity in a world in which they may be mocked and ridiculed, it is critical to note that abductees are, in a sense, participating in a much broader historical moment of, and conversation about, identity politics. The abduction phenomenon has certainly emerged during the same period as identity politics, in the wake and in the midst of different identity-based social movements, such as the women's rights, civil rights, and LGBT rights movements. Abductees indeed view themselves, like these other historically silenced or aggrieved groups, as marginalized by the dominant culture: as other, as queer, indeed as alien in the context of the culture at large. Their sense of a common identity, when it exists, comes from their sense of difference from a rationalist, skeptical culture, one that exists within and expounds what they take to be a limited and limiting view of reality. As a group, they have appropriated many of the strategies of identity politics in order to be heard and taken seriously. As touched upon in my first chapter, they insist on the value of their stories and subjective experiences, of providing accounts of history and reality that they feel have otherwise been silenced or overlooked. Some wear their difference proudly, touting it as the very source of their specialness. Others are concerned, as in other sites of identity politics, with the limits of claiming special status on the basis of cultural difference. They are wary, like George, of the downside of existing only as a particular, qualified subject; they express the desire to exist as universal subjects, and to reap the privileges of that subject position.

Normal Is Boring to Us

> We're taking a lot of hits. We're getting it initially from nonhuman entities, then we're getting it from our own people. It really sucks. It really does.

> This is the best story ever. I get bored quickly, but this keeps me going. Being an artist, you know our minds are pretty expanded as it is, and out there normal is boring to us. That's how we feel.

These two claims, both made by Anthony during the course of the same interview, demonstrate the ambiguity that most abductees express about their abduction experiences. On the one hand, simply put, it sucks. But on the other hand, it is "the best story ever." In Anthony's statement the "we" he refers to are artists. And yet he could just as easily be speaking here for abductees, for while they want us to know that they are sane and normal and that abductions are real, abductees also have a degree of uncertainty and concern about what the value of sanity and normalcy are in the dominant reality, which they reject. While in interviews they stress the pain and disruption these events have visited upon them, their social stigmatization and marginalization, in the same interviews and in written texts they express the sort of pleasure and excitement that Anthony expresses.

While to nonbelievers alleged abductees stress that their experiences are "real," they also engage in a collective effort to revise reality—to propose that there is indeed more to the world around us than meets the eye. In this sense, belief in alien abduction resembles religion in its effort to transcend the worldly, to suggest the existence of mystery, magic, and some sort of higher power or powers. Through this project of imagining other realities, abductees also find a place to express anger and disappointment about the reality in which we do live. As Rusty, an abductee whom I heard speak with John Mack, declares of his abduction, "The experience had made me see that this (this reality) is all a bunch of lies." By embracing the belief that they have, in fact, been abducted by aliens, abductees find a means for circumventing those aspects of normalcy that may indeed be boring or difficult. The alternate realities they construct are ones in which they play featured roles, and in contrast to the passivity of Mike's claim that "reality gets exploded," abductees get to play at collectively attempting to explode reality.

Conclusion
Alien Abduction and the New Face of Terror

Debate about the legitimacy of the alien abduction phenomenon may have reached a high-water mark in 1992 with the MIT Abduction Study Conference at which numerous high-profile scientists, psychologists, and academics (not only believing "ufologists") gathered to share research and views about possible explanations for the phenomenon, including "the ET hypothesis." In the last few years an increasing number of skeptical treatments of the phenomenon, including some scientific investigations that attribute abduction reports to temporal-lobe disturbance and an array of sleep disorders, seem to have pushed abductees and abduction researchers more firmly into the margins of contemporary culture. While in 1997 thousands of people attended the fiftieth anniversary of the alleged flying saucer crash at Roswell, New Mexico, it was an event characterized more by carnivalesque celebration (and commercialization) than by sober scientific inquiry. And in that same year the Heaven's Gate mass suicide pointed to the possible extremism, danger, and cultishness of alien-abduction-related belief.

In 2006 alleged alien abductees remain convinced of the veracity of their extraterrestrial experiences and continue to produce and publish accounts of those experiences where they can. And yet at least online, on message boards and abductee websites, there seems to be a collective throwing up of hands about "going public." In a thread on Virtually Strange.net, for example, abductee Katharina Wilson asked why people no longer post updates about their abduction experiences. One post noted that "it's hard enough to live with abductions, without having other people judging the validity of what you are saying. Most everyone I've told anything to in my life thinks I'm crazy, or making it all up." Another person writes, "I don't feel like I should have to defend myself when I talk about what I have seen and experienced."[1] The sense of weariness at the ridicule that often follows sharing alleged experiences of abduction was certainly present during the interviews I conducted several years ago; it seems only to have deepened for many alleged alien abductees in subsequent years.

What seems most different now, however, just a few short years later, is that popular interest in the alien abduction phenomenon—a widespread willingness to engage the possibility that humans might actually be abducted regularly by extraterrestrials—seems to have dropped off. The last book on alien abduction to be on the *New York Times* bestseller list was John Mack's *Abduction: Human Encounters with Aliens* (1994); the last published by major publishing houses and widely marketed were Budd Hopkins's *Witnessed: The True Story of the Brooklyn Bridge UFO Abduction* (1996), published by a subsidiary of Simon and Schuster, and *Abduction,* published by Charles Scribner's Sons.[2] In 2002 Steven Spielberg's miniseries *Taken* was broadcast on the FX channel, and in 2006 the USA network broadcast *The 4400.* Yet *Taken* uses the alien abduction phenomenon as an excuse for an intergenerational family saga, while *The 4400* aptly concerns itself with the aftermath of alien abduction, following abductees who have been returned to Earth and struggle to reintegrate into the lives from which they were torn away. In the thick of the reality television craze, neither of these shows makes any pretense at reality. Documentaries about the UFO phenomenon do still crop up from time to time, including the History Channel's *UFO Files* series (2005) and Peter Jennings's *UFO: Seeing Is Believing* (2005). But they are generally unanimous in their conclusions that alien abduction is the result of a form of brain disturbance and/or sleep paralysis.

From the perspective of 2007, the alien abduction phenomenon is even more clearly a phenomenon of the late twentieth—not the early twenty-first—century. The period when accounts of abduction by aliens proliferated, and when ample audiences were interested in reading them, watching them, and considering whether or not they might be real was somewhat unusual, hovering as it did between the end of the Cold War and the beginning of the War on Terror. Certainly the September 11, 2001, terror attacks on the United Stated shifted focus to more pressing terrestrial matters. Since 9/11, terror has taken on a new face and meaning.

This is not to suggest that the sorts of felt disempowerment I discuss throughout this book have disappeared. On the contrary, many of the cultural anxieties that I suggest are expressed through accounts of abduction by aliens were dragged to the fore of national consciousness in the wake of 9/11 by the terrorists themselves. The terror attacks on the United States confronted many Americans with the uncomfortable, indeed shocking, reality that some members of the global village take exception to America and that for which it stands, including progress, democratization, capitalism (or infidelism, depending on where you stand.) In attacking the Pentagon and the World Trade Center, Islamic fundamentalists let the world know loudly and clearly that they were attacking the center of economic and military globalization, or imperialism, of U.S. intervention in the Middle East, of the perceived godlessness of Western culture and modernity writ large. Accounts of alien abduction give expression—in an obviously more benign, less overtly politicized fashion—to similar feelings *from within* of exclusion and alienation from national progress and more specifically, from the project of U.S. global expansion and dominance. Close attention to these still relatively marginal accounts of reality demonstrate that not just terrorists, or Islamic fundamentalists, but a good number of American citizens feel not enabled, but rather oppressed, or, at best, left behind, by America's political, technological, and military advantage in the world.

Notes

NOTES TO THE INTRODUCTION

1. The statement by Judith Herman quoted above can be found in Judith Lewis Herman, *Trauma and Recovery* (New York: Basic Books, 1992), 34.

2. This is how Mack described his pre-alien abduction work at a talk I attended at the Seminar Center in New York City, 17 May 2000.

3. I discuss this blurring at length in chapter 8. Authors such as Zecharia Sitchin and Barry Downing, among others, continue to rewrite ancient history and religious history through the lens of belief in aliens. Sitchin claims to be able to read Sumerian clay tablets proving that alien gods from another planet created humans via genetic engineering; his ideas have influenced the recently high-profile Raelian movement, which believes that humans are indeed the result of alien DNA experiments. Downing is more concerned with revisionist Bible history, reinterpreting stories such as the parting of the Red Sea, as the result of alien visitations.

4. Whitley Strieber, *Communion: A True Story* (New York: William Morrow, 1987), 77.

5. The assimilating Borg made its debut in the television series *Star Trek: The Next Generation* (1987–1994) and had a feature role in the movie *Star Trek: First Contact* (1996).

6. Carl Jung, *Flying Saucers: A Myth of Things Seen in the Sky* (New York: Harcourt Brace, 1959).

7. Thomas Bullard, "UFO Abduction Reports: The Supernatural Kidnap Narrative Returns in Technical Guise," *Journal of American Folklore* 102 (1989).

8. Curtis Peebles, *Watch the Skies! A Chronicle of the Flying Saucer Myth* (Washington, DC: Smithsonian Institution Press, 1994), and Benson Saler, Charles A. Ziegler, and Charles B. Moore, *UFO Crash at Roswell: The Genesis of a Modern Myth* (Washington, DC: Smithsonian Institution Press, 1997).

9. Saler, Ziegler, and Moore, 2.

10. Leon Festinger, *When Prophecy Fails: A Social and Psychological Study of a Modern Group That Predicted the Destruction of the World* (New York: Harper and Row, 1956), 22.

11. William James, *The Varieties of Religious Experience: A Study of Human Nature* (Garden City, NY: Dolphin Books, 1960), 55.

12. Elaine Showalter, *Hystories: Hysterical Epidemics and Modern Media* (New York: Columbia University Press, 1997).

13. Susan Clancy, *Abducted: How People Came to Believe They Were Kidnapped by Aliens* (Cambridge, MA: Harvard University Press, 2005).

14. Jodi Dean, *Aliens in America: Conspiracy Cultures from Outerspace to Cyberspace* (Ithaca, NY: Cornell University Press, 1998), 6.

15. Peter Knight, *Conspiracy Nation: The Politics of Paranoia in Postwar America* (New York: NYU Press, 2002), 7.

16. George Lipsitz, *Dangerous Crossroads: Popular Music, Postmodernism, and the Poetics of Place* (New York: Verso, 1994), 3.

17. I share this method of cultural analysis with other work that theorizes the ways in which popular culture, mass media, and new technologies shape the stories we tell ourselves about shared pasts, presents, and futures. See, for example, Michael Rogin, Paige Baty, George Lipsitz, Constance Penley, and Donna Haraway.

18. While I do draw some conclusions about alien abductees as a group, I do not attempt any sort of definitive, quantitative analysis of who alleged alien abductees are, demographically speaking.

19. It has taken hold especially in the United Kingdom and Australia, where communities of UFO investigators and therapeutic experts already exist; and in Mexico and Central America, where rapidly circulating stories of alien abduction seem to resonate and recombine with already existing local belief and folklore, and an industry of local experts is emerging to diagnose and interpret the phenomenon.

20. An oft quoted Roper Poll conducted in 1991 reported that as many as four million people believed they had been abducted; Whitley Strieber's best-selling *Communion* (1987) went out of print in the early 1990s after its eighteenth print run.

21. John Fuller, *The Interrupted Journey: Two Lost Hours Aboard a Flying Saucer* (London: Dial Press, 1966), 92.

22. Strieber, *Communion*, 107.

NOTES TO CHAPTER 1

1. From the program of the Eighth New York Whole Life Expo 1994 Conference, Roosevelt Hotel, New York, 18 November 1994, 29.

2. Budd Hopkins, personal interview, 15 May 1998.

3. As Fuller explains in the book, the Hills were discouraged by a series of unauthorized articles written about them that had appeared in the *Boston Traveller* written by journalist John Lutrell. The first was published on 25 October

1965. The story had been written "without their permission, without their being interviewed by the reporter involved" and the Hills were "extremely upset" at the sensational nature of the account. Fuller, *The Interrupted Journey*, 20. The Hills were familiar with Fuller because he had recently written a series of articles about UFO sightings in New Hampshire, which would be compiled into his first book, *Incidents at Exeter* (New York: Berkley Publishing Group, 1966). Based on what the Hills deemed to be the seriousness of that work, they chose Fuller to chronicle their own mysterious experiences. His version of the Hill story first appeared as a two-part article in *Look* magazine, "Aboard a Flying Saucer," *Look*, 4 and 18 October 1966).

4. Fuller, *The Interrupted Journey*, 47.
5. Fuller, *The Interrupted Journey*, 47.
6. Fuller, *The Interrupted Journey*, xvi.
7. Fuller, *The Interrupted Journey*, 48.
8. Fuller, *The Interrupted Journey*, 49.
9. The original novel and film posit mind control as a means of Communist takeover of the U.S. government. Jonathan Demme's 2004 remake of the film tellingly recasts global capitalism—namely the Manchurian Global Corporation—as agent of external control. I discuss *The Manchurian Candidate*—and the differing conspiracy theories it suggests—further in chapters 6 and 7.
10. Fuller, *The Interrupted Journey*, 47.
11. Fuller, *The Interrupted Journey*, 56.
12. At the same time Fuller omits mentioning that hypnosis was a therapeutic method that had been in dispute among psychologists since the turn of the century. In the late nineteenth century Sigmund Freud, with his colleague Joseph Breuer, as well as Pierre Janet in France, theorized that hysteria was a symptom of psychological trauma. These early psychologists believed that female hysteria was caused by repressed memories of actual trauma—most often sexual experiences. Hypnosis was used to stimulate recall, based on the belief that neuroses were the result of buried psychological trauma. In 1897 Freud abandoned his seduction theory in favor of his Oedipal theory, according to which hysterical women were not repressing memories of real events, but rather expressing fantasies based on their unconscious Oedipal desires. Hypnotism was abandoned in favor of the "talking cure." For a historical overview of this shift, see Herman.
13. Betty Hill, letter to Admiral Donald Keyhoe, 26 September 1961, Center for UFO Studies Archives, Chicago (hereafter cited as CUFOS). On 2 March 1994 Mark Rodeghier, director of the Center for UFO Studies, wrote to Betty Hill to ask why she thought the line had been left out by Fuller. In her response (8 March 1994) she does not answer his question. Both letters in CUFOS.
14. Fuller, *The Interrupted Journey*, viii.
15. Fuller, *The Interrupted Journey*, x.

16. Fuller, *The Interrupted Journey*, xi.

17. Fuller, *The Interrupted Journey*, 104. Simon nonetheless proceeded with hypnosis of the Hills and did have faith that it was "the key to the unlocked room" of amnesia. The remaining 250 or so pages of Fuller's book consist almost entirely of transcripts from the Hills' hypnotic sessions, interspersed with their reflection back on the session, and Fuller's meditations on the nature of memory and forgetting and on the process of hypnosis itself.

18. Simon continued to converse with members of the Mutual UFO Network (MUFON), asserting that "the use of hypnosis directly for the purpose of eliciting 'truth' establishes a contextual atmosphere not conducive to the elicitation of the 'real' facts." Benjamin Simon, letter to MUFON, 29 February 1972, CUFOS. Those on the professedly scientific end of the UFO investigative community rejected abduction because they could not accept the nature of evidence produced under hypnosis. And in 1977 Alvin Lawson, a MUFON investigator, published the findings of a study that showed that the abduction experience could be "induced" hypnotically. Alvin Lawson, "What Can We Learn from Hypnosis of Imaginary Abductees?" in *MUFON Symposium Proceedings*, June 1977, 107. UFO experts thus began a debate about hypnosis as a tool for the retrieval of memories of extraterrestrial contact, that continues today.

19. Religious studies scholars such as Robert Wuthnow support the conventional wisdom that America saw a decline in traditional religious practice during and after the 1960s. Wuthnow attributes the profound change in spiritual practice in the latter half of the twentieth century to a "spirituality of seeking," and a "renewed interest in the inner self as a way of relating to the sacred. See Robert Wuthnow, *After Heaven: Spirituality in America since the 1950s* (Berkeley: University of California Press, 1998), 3, 142.

20. Fuller, *The Interrupted Journey*, 257.

21. Fuller, *The Interrupted Journey*, 264.

22. Fuller, *The Interrupted Journey*, 197.

23. Fuller, *The Interrupted Journey*, 60.

24. Fuller, *The Interrupted Journey*, 76.

25. Fuller, *The Interrupted Journey*, 68.

26. Fuller, *The Interrupted Journey*, 99.

27. Fuller, *The Interrupted Journey*, 114.

28. Fuller, *The Interrupted Journey*, 178.

29. Fuller, *The Interrupted Journey*, 182.

30. Fuller, *The Interrupted Journey*, 238.

31. Fuller, *The Interrupted Journey*, 165, 108.

32. Raymond Fowler, the UFO investigator and author of the *Andreasson Affair*, opens his book, like most subsequent abduction narratives, with a reference back to "the classic UFO abduction case involving Betty and Barney Hill. Raymond Fowler, *The Andreasson Affair: The Documented Investigation of a*

Woman's Abduction Aboard a UFO. (Englewood Cliffs, NJ: Prentice Hall, 1979), 19.

33. Fowler, *The Andreasson Affair*, 20.
34. Fowler, *The Andreasson Affair*, 42.
35. Herman, 11.
36. MUFON was founded in 1969 after the Condon Report recommended that the U.S. government cease funding research into the UFO phenomenon. An offshoot of the National Investigations Committee on Aerial Phenomena (NICAP) and founded in 1956, it was created as a means through which lay people could investigate and explore the possible existence of UFOs.
37. Fowler, *The Andreasson Affair*, 20.
38. Fowler, *The Andreasson Affair*, 42.
39. Fowler, *The Andreasson Affair*, 51.
40. Fowler, *The Andreasson Affair*, 56.
41. Fowler, *The Andreasson Affair*, 95.
42. Fowler, *The Andreasson Affair*, 203.

NOTES TO CHAPTER 2

1. Budd Hopkins, *Missing Time* (New York: Ballantine, 1981), 177.
2. Hopkins, *Missing Time*, 175.
3. Hopkins, *Missing Time*, 178.
4. Hopkins, *Missing Time*, 177.
5. See Debbie Nathan and Michael Snedeker, *Satan's Silence: Ritual Abuse and the Making of a Modern American Witch Hunt* (New York: Basic Books, 1995).
6. See Herman.
7. In the Franklin case, a murder had definitely occurred, and this recovered memory was not the only evidence leading to the conviction. Nonetheless, the decision to include a memory that came to Franklin in the middle of the day, after years of forgetting, was, and continues to be, the source of controversy.
8. Lenore Terr, *Unchained Memories: True Stories of Traumatic Memories Lost and Found* (New York: Basic Books, 1994).
9. Elizabeth Loftus, *Myth of Repressed Memory* (New York: St. Martin's Press, 1994).
10. Hopkins, *Missing Time*, 223.
11. Hopkins, *Missing Time*, 10.
12. Hopkins, *Missing Time*, 12.
13. Hopkins, *Missing Time*, 12.
14. In many respects, Hopkins clearly adheres to many of the formal features of these first two book-length treatments of the phenomenon. His book is structured around transcripts of hypnotic regressions, but in this case of seven

different subjects. The book is written by Hopkins the "investigator" who is witness, initially, to the hypnotic process. Hopkins includes a defense of hypnotic methods, including the obligatory nod to the "classic" Hill case. And Hopkins the investigator works with several mental health professionals who are open to the reality of alien abduction.

15. Hopkins, *Missing Time*, 10.
16. Hopkins, *Missing Time*, 8.
17. Budd Hopkins, *Intruders: The Incredible Visitations at Copley Woods* (New York: Ballantine, 1987), 71.
18. Hopkins, *Missing Time*, 7, 16.
19. Hopkins, *Missing Time*, 11.
20. Hopkins, *Missing Time*, 228.
21. Hopkins, *Missing Time*, 223.
22. David Jacobs, *Secret Life: Firsthand Documented Accounts of UFO Abductions* (New York: Simon and Schuster, 1992), 23.
23. Jacobs, 246.
24. John Mack, *Abduction: Human Encounters with Aliens* (New York: Charles Scribner's Sons, 1994), 22.
25. Mack, 24.
26. Mack, 52.
27. Mack, 20.
28. Jacobs, 255.
29. Http://www.abduct.com/survey.php, 10 August 2004.
30. Hopkins, *Missing Time*, 118.
31. Hopkins, *Missing Time*, 231.
32. Hopkins, *Intruders*, 71.
33. Strieber, *Communion*, 4.
34. Jacobs, 256.
35. Psychologist Janice Haaken makes a similar argument in an article on multiple personality disorder. She writes, "sexual abuse stories have become the officially recognized accounts that both sides can agree are emblematic of trauma itself, eclipsing all other childhood traumas or conflicts in scope and magnitude. . . . Given this context of officially sanctioned stories, victims of various forms of abuse may unconsciously create a sexual abuse narrative in seeking legitimacy for their suffering." Janice Haaken, "Sexual Abuse, Recovered Memory, and Therapeutic Practice: A Feminist Perspective," *Social Text* 40 (fall 1994): 122.
36. Ellen Bass and Laura Davis, *The Courage to Heal* (New York: Harper and Row, 1988), quoted in Showalter, 150.
37. Feminists have debated and continue to debate the politics of categorical belief in the accounts of victims. Psychologist Judith Herman remains a staunch defender of the necessity of believing women and children, insisting that anyone

who would deny the truth of such claims is in denial about the reality of women's lives. Nathan on the other hand is more interested in how "those fantasies exercised an irresistible hold on American society during the 1980s and 1990s," and how "In the absence of conventional evidence, the proof became words obtained via suggestion and coercion." Nathan and Snedeker, 5.

38. Jacobs, 29.
39. Jacobs, 198.
40. Mack, 163.
41. Mack, 155.
42. Hopkins, *Intruders*, 118.
43. Jacobs, 106.
44. Mack, 99.

NOTES TO CHAPTER 3

1. Jean, personal interview, 8 April 1998.
2. Such critiques proliferated during the 1990s. See Charles Sykes, *A Nation of Victims: The Decaying of the American Character* (New York: St. Martin's Press, 1992); Robert Hughes, *The Culture of Complaint: The Fraying of America* (New York: Oxford University Press, 1993), and Wendy Kaminer, *I'm Dysfunctional, You're Dysfunctional* (New York: Perseus Books, 1992). More in line with Elaine Showalter and her theory of *Hystories*, I am interested in how such identification of victimization through alien abduction is a "cultural symptom of anxiety and stress." Showalter, 9. But I want to go one step further than Showalter and try to understand what people gain (attention, chosenness), and what they might lose when the impulse to locate their suffering on the alien draws them away from their social reality.
3. Mack, 132.
4. Mack, 200.
5. Hopkins, *Intruders*, 196.
6. Hopkins, *Intruders*, 191.
7. Strieber, *Communion*, 30.
8. Mack, 68.
9. Mack, 60.
10. Strieber, *Communion*, 83.
11. Strieber, *Communion*, 83.
12. Mack, 59.
13. Jacobs, 205.
14. Mack, 124.
15. Mack, 64.
16. Mack, 64.
17. Denial of pleasure and arousal echo homophobic discourse about "gay

panic" whereby heterosexual men report having been approached, seduced, even attacked by aggressive and threatening transgender or homosexual men. Such narratives are often deployed in the defense of gay-bashing and other forms of violence against LGBTs (lesbians, gays, bisexuals, and transsexuals). This defense was rehearsed not long ago in the explanation for the brutal murder of gay college student Matthew Shepherd by two such "threatened" heterosexual males.

18. Fuller, *The Interrupted Journey*, 66.
19. Fuller, *The Interrupted Journey*, 256.
20. Fuller, *The Interrupted Journey*, 121.
21. Fuller, *The Interrupted Journey*, 181.
22. Strieber goes through requisite steps of admitting that hypnosis may not be "a completely trustworthy tool." But within three pages he has found Dr. Klein, who he is convinced is competent. Strieber, *Communion*, 59, 56.
23. Strieber, *Communion*, 62.
24. Strieber, *Communion*, 154.
25. Strieber, *Communion*, 64.
26. Strieber, *Communion*, 71.
27. Strieber, *Communion*, 66.
28. Strieber, *Communion*, 71.
29. Henry, personal interview, 23 May 1999.
30. As quoted in Herman, 33.
31. Dr. Simon actually concluded after a number of hypnotic sessions with the Hills that their rendering of those two hours was a sort of shared fantasy, or folie à deux. More specifically, he suggested that Betty had, through repeated recounting of an elaborate recurring dream, convinced Barney that he had experienced the same thing. He theorized that this episode may have been triggered by the more general stresses of being an interracial couple.
32. Fowler, *The Andreasson Affair*, 160.
33. Fowler, *The Andreasson Affair*, 198.
34. Fowler, *The Andreasson Affair*, 160, 198.
35. Hopkins, *Intruders*, 51.
36. Hopkins, *Intruders*, 77.
37. Hopkins, *Intruders*, 26.
38. This passage from *Intruders* resembles the even more over-the-top litany of illnesses reported by the wife of a now-deceased conspiracy theorist that I will discuss in chapter 7. Phil Schneider's ailments and death are most likely attributable to his life of work in the atomic southwest, and while he did place blame on the government for his ill health, he could only imagine the government as culpable insofar as it was conspiring with the aliens.
39. Mack, 113.
40. Mack, 145.

41. Mack, 18.
42. Mack, 18.
43. Mack does cite several studies that have explored this connection, including George Ganaway, "Historical versus Narrative Truth: Confronting the Role of Exogenous Trauma in the Etiology of MPD and Its Variants," *Dissociation II* 4 (1989): 205–220; and R. L. Laibow, "Dual Victims: The Abused and the Abducted," *International UFO Reporter* 14, no. 3 (1989): 4–9.
44. Mack, 18.
45. Mike, personal interview, 6 August 1998.
46. Hopkins, *Missing Time*, 50.
47. Betty Hill, Letter to CUFOS, 10 July 1994, CUFOS.
48. The False Memory Syndrome Foundation has in turn been astutely criticized for seeking to discredit all accusations of sex abuse made by women against their relatives.
49. *Frequently Asked Questions* (Philadelphia: False Memory Syndrome Foundation, 1994), 3.
50. Sean Casteel, "Interview with Katharina Wilson," *Mutual UFO Network UFO Journal*, no. 329, 2.
51. Michelle LaVigne, "On-Line Interview with Katharina Wilson," http://www.alienjigsaw.com (6 February 1999).
52. Ann Druffel, *How to Defend Yourself against Alien Abduction* (Three Rivers Press, 1998), x.
53. Showalter, 10.
54. Showalter, 4.
55. Haaken, 34.

NOTES TO CHAPTER 4

1. "Kidnapped by UFOs?" *Nova* Online, http://www.pbs.org/wgbh/nova/aliens/johnvelez, June 1998.
2. Throughout this project I am critical of abduction "experts" who rely often on hypnotherapy in order to elicit detailed accounts of the abuses—often sexual—suffered at the hands of aliens. My criticism is that they essentially exploit their "patients," taking what can seem like a prurient interest in those more shocking facets of the abduction scenario that are apt to sell books. Throughout this project I also argue that abductees take an active part in this process, seeking out and participating, it seems, in this exploitative exchange. Abductees write, gather, circulate, and recirculate stories of their own rape and submission. And so while both experts and abductees participate in this cultural practice, I nonetheless feel uncomfortable asking abductees to repeat their same detailed stories for me. And interestingly, while many acknowledged that they had been subject to the sorts of procedures discussed here, none offered details

about the process of their own sexual/reproductive violation. Their silence was, I suspect, a function of their audience awareness, which I discuss more in chapter 10: most of my informants seemed to edit out those details of their experiences that might have seemed to the academic skeptic excessively "far out," details that many share freely in the writing and speaking they do for and with abductees. Velez's willingness to share these details with *Nova* is unusual, and due to the ways in which he felt it backfired, may also account for his unwillingness to offer me the same sorts of details during our interview.

3. Fuller, *The Interrupted Journey,* 164.
4. Fuller, *The Interrupted Journey,* 299.
5. Fuller, *The Interrupted Journey,* 123.
6. Fuller, *The Interrupted Journey,* 117.
7. Fuller, *The Interrupted Journey,* 123.
8. Rutherford Platt, "The Wondrous Inner Space of Living Cells," *Reader's Digest,* June 1964, 195.
9. Platt, 195.
10. Platt, 196. For more on how popular culture and science interact to imbue DNA with meaning and agency, see Dorothy Nelkin, *The DNA Mystique: The Gene as Cultural Icon* (New York: W. H. Freeman, 1995).
11. "Control of Life," *Life,* 10 September 1965, 76.
12. For discussion and debate between feminist historians on the relative empowerment of women in the face of medical expertise, see Barbara Ehrenreich and Deirdre English, *For Her Own Good: 150 Years of the Experts' Advice to Women* (Garden City: Anchor Press, 1978); Carroll Smith Rosenberg, *Disorderly Conduct: Visions of Gender in Victorian America* (New York: Knopf, 1985), especially her chapter on the American Medical Association; Elaine Tyler May, *Homeward Bound: American Families in the Cold War Era* (New York: Basic Books, 1988); Regina Morantz-Sanchez, *Sympathy and Science: Women Physicians in American Medicine* (New York: Oxford University Press, 1985).
13. "The Secret World of the Unborn," *McCalls,* May 1963, 75.
14. "Control of Life," 64.
15. "Control of Life," 62.
16. "Control of Life," 62.
17. In *Disorderly Conduct,* Smith Rosenberg considers the historical emergence of this particular redistribution of power in the nineteenth century. Smith Rosenberg notes that, the American Medical Association then succeeded in creating, "a new Oedipal triangle, linking the male physician with the female fetus against the mother." 242.
18. Rosalind Petchesky, *Abortion and Woman's Choice: The State, Sexuality, and Reproductive Freedom* (New York: Longman, 1984), 273.
19. Nelkin, 34. Nelkin argues that hereditary material has since the beginning of the century been held to be "the determiner of character and personal-

ity, the source of social order. 20. Popular interest in eugenics had its heyday from 1900–1935, and "promoters were drawn to its potential for transforming the human condition and for eliminating the everyday human suffering caused by physical or mental disability." 32.

20. Fuller, *The Interrupted Journey*, 159.
21. Fuller, *The Interrupted Journey*, 299.
22. In chapter 3 I make a related argument about the ways in which male abduction experts have appropriated feminist rhetoric about victimization in order to shore up their own authority. Here I am more interested in understanding what is at stake for alleged male abductees in identifying as such.
23. Fuller, *The Interrupted Journey*, 93; Strieber, *Communion*, 15.
24. Fuller, *The Interrupted Journey*, 187.
25. See Carol Clover, *Men, Women, and Chainsaws: Gender in the Modern Horror Film* (Princeton, NJ: Princeton University Press, 1992), and Kaja Silverman, *Male Subjectivity at the Margins* (New York: Routledge, 1992) for examples of how feminist film theorists have begun to challenge the argument that the filmic gaze is always a male gaze with which spectators identify, thus collaborating in the objectification of the female body. The locus classicus of this argument is Laura Mulvey's "Visual Pleasure and Narrative Cinema," *Screen* 16 (1975): 6–18.
26. Medical institutions have long been sites of power, and the gaze of the doctor—his ability to look in and through mere mortal flesh—has long been the coordinator of this power. See Michel Foucault, *Birth of the Clinic: An Archaeology of Medical Perception* (New York: Vintage, 1973). Foucault observes of eighteenth-century medical discourse that, "in medical space . . . one began to conceive of a generalized presence of doctors whose intersecting gazes form a network and exercise at every point in space and at every moment in time, a constant, mobile, differentiated supervision." 31.
27. Fuller, *The Interrupted Journey*, 89.
28. See, for example, Ellen Herman, *The Romance of American Psychology: Political Culture in the Age of Experts, 1940–1970* (Berkeley: University of California Press, 1995); Stuart Leslie, *The Cold War and American Science: The Military-Industrial-Academic Complex at MIT and Stanford* (New York: Columbia University Press, 1993); *The Cold War and Expert Knowledge: New Essays on the National Security State, Radical History Review* 63 (fall 1995).
29. For defenses of technocratic neutrality and objectivity from the first half of the century, see Frederick Winslow Taylor, *The Principles of Scientific Management* (New York: Norton, 1911); Thorstein Veblen, *The Engineers and the Price System* (New York: B. W. Huebsch, 1921). For a postwar, postindustrial version of the same, see Daniel Bell's *The Coming of Post-industrial Society: A Venture in Social Forecasting* (New York: Basic Books, 1976). For critiques of technocracy see C. Wright Mills, *The Power Elite* (New York: Oxford Univer-

sity Press, 1956); Theodore Roszak, *The Making of a Counter Culture: Reflections on the Technocratic Society and Its Youthful Opposition* (Berkeley: University of California Press, 1968). For discussions of growing popular criticism of scientific and medical authority in general, see Charles Rosenberg, *No Other Gods: On Science and American Social Thought* (Baltimore: Johns Hopkins University Press, 1997), and Malcolm Goggin, *Governing Science and Technology in a Democratic Society* (Knoxville: University of Tennessee Press, 1986).

NOTES TO CHAPTER 5

1. While a handful of alien abductions were reported during the late 1960s and early 1970s, UFO investigators deployed from organizations such as the Mutual UFO Network dismissed many of them as hoaxes. In their quest for legitimacy and acceptance by the scientific community, many such organizations sought in particular to distance themselves from those abductees who sold their stories to tabloids such as the *National Enquirer*. The next book-length treatment of alien abduction, Fowler's *Andreasson Affair* (1979) reintroduced the theme of explicitly reproductive experimentation hinted at in *The Interrupted Journey*. The *Andreasson Affair* combines religious/spiritual imagery with a clinical scenario similar to that reported by Betty Hill. Under hypnosis Betty Andreasson remembered that, "there's a big block-thing they had me on, and . . . lights coming from the walls, and . . . wires, needle wires." Andreasson also recalled, unlike Hill, that the aliens removed an implant from her nose. The implant is now a standard feature of most abduction scenarios, an extrapolation of the notion that abductees are human test subjects who, like wild animals, are tagged and tracked by extraterrestrial scientists. They also, however, tell her that they have to "measure [her] for procreation." Under hypnosis she remarks of this procedure, "Oh! He's pushing that again . . . around, feeling things. . . . I don't like this! . . . Feels like he's going right around my stuff inside—feeling it, or something with that needle." Andreasson elaborates Hill's notion that abduction is at least in part an occasion for forced and uninvited gynecological examination. Fowler, *The Andreasson Affair*, 77–79.

2. Hopkins, *Intruders*, 115.

3. Hopkins, *Intruders*, 187.

4. Hopkins, *Intruders*, 18.

5. For more on Steptoe and Edwards, see Gina Maranto, *The Quest for Perfection: The Drive to Breed Better Humans* (New York: Charles Scribner's Sons, 1996).

6. Lesley Brown and John Brown, *Our Miracle Called Louise* (New York: Paddington Press, 1979), 106.

7. Raymond Fowler, *The Watchers: The Secret Design behind UFO Abduction* (New York: Bantam Books, 1990), 120.

8. Jacobs, 308.
9. Jacobs, 107.
10. Jacobs, 107.
11. Mack, 82.
12. Mack, 99.
13. Mack, 414.
14. Mack, 132.
15. Hopkins, *Intruders*, 118.
16. Nelkin, 40, 56.
17. Andrew Ross. "Dr. Frankenstein, I Presume?" *Salon*, February 1997, http://www.salon.com/feb97/news/news2970224.html.
18. The Raelian Movement, a Montreal-based group founded in 1973, believe that humans are cloned from alien DNA. In 2002 the Raelians received a flurry of media attention when they claimed that scientists working for their organization, Clonaid, had successfully cloned a human infant. Evidence was not forthcoming and public interest in then faded quickly.
19. Hopkins, *Intruders*, 118.
20. Hopkins, *Intruders*, 79.
21. Hopkins, *Intruders*, 168.
22. Jacobs, 114.
23. Jacobs, 118–120.
24. For discussion of the ways in which new reproductive technologies, especially fetal imaging technologies, have influenced ideas about fetal and maternal agency see Ann Oakley, *The Captured Womb: A History of the Medical Care of Pregnant Women* (New York: B. Blackwell, 1984); Sarah Franklin, *Embodied Progress: A Cultural Account of Assisted Conception* (New York: Routledge, 1997); Marilyn Strathern, *Reproducing the Future: Essays on Anthropology, Kinship, and the New Reproductive Technologies* (New York: Routledge, 1992); Rosalind Petchesky, *Abortion and Woman's Choice: The State, Sexuality, and Reproductive Freedom* (New York: Longman, 1984); Faye Ginsburg and Rayna Rapp, eds., *Conceiving the New World Order: The Global Politics of Reproduction* (Berkeley: University of California Press, 1995).
25. See Janelle Taylor, "The Public Fetus and the Family Car: From Abortion Politics to a Volvo Ad," *Public Culture* 4, no. 2 (1992): 47–59. As cited in Taylor, during the 1980s the number of women getting ultrasounds for pregnancy increased drastically—from 35.5% to 78.8% between 1980 and 1987 alone. 23.
26. Since the 1980s, the fetus has been redefined as person not only in scientific discourse but also in legal discourse and anti-abortion legislation, oftentimes itself informed by scientific authority. In "Containing Women: Reproductive Discourse in the 1980s," Valerie Hartouni details how abortion became a centerpiece during the 1980s for a wider-ranging campaign to "revitalize the

country politically and rehabilitate it morally." See Hartouni's essay in *Technoculture*, ed. Constance Penley and Andrew Ross (Minneapolis: University of Minnesota Press, 1991), 33. The official legislative campaign to chip away at abortion rights began in 1981 when Senator Orrin Hatch spearheaded Senate Judiciary Subcommittee hearings, the goal of which was to locate life at the moment of conception and thus legally define the fetus as person. In 1989, as a result of this campaign, the Supreme Court's decision in *Webster v. Reproductive Health Services* declared the fetus a person with rights.

27. Fuller, *The Interrupted Journey*, 260.
28. Mack, 132.
29. Jacobs, 153, 167.
30. Jacobs, 162.
31. Hopkins, *Intruders*, 240.
32. Cassie, personal interview, 18 February 2000.
33. Hopkins, *Intruders*, 226.
34. "Kidnapped by UFOs?"
35. Jane, personal interview, 7 July 1999.
36. From a flyer about her experiences that Jane typed up and distributes at conferences.
37. [Maureen], "Sands of Time: The Montauk Project," http://hometown.aol.com/nymush/sands, 1 September 1999.
38. I discuss this further in chapter 7.
39. Maureen, personal interview, 13 August 1999.
40. Popular television shows like *Buffy the Vampire Slayer* and *Roswell* play with the literalization of teenage alienation through the alien teen.
41. Mack, 60.
42. Fuller, *The Interrupted Journey*, 207.
43. I discuss the extent to which abductees claim to feel "chosen" at length in chapter 9.

NOTES TO CHAPTER 6

1. Despite their geographic and allegedly experiential proximity, John and Anthony do not know each other.
2. Anthony, personal interview, 15 July 1999.
3. Valdemar Valerian, ed., *Matrix II: The Abduction and Manipulation of Humans Using Advanced Technologies* (Yelm, WA: Leading Edge Research, 1991).
4. Richard Hofstadter, *The Paranoid Style in American Politics and Other Essays* (New York: Knopf, 1965), 29.
5. Timothy Melley, *Empire of Conspiracy: The Culture of Paranoia in Postwar America* (Ithaca: Cornell University Press, 2000), 7.

6. Knight, *Conspiracy Nation*, 5.

7. Frederic Jameson, "Cognitive Mapping," in *Marxism and the Interpretation of Culture*, ed. Cary Nelson and Lawrence Grossberg (Basingstoke, England: Macmillan, 1988), 356.

8. Frederic Jameson, *The Global Aesthetic: Cinema and Space in the World System* (Bloomington: Indiana University Press, 1992), 3.

9. Jonathan Alter, "The Weird World of Secrets and Lies," *Newsweek*, 22 June 1998, 76.

10. This tendency to either dismissiveness or alarmism can be seen in a number of more recent academic treatments of conspiracy theory, including Daniel Pipes, *Conspiracy: How The Paranoid Style Flourishes and Where It Comes From* (New York: Free Press, 1997); and Showalter.

11. See, for example, Dean; Mark Fenster, *Conspiracy Theories: Secrecy and Power in American Culture* (Minneapolis: University of Minnesota Press, 1999); Peter Knight, *Conspiracy Culture From Kennedy to the X Files*, (London: Routledge, 2000); Knight, *Conspiracy Nation*; Melley; Patricia Turner, *I Heard It through the Grapevine: Rumor in African American Culture* (Berkeley: University of California Press, 1993).

12. Melley, 8.

13. Knight, *Conspiracy Nation*, 6.

14. In the *X Files*, the elite in control are a small group of shady, suit-wearing bureaucrats known as "the Syndicate."

15. In part I refer here to the multiple congressional inquiries into intelligence violations, many of which I detail in the body of this chapter. These revelations were followed by a spate of work by journalists and scholars in the late 1970s and early 1980s that considers the extent to which intelligence is tenable in a democratic society, a project begun by intelligence scholar Harry Howe Ransom in the 1950s. See, for example, David Wise, *The American Police State: The Government against the People* (New York: Random House, 1976); Morton Halperin, *The Lawless State: The Crimes of the U.S. Intelligence Agencies* (New York: Penguin, 1976); William Corson, *The Armies of Ignorance: The Rise of the American Intelligence Empire* (New York: Dial Press, 1977); and, for discussion of FBI abuses specifically, Richard Morgan, *Domestic Intelligence: Monitoring Dissent in America* (Austin: University of Texas Press, 1980). For more recent treatments of post-Watergate congressional inquiries into intelligence abuses, see Loch K. Johnson, *America's Secret Power: The CIA in a Democratic Society* (New York: Oxford University Press, 1989); Gregory Treverton, *Covert Action: The Limits of Intervention in the Postwar World* (New York: Basic Books, 1987). For work that focuses on the CIA's LSD experiments in particular, see Martin A. Lee and Bruce Shlain, *Acid Dreams: The CIA, LSD, and the 60s Rebellion* (New York: Grove Press, 1985). For recent treatments of the U.S. government's program in recruiting Nazi scientists after WWII, and on

the involvement of those scientists in mind control and other experiments on U.S. citizens, see Tom Bauer, *The Paperclip Conspiracy: The Hunt for the Nazi Scientists* (Boston: Little, Brown, 1987); Linda Hunt. *Secret Agenda: The U.S. Government, Nazi Scientists, and Project Paperclip, 1945–1990* (New York: St. Martin's Press, 1991). For consideration of the wide-ranging social and cultural effects of radioactivity testing, and more general anxiety about radioactivity and the atom bomb, see Robert Williams and Philip Cantelon, *The American Atom: A Documentary History of Nuclear Policies* (University of Pennsylvania Press, 1984); Carol Gallagher, *American Ground Zero: The Secret Nuclear War* (Cambridge, MA: MIT Press, 1997); Thomas Englehardt, *The End of Victory Culture: Cold War America and the Disillusioning of a Generation* (Amherst: University of Massachusetts Press, 1998); Margot Henriksen, *Dr. Strangelove's America: Society and Culture in the Atomic Age* (Berkeley: University of California Press, 1997).

16. David Wise and Thomas Ross, *The Invisible Government* (New York: Random House, 1964), 18.

17. Wise and Ross, 18.

18. "Secrecy, Human Radiation Experiments, and Intentional Releases," chapter 13 in *Final Report: Department of Energy Openness: Human Radiation Experiments,* by Advisory Committee on Human Radiation Experiments, http://www.eh.doe.gov/ohre/roadmap/achre/report.html, published 21 October 1994, accessed 10 June 1999.

19. This possibility had been taken up in Richard Condon's 1959 novel *The Manchurian Candidate,* from which Marks borrowed the term. Both Condon's novel and the 1962 John Frankenheimer movie of the same name are set in the wake of the Korean War.

20. Among the more bizarre and sensational details about MKUltra was the revelation that LSD had been administered to unwitting subjects in social settings, and that the CIA employed prostitutes in a safehouse experiment to spike the drinks of customers, whereupon CIA operatives observed and recorded them. A 1994 *U.S. News* article, "The Cold War Experiments," prompted by inquiry into human radiation experiments, reviewed the sordid details of the MKUltra program, reporting that some of the unwitting drug testing was carried on in safehouses in San Francisco and New York City. Testing took place on criminal sexual psychopaths confined to a state hospital. These CIA-funded experiments extended outside of U.S. borders. One such notable example is the study undertaken by Dr. Ewen Cameron, through a grant provided by the Society for Human Ecology, a front set up by the CIA to support behavior-control research. At Allen Memorial Institute at McGill University, Cameron worked with psychotic patients to "depattern" their behavior through electroshock and repeated doses of LSD, sensory deprivation, and forced listening to a tape-recorded message. His work was aimed at "inactivating the patient." For one

subject this included thirty electroshock sessions followed by fifty-six days of drug-induced sleep which left her incontinent. Other subjects "suffered permanent brain damage, lost their jobs, or otherwise deteriorated." "The Cold War Experiments," *U.S. News,* 24 January 1994, 32. See also Lee and Shlain.

21. Senate Select Committee Report on MKUltra, 1977, http://www.parascope.com/ds/documentslibrary, Appendix A, 93.

22. The 1980s and 1990s saw a rise in antigovernment sentiment on the right, embodied in its most extreme form in growing white pride and Christian identity groups such as Aryan Nation. Standoffs between U.S. agents and citizens in Ruby Ridge and Waco created instant evidence for those increasingly visible numbers of Americans who suspected the government of working against rather than for the American people. Such groups seemed to take their cue, somewhat paradoxically, from a brand of conservatism newly invigorated by Ronald Reagan and George H. W. Bush, who called for a paring down and decentralization of federal government, including deregulation and a return to states' rights. So too did Reaganist rhetoric stress personal rights and responsibilities, volunteerism as a vehicle of social change rather than systematic, institutional change. Finally, Reaganist conservatives pointed the finger at the new social movements of the 1960s and 1970s, harbingers, they claimed, of social decay.

23. The government did officially investigate UFOs from 1947–1969. During the 1940s and 1950s Presidents Truman and Eisenhower sponsored a number of projects to investigate the UFO phenomenon through the Air Force and the then newly formed CIA. Project Sign was initiated in 1947. In 1949 the Air Force downgraded Project Sign to Project Grudge, which was later stepped up again in response to a nationwide wave of sightings in 1952 and 1953. In response to the same UFO "flap," the CIA formed the Robertson Panel in 1953. It concluded that UFOs were not fact but fantasy, that it was the responsibility of government projects to demystify misidentifications of natural occurrences and to unveil hoaxes, and that UFO investigations should be stripped of special status. Despite this conclusion, Project Blue Book, the third and last government-sponsored investigation of the UFO phenomenon, continued until 1969, when the Condon Committee concluded that UFOs were not of extraterrestrial origin, and not worthy of further investigation.

24. Peter Gersten, "CAUS Position on Congressional Hearings, Immunity, and Amnesty," http://www.caus.org, 26 July 1999.

25. "Stop the Cosmic Watergate!" Transcript, CNN news, 6 July 1993, 1.

26. Charles Berlitz and William Moore, *The Roswell Incident* (New York: Berkeley Books, 1980), 4.

27. Berlitz and Moore, 147.

28. William Broad, "Wreckage in the Desert Was Odd but Not Alien," *New York Times,* 8 September 1994, A1.

29. I consider the cultural practice of alien abduction extensively in chapter 10.

30. Strieber, *Communion*, 233.

31. Whitley Strieber, *Transformation: The Breakthrough* (New York: HarperCollins, 1988). *Transformation* includes a story very much like the story of Shandera and Moore's, "discoverers" of the Roswell–Majestic 12 documents and many others found throughout the vast literature of UFO investigation. According to Strieber, a documentary filmmaker who comes to visit his summer home reports that in 1986, the filmmaker had a very unusual encounter with a man who identified himself as a member of the air force. Their meeting was held at an air force base in connection with a documentary the filmmaker was preparing. The filmmaker was allowed to read a briefing paper concerning crashed disks and retrieval of the bodies of nonhuman beings. The typed pages he read were titled "Briefing Paper for the President of the U.S." There was no specific president mentioned, and the filmmaker didn't remember a specific date. He was not allowed to take notes on the spot, but he recorded his recollections later in detail. The controversial document surfaced in 1987, and the filmmaker's memory "proved" to be accurate. The agent told the filmmaker that he was being shown the document and given the information because the government intended to release to him several thousand feet of film taken between 1947 and 1964 showing crashed disk and ET bodies as historic footage to be placed in his documentary. He never received the footage. 117.

32. Strieber, *Transformation*, 271.

33. Advisory Committee on Human Radiation Experiments, *Final Report of the Advisory Committee on Human Radiation Experiments* (New York: Oxford University Press, 1996).

34. Advisory Committee, *Final Report*, xvii.

35. Advisory Committee, *Final Report*, xvii.

36. "Clinton Offers Apology; Says Tuskegee Syphilis Study Was Shameful," *Boston Globe*, 17 May 1997, A1:1

37. Gallagher, xix.

38. "Redressing a Past of Shameful Experiences," *San Francisco Chronicle*, 22 December 1996, Editorial, A15.

39. "Soldier Given LSD in '58 Settles Suit for $400,000," *Los Angeles Times*, 6 March 1996, 9.

40. "CIA, Army Must Pay for Giving Soldiers LSD," *Times Picayune*, 6 March 1996, A2.

41. The need for public coming clean was not restricted to America. In 1997 British Prime Minister Tony Blair apologized to the Irish for the Potato famine. In 1998 the Vatican issued an apology for its passivity in the face of the Holocaust, as did the French Government for Vichy participation in enabling of the Holocaust.

42. "Soldier Given LSD."

43. Though President Clinton has apologized, for, as summarized in one news magazine, "involvement in the slave trade, coddling of African dictators, neglect of the continent, complicity in apartheid, and failure to stop the slaughter in Rwanda, he has, to the chagrin of many African Americans, stopped short of apologizing to them for their past enslavement." Ronald Steel, "Sorry about That," *New Republic,* 20 April 1998, 22.

44. For further information on Gulf War illness studies, see http://www.cdc.gov/nceh/veterans.

NOTES TO CHAPTER 7

1. Anthony, personal interview, 15 July 1999.

2. Maureen, personal interview, 13 August 1999. All of Maureen's statements I report here were made in this interview.

3. Valerian, 131.

4. Strieber, *Transformation,* 234.

5. *Matrix III* is on "The Psychosocial, Chemical, Biological, and Electromagnetic Manipulation of Human Consciousness," 2 vols. (Yelm, WA: Leading Edge Research, 1992); *Matrix IV* takes as its focus "Paradigms and Dimensions of Human Evolution and Consciousness" (Yelm, WA: Leading Edge Research, 1994). There doesn't seem to have been a *Matrix I.* A Leading Edge Information Package (flyer) states the group's philosophy as follows: "all life forms and states of consciousness should have the right and opportunity to have an existence which is endowed with the freedom to produce the maximum number of probable lines of reality in an evolving direction, through uncoerced choice, and without repression of awareness or manipulation of physical, mental, or spiritual aspects."

6. Valerian, 2.

7. Valerian, 3.

8. Valerian, 137.

9. Collusion and interconnectedness are defining characteristics of all conspiracy theories, most of which posit the existence of networks of controlling elites. Theories, for example, about the Masons, or the Illuminati, often focus on financial power and access to and control of capital. UFO conspiracy theory is somewhat unique for its focus on military/scientific elites.

10. This same supplantation of historical processes by individual agency is seen in a season four episode of *The X Files* in which Cigarette Smoking Man—a key member of the Syndicate—is revealed to have been involved in, or responsible for, many of the key moments in Cold War American history, from the assassination of John F. Kennedy to the outcome of the Anita Hill Senate hearings.

11. Valerian, 195.

12. Valerian, 174.

13. Valerian, 200.

14. Valerian, 200.

15. It precedes by two years, and therefore does not make use of, *The X Files*.

16. In 1944 Richard Shaver, a welder from Pennsylvania, sent his "true" story about visiting the center of the hollow earth to *Amazing Stories* editor Ray Palmer. Palmer dismissed Shaver as a paranoid schizophrenic and rewrote his story as "I Remember Lemuria!" Circulation of the magazine soared, and *Amazing Stories* received letters from people claiming to have had the same experience. The broader idea that humans may actually be enslaved or controlled by external, perhaps alien, forces was also prominent in the copious writings of Charles Fort, an avid chronicler of unexplained phenomena during the early decades of the century, whose findings also inspired many pulp sci fi and fantasy stories. Fort put a rather dark spin on traditionally religious notions of the involvement of higher beings in the lives of humans, when he wrote, "I think we're property." Charles Fort, *The Book of the Damned* (New York: Horace Liveright, 1919), 312.

17. Valerian, 202.

18. Rhonda Francis, "Paul Bennewitz," http://www.shadowmag.com, 10 January 2001.

19. Helmut Lammer, "Further Findings of Project MILAB: Looking behind the Alien/Military Abduction Agenda," http://members.aol.com/nymuch/correcte.txt, 2 August 1999.

20. Not surprisingly MILAB lore incorporates Nazi doctors as evil rogue technocrats. This feature of alien-government conspiracy theory makes use of disclosures during the 1980s that the recruitment of Nazi scientists and technicians after World War II was more extensive and long-term than Americans had originally been told; and that their vowed disaffiliation from the Nazi party was often assumed rather than investigated.

21. Valerian, 166.

22. Comedian Stephen Colbert, host of the faux news commentary show *The Colbert Report,* has coined the term "truthiness" to describe the quality of an event or claim that feels true, despite facts to the contrary. There is certainly an element of "truthiness" to many claims of alien abduction—while evidence of the facts of what happened during alien abduction are often absent, the larger truth of the story they tell makes sense—they could happen and so perhaps they have.

23. Francis.

24. Schneider claimed that his father, Oscar Schneider, was a captain in the U.S. Navy, helped design the first nuclear submarine, and was part of Operation

Crossroads, which was responsible for the testing of nuclear weapons in the South Pacific.

25. "The Mysterious Life and Death of Philip Schneider," http://www.think-aboutit.com/underground, 10 January 2001. Among Schneider's claims were that "the Star Wars program is there solely to act as a buffer to prevent alien attack; it has nothing to do with the 'Cold War,' which was only a toy to garner money from all the people," and that the federal government is building black helicopters at the rate of one per hour in order, most likely "to enslave us." "The Mysterious Life."

26. Http://www.shadowmag.com, 10 January 2001.

27. Http://www.think-aboutit.com, 15 January 2001.

28. Stuart Swerdlow, *Montauk: The Alien Connection* (Westbury, NY: Sky Books, 1998), 10.

29. Swerdlow, 45.

30. Swerdlow, 12.

31. Swerdlow, 55.

32. For discussion of the sort of moral gender panic that has fueled much of the Satanic ritual abuse phenomenon, see Nathan and Snedeker, as cited in chapter 2.

33. John Quinn, "Montauk Air Force Station Active or Not?" http://mindcontrolforum.com/MCF/Montauk.htm, 15 September 1999. Subsequent quotations of Quinn are also from this source.

34. Tanya, personal email, 27 August 1999. Subsequent quotations of Tanya are also from this source.

35. According to Tanya, "they used all sorts of mainstream songs and classical music. I can only tell you the ones that are known publicly. For example, for the time travel prep, one of the symphonies from Swan Lake was used. For LSD-like experiments, the Rolling Stones 'Gimme Shelter' was used. Usually 60s/70s possibly 80s music was/is used. . . . The thing is that listening to them on radio or tape or CD reinforces or can trigger the programming. Insidious, no?"

36. Jason Vest, "Alien Toxins," *Village Voice*, 10–16 November 1999, 28–29.

NOTES TO CHAPTER 8

1. Budd Hopkins, *Witnessed: The True Story of the Brooklyn Bridge UFO Abductions* (New York: Pocket Books, 1996), 110.

2. Hopkins, *Witnessed*, 124.

3. Hopkins, *Witnessed*, 111.

4. Hopkins, *Witnessed*, 196.

5. Hopkins, *Witnessed*, 197.

6. De Cuellar issued this response in February 1996, reprinted in the *Skeptics UFO Newsletter*, no. 43 (January 1997): 4: "I cannot but strongly deny the claim that I have had an abduction experience at any time. On several occasions, when questioned about that matter, I reiterated that these allegations were completely false and I hope that this statement will definitely put an end to these unfounded rumors."

7. Hopkins, *Witnessed*, 428.

8. Hopkins, *Witnessed*, 127.

9. There is critical consensus about this movement among UFO investigators which was corroborated by my review of the National Investigative Committee for Aerial Phenomena (NICAP) archives housed at the Center for UFO Studies (CUFOS) in Chicago. NICAP was the civilian offshoot of official government investigations of UFOs and related phenomena. While government investigation ended with Project Blue Book in 1969, NICAP continued to be active up through the early 1980s.

10. Claims by contactees that extraterrestrials may act as caretakers whose function it is to save humanity from itself are not unprecedented. First, the comparison to all variety of gods, demigods, and angels from a variety of world religions is somewhat obvious: entities that exist "above" us observe, monitor, and perhaps control human activity from on high, intervening when necessary to alter the course of human events, or to redeem humankind from sin. In addition, the wish for benevolent intervention by extraterrestrials to save us from ourselves is a science fiction commonplace, an extension of such stories of divine intervention for a secular age. During the 1950s in movies, such as *The Day the Earth Stood Still* and *It Came from Outer Space*, robotic aliens brought messages of peace to otherwise war-mongering humans, the aliens assuring humans that, "we have souls and minds and we are good." *The Day the Earth Stood Still*, Robert Wise, dir. (1951). Movies such as these complemented the host of malevolent invasion films listed in chapter 1. In all of these accounts however, the notion of benevolence is not untroubled, and "true" stories of contact with aliens in particular underscore that the good/bad dichotomy is not so neat. Both the alien bearers of messages and the messages they bring about the earth and humankind have the potential to upset the status quo by forcing us to confront our own earthly oversights, limitations, and excesses.

11. Blurring between science and spirituality is at the heart of UFO belief, based as it is on a sort of hybridization of Western metaphysical and spiritual belief, Christian symbolism, and science fiction. In this blending, early contactees—members as they were of "occult scenes" and flying saucer clubs, were precursors to the New Age movement, which gained steam after the 1960s and cohered into an industry in the 1980s and 1990s. Early New Agers drew on the longer Western metaphysical tradition of spiritualism, including theosophy

which offered revisions of, or an alternative to, Christianity. During the nineteenth century spiritualists thrived because of science and the alternative ways of knowing that it enabled. In the mid-twentieth century, in the wake of two world wars and the atom bomb, contactees and others involved in ufology—often also fans, consumers, and producers of science fiction—marked a shift in the evolving relationship between mysticism and science. This shift reflects ambivalence about the mystical qualities of science and technology and the modes of transformation it offers. For more on the ambivalent relationship between New Agism and science see Andrew Ross, "New Age—A Kinder, Gentler Science?" in *Strange Weather: Culture, Science, and Technology in the Age of Limits* (New York: Verso, 1991), 15–74.

12. Jerome Clark, *UFO Encyclopedia*, vol. 2, *Emergence of a Phenomenon* (Detroit: Omnigraphics, 1996), 47.

13. Clark, 2.

14. George Adamski, *The Flying Saucers Have Landed* (London: Werner Laurie, 1953), 194.

15. Jerome Clark, *UFO Encyclopedia*, vol. 2, *Emergence of a Phenomenon* (Detroit: Omnigraphics, 1996), 48.

16. Quoted in Clark 2:49.

17. Adamski, 198.

18. In 1958 the newly formed National Aeronautics and Space Administration (NASA) would detonate several nuclear devices in space three hundred miles above the South Atlantic during Project Argus. They did so in an effort to test whether the large number of electrons released in such explosions would become trapped in the magnetic field forming an artificial radiation belt. The discovery of the Van Allen radiation belts resulted.

19. Adamski, 199.

20. Adamski, 210.

21. Adamski, 207.

22. Clark 2:49.

23. It is the dominance of this worldview that, according to John Mack, has led aliens to intervene on our behalf. Mack's critique is one shared by many in various New Age communities, not all of which include belief in aliens. Mack, 4.

24. Proponents of space spending in science and government exploited the magical qualities of space travel in the effort to gain popular acceptance of a program that was met initially with resistance and criticism from a variety of sources. Vannevar Bush, head of the Office of Research and Development during World War II called the man-in-space program "a vastly overrated stunt" and other science advisory committee members agreed. So too did "top military planners" including members of the Senate Armed Services committee and the Joint Congressional Committee on Atomic Energy, including both Democrats

and Republicans, oppose space spending as "senseless." Both opposing positions were summarized by *Reader's Digest* as part of an ongoing "debate" in that periodical about whether or not to "Stop the Race to the Moon." See "The Senseless Race to Put Man in Space," *Readers Digest,* May 1961; and "We're Running the Wrong Race with Russia!" *Readers Digest,* August 1963.

25. In September 1965, Gemini 5 took pictures of Earth "from 100 miles up" that graced the cover of *Life,* affording "the most remarkable view of earth ever recorded." As astronaut Pete Conrad reflected, the view of Earth "was so vast, so beautiful and so overpowering that somehow man and all his problems seemed insignificant." The perceived beauty of the planet erases—at least temporarily—terrestrial imperfections. Indeed, from space, things look better, as Conrad exclaims during reentry, "Christmas! It looks better than it did for real!" 84. This text appears on an unnumbered page that is part of a fold-out front cover.

26. For a more extensive inquiry into the ways in which the space program's dependence on witnesses for credibility contributed to the alien abduction phenomenon, see Dean. Dean reads abduction as "the dark underside of official space, as a return of the repressed dimensions of astronaut heroics" originally orchestrated to "present a particular image of freedom." 121, 90.

27. Arthur C. Clarke, "Space Flight and the Spirit of Man," *Astronautics,* October 1961, 76.

28. Edgar Mitchell, *The Way of the Explorer: An Apollo Astronaut's Journey through the Material and Mystical Worlds* (New York: G. P. Putnam's Sons, 1996), 3–4.

29. Mitchell, 4.

30. John Fuller, *The Interrupted Journey,* 285.

31. Fuller, *The Interrupted Journey,* 287.

32. Fowler, *The Andreasson Affair,* 14.

33. Fowler, *The Andreasson Affair,* 99.

34. Fowler, *The Andreasson Affair,* 100.

35. Fowler, *The Andreasson Affair,* 200.

36. Fowler, *The Andreasson Affair,* 77, 83.

37. Fowler, *The Andreasson Affair,* 99.

38. Fowler, *The Andreasson Affair,* 104.

39. Fowler, *The Andreasson Affair,* 32.

40. Fowler, *The Andreasson Affair,* 200.

41. Fowler, *The Andreasson Affair,* 30.

42. Fowler, *The Andreasson Affair,* 54.

43. James Lovelock, *Gaia: A New Look at Life on Earth* (New York: Oxford University Press, 1979), 1.

44. Quoted in Lawrence Joseph, *Gaia: The Growth of an Idea* (New York: St. Martin's Press, 1990), 336.

45. Lovelock's ideas about the earth as living entity were solidified for him by the new view of Earth made possible via the space program. He writes, "for the first time in human history we have had a chance to look at earth from space, and the information gained from seeing from the outside our azure-green planet in all its global beauty has given rise to a whole new set of questions and answers." 8. During the early 1960s Lovelock worked as a consultant at the Jet Propulsion Laboratories of the California Institute of Technology in Pasadena. Lovelock, part of a team working on ways to detect life on Mars, was instrumental in the invention of something called the electron capture detector, a device that worked to detect traces of chemical substances in various materials. As Lovelock notes, "this sensitivity first made possible the discovery that pesticide residues were present in all creatures of the earth from Penguins in Antarctica to the milk of nursing mothers in the USA." Viii. It was this device, Lovelock adds, that facilitated the writing of *Silent Spring* by providing the evidence necessary to support Rachel Carson's claims about "the ubiquitous presence of these toxic chemicals." Viii.

46. Quoted in Maurice Strong, ed., *Who Speaks for Earth?* (New York: Norton, 1973), 92.

47. "Have We Reached the Limits of Pollution?" *Time Magazine*, 19 May 1968, 153–154, 153.

48. Other films from the same period rendering the dystopian possibilities of environmental collapse included *Doom Watch* (1972), *Soylent Green* (1973), *Logan's Run* (1976), and the Road Warrior movies, beginning with *Mad Max* in 1980.

49. Adlai Stevenson III, in *Earth Day—The Beginning: A Guide to Survival*, by National Staff of Environmental Action (New York: Arno Press, 1970), 76.

NOTES TO CHAPTER 9

1. Jean, personal interviews, 8 April 1998, 18 September 1998.
2. Mack, 4.
3. Mack, 3.
4. For more information on SDI, see the Federation of American Scientists website at http://www.fas.org.
5. Mack, 40.
6. Jacobs, 136.
7. Jacobs, 137.
8. Jacobs, 148.
9. Strieber, *Communion*, 64.
10. Strieber, *Communion*, 69.
11. Strieber, *Communion*, 65.
12. Strieber, *Communion*, 107.

13. Strieber, *Communion*, 57.
14. Strieber, *Communion*, 57.
15. Strieber, *Communion*, 253.
16. Mack, 53.
17. Mack, 54.
18. Mack, 60.
19. Mack, 61.
20. Strieber, *Communion*, 265.
21. Fowler, *The Watchers*, 341.
22. Fowler, *The Watchers*, xvi.
23. Fowler, *The Watchers*, 119.
24. Fowler, *The Watchers*, 22.
25. Fowler, *The Watchers*, 349.
26. Strieber, *Communion*, 83.
27. Strieber, *Communion*, 288.
28. Casteel, 31.
29. Even within some sectors of the abduction community it is hard to be heard, or taken seriously if you propose revelations, if the "message" you impart is perceived to be too far out. There's an ironic intolerance for New Age belief among some abduction experts, particularly those, like Budd Hopkins and David Jacobs, who are heavily invested in establishing the legitimacy of abduction accounts and their own investigations, the normalcy and credibility of abductees.
30. Jane, personal interview, 10 July 1999.
31. Henry, personal interview, 23 May 1999.
32. George, personal interview, 8 August 1998.
33. George, personal interview, 8 August 1998.
34. Anthony, personal interview, 15 July 1999. Subsequent quotations of Anthony are from this interview as well.
35. Mack, 4.
36. Jean, personal interview, 18 September 1998.
37. Manuel Castells, *Informational Cities: Information Technology, Economic Restructuring, and the Urban-Regional Process* (New York: Basil Blackwell, 1989), 307.
38. Castells, 347.
39. Castells, 349.
40. Economic globalization has escalated, as has the abduction phenomenon, since the 1980s. The restructuring of capitalism in the late 1970s and 1980s was in part prompted by the oil crises of the mid- to late 1970s. Though internationalization of the economy had begun after World War II with the formation of the International Monetary Fund and other international institutions,

post–oil crisis restructuring was an opportunity for such organizations to step in and impose a global economy.

41. Henry, personal interview, 23 May 1999. Subsequent quotations of Henry are also from this interview.

42. This is the group with which I open my introduction.

NOTES TO CHAPTER 10

1. When I interviewed Hopkins in his home in the spring of 1998 he wanted, among other things, to convince me that alien abduction is not the result of what he calls "media contamination." He holds up as evidence of this point a Roper Survey, then underway and with which he was involved. The survey indicates that since the television series the *X Files* first aired in 1993, the number of people reporting their abduction by aliens has not increased. He and other proponents of the "ET hypothesis" insist that there is, in his words, a "disconnect" between "visual data" and our idea of outer space, between popular imagery of alien abduction and reports of actual abductions.

2. George, personal interview, 8 August 1998. Subsequent quotes of George are also from this interview.

3. Mike, personal email, 4 May 2000.

4. Cassie, personal interview, 2 February 2000.

5. Maureen, personal interview, 13 August 1999.

6. Henry, personal interview, 23 May 1999.

7. Anthony, personal interview, 15 July 1999.

8. Zecharia Sitchin's books include *Genesis Revisited: Is Modern Science Catching Up with Ancient Knowledge?*; *When Time Began*; *Divine Encounters: A Guide to Visions, Angels, and Other Emissaries*; and *The Lost Realms*.

9. A Fortean, after Charles Fort, is an investigator of anomalous phenomena.

10. Some want to underscore that they are not writing books, wary of accusations that they are feigning abduction in order to get rich on royalties. Mike writes, "I'm not writing a book. That's not what I'm interested in or about," while Anthony insists, "we're not getting rich, that's not what this is about."

11. Jean, personal interview, 8 April 1998.

12. *SPACE Explorer* 8, no. 2 (summer 1999), issue 66.

13. Http://www.virtuallystrange.com.

14. Jane, personal interview, 7 July 1999.

15. The Bordentown conference turned out to be an excellent source for finding out-of-print UFO books. The exhibits area at the conference—about four tables' worth—was manned by collectors and sellers as well as some local UFO photographers and their collections.

16. Chupacabras are the blood-sucking alien entities believed to be responsible for the ex-sanguination of animals—usually goats—throughout Central America.

17. Program for Extraordinary Experience Research (PEER), Cambridge, MA (Mack's group); Intruders Foundation, New York (Hopkins's group); Organization for Paranormal Understanding and Support (OPUS), Concord, CA; Treatment and Research of Experienced Anomalous Trauma (TREAT), Ardsley, NY; Close Encounters Investigation Team (CEIT), Santa Barbara, CA; Long Island Abductee Support Network, Point Lookout, NY; Close Encounters Research Organization (CERO), Verdugo City, CA; SPACE, Brooklyn, NY; Midwest Abductee Research and Support System (MARS), Fremont, IA; East Bay Contact and Support Network, Oakland, CA; and one in Germany, Projekt Austausch.

18. Henry, personal interview, 23 May 1999.

19. *SPACE Explorer* 8, no. 2 (summer 1999), issue 66.

20. A 6 July 1999 *New York Times* article (Nicholas Kristoff, "Alien Abduction? Science Calls It Sleep Paralysis") reports that a Japanese psychologist has concluded that ancient reports of attacks by witches and stories of alien abduction can be explained as symptoms of sleep paralysis. This is a condition during which "the body is in REM sleep and so is paralyzed, disconnected from the brain, while the brain has emerged from sleep." F2. Anthony and Adam also quickly dismissed this new theory as just another example of U.S. media blackout on the truth of alien abduction.

21. Mike, personal email, 4 May 2000.

22. Anthony, personal interview, 15 July 1999.

23. "Kidnapped by UFOs?"

24. [Maureen], "Sands of Time."

25. John Velez, personal email, 5 May 2000.

26. Adam, personal interview, 14 May 2000.

NOTES TO THE CONCLUSION

1. Http://www.virtuallystrange.net/ufo/updates/2002, 8 August 2002.

2. Books do continue to get published, but by much smaller presses with lists largely devoted to New Age and paranormal phenomena. In the last several years, for example, the following: Dolores Cannon, *The Custodians: Beyond Abduction* (Huntsville, AR: Ozark Mountain Publishing, 1998); Constance Clear, *Reaching for Reality: Seven Incredibly True Stories of Alien Abduction* (San Antonio: Consciousness Now, 1999); Dana Redfield, *Summoned: Encounters with Alien Intelligence* (Norfolk, VA: Hampton Roads, 1999); and Marcia Schafer, *Confessions of an Intergalactic Anthropologist* (Phoenix: Cosmic Destiny Press, 1999).

Bibliography

Adam. Personal Interview. 14 May 2000.

Adamski, George. *The Flying Saucers Have Landed*. London: Werner Laurie, 1953.

Advisory Committee on Human Radiation Experiments. *Final Report of the Advisory Committee on Human Radiation Experiments*. New York: Oxford University Press, 1996.

Anthony. Personal Interview. 15 July 1999.

Berlitz, Charles, and William Moore. *The Roswell Incident*. New York: Berkeley Books, 1980.

Broad, William. "Wreckage in the Desert Was Odd but Not Alien." *New York Times*, 8 September 1994, A1.

Brown, Lesley, and John Brown. *Our Miracle Called Louise*. New York: Paddington Press, 1979.

Carson, Rachel. *Silent Spring*. Boston: Houghton Mifflin, 1962.

Cassie. Personal Interview. 4 March 2000.

Casteel, Sean. "An Interview with Katharina Wilson." *Mutual UFO Network Journal*, No. 329 (1995).

Castells, Manuel. *Informational Cities: Information Technology, Economic Restructuring, and the Urban-Regional Process*. New York: Basil Blackwell, 1989.

"CIA, Army Must Pay for Giving Soldiers LSD." *Times Picayune*, 6 March 1996, A2.

Clancy, Susan. *Abducted: How People Came to Believe They Were Kidnapped by Aliens*. Cambridge, MA: Harvard University Press, 2005.

Clark, Jerome. *The UFO Encyclopedia*. Vols. 1–3. Detroit: Omnigraphics, 1996.

Clarke, Arthur C. "Space Flight and the Spirit of Man." *Astronautics*, October 1961.

"Clinton Offers Apology; Says Tuskegee Syphilis Study Was Shameful." *Boston Globe*, 17 May 1997, A1:1.

"Cold War Experiments." *U.S. News and World Report*, 24 January 1994, 32.

"Control of Life." *Life*, 10 September 1965, 59–79.

Dean, Jodi. *Aliens in America: Conspiracy Cultures from Outerspace to Cyberspace.* Ithaca, NY: Cornell University Press, 1998.
Druffel, Ann. *How to Defend Yourself against Alien Abduction.* New York: Three Rivers Press, 1998.
Edwards, Robert, and Patrick Steptoe. *A Matter of Life: The Story of a Medical Breakthrough.* New York: William Morrow, 1980.
"An Experiencer's Guide to Therapy." Program for Extraordinary Experience Research, Cambridge, MA: Harvard Medical School, 1994.
"Explosion of Science." *Life,* 26 December 1960, 26–28.
Festinger, Leon. *When Prophecy Fails: A Social and Psychological Study of a Modern Group That Predicted the Destruction of the World.* New York: Harper and Row, 1956.
Fowler, Raymond. *The Andreasson Affair: The Documented Investigation of a Woman's Abduction Aboard a UFO.* Englewood Cliffs, NJ: Prentice Hall, 1979.
———. *The Watchers: The Secret Design behind UFO Abduction.* New York: Bantam Books, 1990.
Frequently Asked Questions. Philadelphia: False Memory Syndrome Foundation, 1994.
Fuller, John. *The Interrupted Journey: Two Lost Hours Aboard a Flying Saucer.* London: Dial Press, 1966.
Gallagher, Carole. *American Ground Zero: The Secret Nuclear War.* Cambridge, MA: MIT Press, 1997.
George. Personal Interview. 8 August 1998.
Gersten, Peter. "CAUS Position on Congressional Hearings, Immunity, and Amnesty," http://www.caus.org. 26 July 1999.
Haaken, Janice. "Sexual Abuse, Recovered Memory, and Therapeutic Practice: A Feminist Perspective." *Social Text,* 40 (fall 1994): 115–145.
"Have We Reached the Limits of Pollution?" *Time Magazine,* 19 May 1968, 153–154.
Henry. Personal Interview. 23 May 1999.
Herman, Judith Lewis. *Trauma and Recovery.* New York: Basic Books, 1992.
Hill, Betty. Letter to Major Donald Keyhoe. 26 September 1961. Center for UFO Studies Archives, Chicago (hereafter cited as CUFOS).
———. Letter to Mark Rodeghier. 8 March 1994. CUFOS.
———. Letter to Mark Rodeghier. 10 July 1994. CUFOS.
Hopkins, Budd. Personal Interview. 15 May 1998.
———. Personal interview. 9 November 2000.
———. *Intruders: The Incredible Visitations at Copley Woods.* New York: Ballantine, 1987.
———. *Missing Time.* New York: Ballantine, 1981.

———. *Witnessed: The True Story of the Brooklyn Bridge UFO Abductions.* New York: Pocket Books, 1996.
Jacobs, David. *Secret Life: Firsthand Documented Accounts of UFO Abductions.* New York: Simon and Schuster, 1992.
James, William. *The Varieties of Religious Experience: A Study of Human Nature.* Garden City, NY: Dolphin Books, 1960.
Jane. Personal Interview. 10 July 1999.
Jean. Personal Interview. 8 April 1998.
———. Personal Interview. 18 September 1998.
Jenkins, Henry. "Star Trek Rerun, Reread, Rewritten." In *Close Encounters: Film, Feminism, and Science Fiction,* Ed. Constance Penley, Elisabeth Lyon, Lynn Spigel, and Janet Bergstrom. Minneapolis: University of Minnesota Press, 1991.
Joseph, Lawrence. *Gaia: The Growth of an Idea.* New York: St. Martin's Press, 1990.
Jung, Carl. *Flying Saucers: A Myth of Things Seen in the Sky.* New York: Harcourt Brace, 1959.
"Kidnapped by UFOs?" *Nova* Online, http://www.pbs.org/wgbh/nova/aliens/johnvelez. 10 June 1998.
Knight, Peter. *Conspiracy Nation: The Politics of Paranoia in Postwar America.* New York: NYU Press, 2002.
Lammer, Helmut. "Further Findings of Project MILAB: Looking behind the Alien/Military Abduction Agenda," http://www.members.aol.com/nymush/correcte.txt. August 1999.
LaVigne, Michelle. "On-Line Interview with Katharina Wilson," http://www.alienjigsaw.com. 6 February 1999.
Lovelock, James. *Gaia: A New Look at Life on Earth.* New York: Oxford University Press, 1979.
Mack, John. *Abduction: Human Encounters with Aliens.* New York: Charles Scribner's Sons, 1994.
Maureen. Personal Interview. 13 August 1999.
[———]. "Sands of Time: The Montauk Project." Http://hometown.aol.com/nymush/sands.
Mike. Personal Email. 4 May 2000.
———. Personal Interview. 10 July 1998.
Mitchell, Edgar. *The Way of the Explorer: An Apollo Astronaut's Journey through the Material and Mystical Worlds.* G. P. Putnam's Sons, 1996.
"The Mysterious Life and Death of Philip Schneider," http://www.think-aboutit.com/underground. 10 January 2001.
Nathan, Debbie, and Michael Snedeker. *Satan's Silence: Ritual Abuse and the Making of a Modern American Witch Hunt.* New York: Basic Books, 1995.

National Staff of Environmental Action, *Earth Day—The Beginning: A Guide to Survival*. New York: Arno Press, 1970.

Nelkin, Dorothy. *The DNA Mystique: The Gene as Cultural Icon*. New York: W. H. Freeman, 1995.

Nicholls, Preston B., with Peter Moon. *The Montauk Project: Experiments in Time*. Westbury, NY: Sky Publishers, 1992.

Petchesky, Rosalind. *Abortion and Woman's Choice: The State, Sexuality, and Reproductive Freedom*. New York: Longman, 1984.

Platt, Rutherford. "The Wondrous Inner Space of Living Cells." *Reader's Digest*, June 1964, 195–198.

Quinn, John. "Montauk Air Force Station Active or Not?" Http://mindcontrol forum.com/MCF/Montauk.htm, 15 September 1999.

"Redressing a Past of Shameful Experiences." *San Francisco Chronicle*, 22 December 1996, Editorial, A15.

Saler, Benson, Charles A. Ziegler, and Charles B. Moore, *UFO Crash at Roswell: The Genesis of a Modern Myth*. Washington, DC: Smithsonian Institution Press, 1997.

"The Secret World of the Unborn." *McCalls*, May 1963, 75.

Showalter, Elaine. *Hystories: Hysterical Epidemics and Modern Media*. New York: Columbia University Press, 1997.

"Soldier Given LSD in '58 Settles Suit for $400,000." *Los Angeles Times*, 6 March 1996, 9.

SPACE Explorer vol. 8, no. 2 (summer 1999), issue 66.

"Stop the Cosmic Watergate!" Transcript, CNN news, 6 July 1993.

Strieber, Whitley. *Communion: A True Story*. New York: William Morrow, 1987.

———. *Transformation: The Breakthrough*. New York: HarperCollins, 1988.

Strong, Maurice, ed. *Who Speaks for Earth?* New York: Norton, 1973.

Swerdlow, Stewart. *Montauk: The Alien Connection*. Westbury, NY: Sky Books, 1998.

Tanya. Personal Email. 27 August 1999.

Valerian, Valdemar, ed. *Matrix II: The Abduction and Manipulation of Humans Using Advanced Technologies*. Yelm, WA: Leading Edge Research, 1991.

Wilson, Katharina. *Puzzle Pieces: A Self-Help Guide for Abductees*. Portland: Puzzle Publishing, 1994.

Wise, David, and Thomas Ross. *The Invisible Government*. New York: Random House, 1964.

Index

Abduction: Human Encounters with Aliens, and interspecies breeding project, 88–89
Adamski, George, 145–150
Alter, Jonathan, 103–104
Andreasson Affair: The Documented Investigation of a Woman's Abduction Aboard a UFO, 32–36, 154–155
Andreasson, Betty, 33–36, 57, 60, 166–167
Angelluci, Orfeo, 145–150

Bennewitz, Dr. Paul, 132–133
Biotechnology, anxiety about, 5, 70–82
Body marks, as proof of alien abduction, 46, 71, 192–194
Bush, President George H. W., 117
Bush, President George W., 120

Carson, Rachel, 156, 164
Center for UFO Studies (CUFOS), 66
Charcot, Jean-Martin, 34
Chariots of the Gods, 5–6
Chosenness, alien abductee feelings of and about, 15, 17, 167–169
Citizens Against UFO Secrecy (CAUS), 111–112
Clancy, Susan A., 9–10
Clarke, Arthur C., 150–151
Clinton, President William J.: and call for national healing, 19, 118–119; and human radiation experiments, 116
Close Encounters of the Fourth Kind, 6, 46
Close Encounters of the Third Kind, 5
Cold War, 18; and arms race, 18; conspiracy theory as revisionist history of, 105–120, 126, 144–145; and state sponsored science, 74
Communion, 54–55, 57; and alien abduction, 83; as trigger to alien abduction memories, 178–179
Condon Report, 111
Conferences, UFO and alien abduction themed, 183–185
Conspiracy theory: and anti-government sentiment, 227n22; and government cover-up of alien abduction, 4, 100–102, 121–141; and government secrecy, 108–110; and military abductions, 121–124; and national "healing," 19; scholarship about, 10–11, 102–104
Cortile, Linda, 142–145
Crowell, Cynthia, 126
Cultural practice, alien abduction as, 18, 177–206

Dark Side Hypothesis, 17, 124–141
Davis, Kathie, 61–62; and hybrid baby, 96
Dean, Jodi, 10–11
Druffel, Ann, 68
Dulce Underground Base, 128–135

Earth: concern about state of the planet as expressed in alien abduction accounts, 17
Environmental apocalypse, anxieties about, as expressed in alien abduction accounts, 157–159, 160–176
Environmentalism: activism among alien abductees, 173–176; history of, 1970s to 1990s, 155–159, 162; as result of alien abduction, 142–145

243

244 | Index

Experts, alien abduction, and role in shaping alien abduction phenomenon, 15, 37–51
Extraterrestrials: different types of, 188; in early sightings, 146; Greys, 6, 14, 92–98, 122–123, 126, 141, 198; reptilians, 123, 141

False Memory Syndrome Foundation (FMSF), 66–67
Festinger, Leon, and social-psychological explanations of belief in aliens, 8–10
Fetal personhood, 92; and appearance of abducting aliens, 92
Fetuses, and imaging technologies, 75–82, 91–92
Fowler, Raymond, 33–36, 60; and environmental apocalypticism, 166–167
Fuller, John, 25–32, 60

Genetic engineering, anxieties about, as expressed in alien abduction accounts, 74–75, 79, 88–89
Globalization, 5, 172–173
Grey, alien type: 6, 14, 122, 126, 141, 198; fetal appearance of, 92–98

Haaken, Janice, 69
Healing, call for national, 19
Herman, Judith, 60
Hill, Betty and Barney, 19, 25–32, 56–57; description of extraterrestrials, 98–99, 153; and physical violation by extraterrestrials, 71–73, 79–80
Hopkins, Budd: abductee critiques of, 180, 199, 204; and claims at expertise, 30, 67; and debate over meaning of alien abduction, 3; defining alien abduction as trauma, 37, 40–43, 45, 49–51, 61–62, 66, 193; interspecies breeding experiment, 89; professional history, 21–25; use of hypnosis to treat alien abductees, 37, 40–43, 45, 49–51, 52, 142–143, 215n14
Human radiation experiments (HRE), 116–119
Hybrid babies, 92–99, 198
Hypnosis: as method for recovering memories of alien abduction, 15, 24, 27–36, 41–45, 56–58, 122–124; backlash against, 66–67; debate over reliability as evidence, 214n18; and gender, 34–35; history of, 213n12
Hysteria: explanation of alien abduction as, 9, 28; history of, 34, 213n12; *Hystories* (Elaine Showalter), 68–69, 119

Incest Survivor Movement (ISM), 48–49
Interrupted Journey: Two Lost Hours Aboard a Flying Saucer, 19, 25–32, 72, 80
Interspecies breeding program, 70–71, 83–99
Intruders: The Incredible Visitations at Copley Woods, 21, 47, 61; and alien abduction boom, 83, and interspecies breeding project, 84–85, 88–89

Jacobs, David, 42–45, 47, 49–51; abductee critiques of, 180; and interspecies breeding project, 90
Jameson, Frederic, 103–104
Jung, Carl, and mythic explanation of UFOs, 7–10

Keyhoe, Major Donald, 28
"Kidnapped by UFOs?" (*Nova*), 70–71, 200
Knight, Peter, 10–11

Life, and "explosion of science," 74–82
Lipsitz, George, 11

Mack, John, 3, 42, 44–45, 49–51; abductee critiques of, 180, 204; and environmental apocalypticism, 161, 165, 170–171, 176; and interspecies breeding experiment, 88–89; and victim identity of subjects, 62–63
Manchurian Candidate: conspiracy theory about actual creation of, 27, 109, 129, 137, 140; the film(s), 27, 213n9; the novel, 27, 226n19
Melley, Timothy, 104
Memory: of alien abduction retrieved through hypnosis, 25–33, 66; debate over repressed, 39–40, 47
Military abductees (MILABS), 121–124; origin of term, 130
Missing Time, 21, 37, 40–42, 45–46, 65;

as trigger to alien abduction memories, 52, 178, 197
MKUltra, 108–112, 117–118, 226n20; as conspiracy theory touchstone, 129, 136
Montauk Project, 121–124, 135
Mutual UFO Network (MUFON), 34, 53, 67, 123; history of, 215n36
Myth, explanation of alien abduction as, 7–10

National Aeronautics Space Administration (NASA), 151, 153
National Investigations Committee on Aerial Phenomena (NICAP), 26, 111; history of, 215n36, 232n9
New Age: and belief in extraterrestrials, 171, 232n11; explanations of alien abduction, 3, 4, 161; movement and hypnosis, 39, 45
Nixon, President Richard M., 157

Physical examination, as part of alien abduction, 16, 155, 163–164, 222n1
Post Abduction Syndrome (PAS), 43–44
Post Traumatic Stress Disorder (PTSD): and alien abductees, 44, 59; and repressed memory debate, 39
Program for Extraordinary Experience Research (PEER), 44
Psychological explanations for alien abduction, 7–10

Racial identity of alien abductees, 12, 25, 60
Rape: equation of alien abduction with, 4, 47–48, 55, 58
Reagan, President Ronald: and apocalypticism, 103; and rise of conservatism, 19; and Strategic Defense Initiative (SDI), 162
Religion: decline of traditional practice and belief in aliens, 30, 214n19; spiritual transformation and alien abduction, 3, 6; Christian themes in abduction accounts and related literature, 147, 154–155, 211n3; belief among alien abductees, 160, 188–189
Representations of alien abduction: in fiction, 73, 129; in film, 73, 232n10; on television, 129–130, 208

Reproductive choice, anxieties about, as expressed in alien abduction accounts, 90–99, 223n26
Reproductive technologies, anxieties about, as expressed in alien abduction accounts, 16, 70–82, 85–99, 222n1
Roswell, New Mexico, and UFO conspiracy theory, 112–115, 148

Satanic Ritual Abuse (SRA): and alien abduction, 9, 137; and debate over repressed memory, 39–40, 47, 66
Schneider, Philip, 130, 133–135
Science fiction, extraterrestrials in, 73–74, 129
Scientific progress, anxiety about as expressed in alien abduction accounts, 5, 14, 150, 161
Search Project for Aspects of Close Encounters (SPACE), 1–4, 18, 175, 177, 183, 185–187
Secret Life: Firsthand Documented Accounts of UFO Abductions, 43; and interspecies breeding project, 87
Self-help movement, and resisting alien abduction, 67–68
September 11, 2001, 120, 208–209
Sexual abuse: of alien abductees, 62–63, 219n2; anal probes, 80; claims of abuse by extraterrestrials, 5, 49–51, 54–56, 123–124
Sexual submission to extraterrestrials, 56–58
Simon, Dr. Benjamin, 27–32, 57, 60
Social engineering, anxieties about, as expressed in alien abduction accounts, 16, 100–102
Socio-economic status of alien abductees, 12–13
Space Age, rhetoric and belief in alien abduction, 5, 77, 81, 149–153, 171, 234n25
Strieber, Whitley, 6, 19, 47; and sexual violation by extraterrestrials, 54–55, 57–59; and conspiracy theories of alien abduction, 114–116, 124–125; and environmental apocalypticism, 163–168
Support groups, 1–5, 138, 185–187, 204
Symptoms of alien abduction, 45–48

Tilton, Christa, 128, 131
Transformation: The Breakthrough, and conspiracy theories of alien abduction, 115–116
Trauma: alien abduction as, 15, 24–25, 38, 40–44; and sexual abuse, 48–49, 213n12; and shell shock, 27–28, 48
Tuskegee experiments, 117–118

Underground Bases, 127–141

Velez, John, 70–71, 88–89
Victim identity, 3, 4, 38, 52–53, 139–140; believe the victims movement, 38, 48–51, 216n37; conservative critique of, 53–54, 217n2; and gender, 12, 217n17; and status, 59–60, 203; debate among abductees about, 201–206

Watchers: The Secret Design behind UFO Abductions, 35; and interspecies breeding project, 87; as trigger to memories of alien abduction, 179
Webb, Walter, 26
Whole Life Expo, 21, 23, 46, 193
Wilson, Katharina, 67–68, 168, 207
Witnessed: The True Story of the Brooklyn Bridge UFO Abductions, 21, 142–145

X Files: the movie, 103: the television show, 104–105, 229n10, 237n1

Zeta Reticulans, or Greys (abducting aliens), 6, 14, 126; and fetal appearance, 92–99

About the Author

Bridget Brown teaches writing at Montclair State University. She received her Ph.D. in American Studies from New York University.